The Creolization of Theory

THE CREOLIZATION OF THEORY

Edited by Françoise Lionnet & Shu-mei Shih

DUKE UNIVERSITY PRESS
Durham & London 2011

Printed in the United States of America on acid-free paper ∞
Designed by Jennifer Hill. Typeset in Minion Pro by Tseng Information Systems, Inc.

Library of Congress Cataloging-in-Publication Data
appear on the last printed page of this book.

CONTENTS

ACKNOWLEDGMENTS

Our foremost thanks go to the contributors in this book for their deep engagement with the issues that concern all of us, and Julin Everett for her intellectual input as an interlocutor and translator, not to mention her much-appreciated help with editing and compiling the manuscript. We also thank Rachelle Okawa, who stepped in at the last minute for final editing and technical help.

Ken Wissoker at Duke University Press has been a most supportive editor, and we are grateful to Mandy Earley, Rebecca Fowler, and William G. Henry for their invaluable assistance.

Many colleagues at different institutions in the United States and abroad have invited us to present our work-in-progress and engaged with its ideas; the members of our UC-wide Multicampus Research Group (MRG) in Transnational and Transcolonial Studies inspired our first collective volume, *Minor Transnationalism*; and the University of California Office of the President provided initial funding for the workshop during which the ideas in this book were first developed. At UCLA, Pauline Yu, then dean of humanities; Don Nakanishi, director of the Asian American Studies Center; and the deans of International Institute provided additional financial contributions, as did the Cultural Services of the French Consulate in Los Angeles. The UCLA Center for Modern and Contemporary Studies supplied the needed space and staff support.

Shu-mei would especially like to mark the visual contribution by her uncle Hung Chang, whose artistic itinerary between Fushan, Seoul, Taipei, Paris, New York, and San Francisco exemplifies multiple processes of geo-historically specific creolization in his artwork, one of which from the Paris period graces the cover of this book. She would like to thank him for his art and for being such a great artist-uncle. He is one of two artists in her large maternal Chang clan, whose members have remained connected despite being scattered to different parts of the world by the Chinese civil war, the Korean War, and the cold war.

Artists, musicians, travelers, and storytellers have echoed one another across the colonial worlds of the Creole Atlantic and Indian Ocean, linking contact zones in which identities are woven into a thick cosmopolitan fabric made of the tangled knots of diverse memories. Françoise thanks her Mauritian family, especially the Mauritian linguist, poet, and dramatist Dev Virahsawmy and the scholar Danielle Tranquille for showing the way by writing and translating *Kreol Morisien*. Creolizing cultures are oriented toward the future and cannot afford to dwell on the lacunae of memory, but knowing that *detwra tipetal rouz pa fer banane* serves to put both past and future into perspective.

We both thank the Aacqumeh Native American poet Simon Ortiz for allowing us to use the poem that opens this collection.

INTRODUCTION

✵

THE CREOLIZATION OF THEORY

Shu-mei Shih and Françoise Lionnet

> This America
> has been a burden
> of steel and mad
> death,
> but, look now,
> there are flowers
> and new grass
> and a spring wind
> rising
> from Sand Creek
>
> Simon J. Ortiz, *From Sand Creek*
>
> Tu dimunn pu vini kreol
> Mauritian popular saying[1]

Creolization commonly refers to a historical process specific to particular colonial sites and moments of world history, especially in the Caribbean and the Indian Ocean. Today, however, it is increasingly being used to describe many forms of cultural contact, including both reciprocal and asymmetrical exchanges across a wide range of cultural formations. Scholars such as the anthropologist Stephan Palmié (2006) have warned against facile appropriations of the concept. While we too argue in this book against the easy universalization of the notion of creolization, we are interested in putting the notion to more general use. Our goal here is twofold: to raise questions about the forms of intellectual and political entanglements that have marked disciplinary formations in the academy, and to bring into productive conversation a set of theoretical approaches that can enable us to move past the increasingly melancholic tone adopted in the past decade by the aging field of Euro-American Theory.

How can a focus on creolization help achieve such a goal? Emerging first in fields such as sociolinguistics and anthropology, the creolization model is used when referring to the mixing of cultures and languages in parts of the early colonial world. It describes a straightforward empirical reality in which cultural and ideological entanglements abound. It is also used as a flexible hypothesis that allows researchers to map different relationships, modes of contact, and migration patterns in and among diverse ethnic and linguistic communities. As a concept creolization is simultaneously descriptive and analytical: it emerges from the experiential but provides a theoretical framework that does justice to the lived realities of subaltern subjects, while explaining their experiences in terms of an epistemology that remains connected to those realities. Creolization indexes flexibility, welcomes the test of reality, and is a mode of theorizing that is integral to the living practices of being and knowing. It is a mode shared by all cultures in contact. A foundational theoretical concept, it thus emerges from a productive engagement with the living dynamics of an uneven but interdependent world. But it is not the "Theory" most familiar to, and at times most vilified by, scholars in the United States.

Our academic division of labor remains such that we generally fail to account for the degree to which our politics of knowledge, disciplinary formations, and social inequalities are mutually constituted. To think about the genealogies of our specialized disciplines is to recognize that, far from being discrete entities, they are much more interconnected and entangled than we generally concede. Objects of study that might first seem antithetical are often historically imbricated, just like creolized cultures or transnational intellectual movements.

The intersections of an array of intellectual currents in the 1960s form our case in point. We are interested in these currents as they emerged from or traveled to Europe, Africa, Asia, and the Americas. In France, Maoism, structuralism, poststructuralism, and the student protests of 1968 led to what has since been termed *la pensée 68* and eventually to what became known as "French Theory." In the United States, the sixties were marked by the Cold War and the development of area studies, as well as the civil rights movement and the creation of ethnic studies programs. The sixties are also the era of decolonization, the Algerian War, the Vietnam War, and the Six-Day War in the Middle East, which in turn gave rise to new forms of Arab anti-Semitism. It is the period during which the works of Frantz Fanon and Aimé Césaire were first translated into English and appropriated by political movements of liberation around the world, by African American thinkers and later by postcolonial theorists.[2] The challenge, as we see it, is to think theoretically and comprehensively about all these historical events and to underscore that they provide the primary ground for the interrelated global disciplinary questions that concern us now.

The Creolization of Theory is our response to this challenge. It is our attempt to think through the notion of theory in an age when its death is frequently announced and prematurely mourned. Our goal is to theorize relationality in a way that can encourage scholars to see historical, social, political, and cultural issues as forming part of a creolized system of knowledge. Our project is thus part intellectual history, part critique of the exclusiveness of Theory—or more specifically of that theoretical discourse that has, of late, become asphyxiated in its own abstract universe, and whose death is chronically being foretold.

A Chronicle of Theory's Death

Indeed, we seem to be living in a time when the death of theory is repeatedly pronounced. This is, of course, not the first time theory has died. Theoretical paradigms have their life cycles; they come into being, live (prosperously or perilously), wane, die, and perhaps are resurrected. The pronouncements of the death of theory since the 1980s are directed specifically against the American version of French poststructuralism as a hegemonic theory with a capital *T* that has gradually lost dominance, and hence relevance. John Scad, in a short preface to *Life after Theory* (2003), describes the moment in a lighthearted fashion:

> If [theory] can be said (speaking very roughly) to have begun in Paris in the late 1960s, and peaked in Yale in the 1970s and 1980s, then it has been busy declining in a university "near you" in the second half of the nineties. Indeed, in the last few years, there have been a number of books marking this passing—witness, for example, Thomas Docherty's *After*

Theory (1996), Wendell Harris's *Beyond Poststructuralism* (1996) and Martin McQuillan's *Post-Theory* (1999). (Scad 2003, ix–x)

In the same year, 2003, seven years after the publication of Docherty's *After Theory*, Terry Eagleton published a book with the same title, *After Theory*. Eagleton's tone is ironic, his humor acerbic. He begins:

> The golden age of cultural theory is long past. The pioneering works of Jacques Lacan, Claude Lévi-Strauss, Louis Althusser, Roland Barthes and Michel Foucault are several decades behind us. So are the path-breaking early writings of Raymond Williams, Luce Irigaray, Pierre Bourdieu, Julia Kristeva, Jacques Derrida, Hélène Cixous, Jürgen Habermas, Fredric Jameson and Edward Said. Not much that has been written since has matched the ambitiousness and originality of these founding mothers and fathers. Some of them have since been struck down. Fate pushed Roland Barthes under a Parisian laundry van, and afflicted Michel Foucault with AIDS. It dispatched Lacan, Williams, and Bourdieu, and banished Louis Althusser to a psychiatric hospital for the murder of his wife. It seemed that God was not a structuralist. (Eagleton 2003, 1)

Eagleton draws up a list of theorists (those he calls postmodernists) and a list of heroes (mostly theorists on the left) and calls for a return to classical philosophical values such as truth, virtue, objectivity, love, and morality, in combination with a return to what he calls the "materialist ethics" of radical Marxism. In the course of what David Simpson calls a petulant argument, full of "spleen" and "polemical reductionism" (2006, 131, 133), Eagleton throws into the same dustbin of theory what he calls the "Cult of the Other" (2003, 21), referring to all the developments that may otherwise be seen as generally positive developments in academia: postcolonial studies, ethnic studies, gender studies, cultural studies, sexuality studies, and multiculturalism. Any discourse that might celebrate difference and heterogeneity is taken to be the symptom of the depoliticized 1980s and 1990s. Theory as the postmodernist cult of the other is thus complicit with global capitalism, which fetishizes and marketizes culturalist difference and heterogeneity with glee and élan. For Eagleton, the cult of the other is merely the academic manifestation of the final victory of global capitalism, which denies the classical virtues he values most.

Contemporary calls for the death of Theory come from at least three other positions. One might be identified as the loosely associated liberal humanist camp that includes the work of Anthony Appiah, from the tradition of analytical philosophy, and the late Edward Said, who called for a return to humanism and philology (Appiah 2005; Said 2003). The second camp might be so-called postpositivist theorists such as Satya Mohanty who claim a solid ground for identity and knowledge against what they perceive to be poststructuralist relativism, which has trivialized experience-based struggles for identity and their significance for politics (Moya and Hames-Garcia 2000). The third camp, the most obvious and polemical one, is the ceaseless neoconservative backlash against Theory, including those who, for instance, have organized themselves around a thick volume titled *Theory's Empire* (2005), a compendium of antitheory writings from the preceding few decades. The volume's editors profess an "affection for literature" and aim to "redeem the study of literature as an activity worth pursuing in its own right" (Patai and Corral 2005, 14, 13). To them, theory with a capital *T* not only is excessive and nihilistic but also lacks logic, reason, consistency, and evidence. Theory consistently commits "textual harassment" on literature while promoting the "stardom" (8) of theorists who are full of "political pretenses" (12). Theory, in short, has become a gospel, an imperialist dogma, hence the word "empire" in the title. If we identify Terry Eagleton (a former theory proponent who is now grumpy about it) and his followers as the fourth camp, then we have the historical convergence of four different critical positions against Theory, and there are probably more. Even if the validity of these positions is open to varying degrees of elaboration and questioning, this convergence has obviously been very much the symptom of the times.

The most powerful critique against Theory, it can be argued, comes from the critics on the left who take a more historically materialist perspective than Eagleton in their examination of the political economy of the production of knowledge. Poststructuralism, seen historically as a knowledge formation in the last four decades of the twentieth century, when global capitalism reached its greatest height, has been criticized as the cultural symptom of global capitalism and its neoliberalizing impulse. The decentered world, here, is not the decentered world of power but that of capital. The world of capital is borderless. However, such is not the case for the world of the dispossessed and perennially oppressed in the highly stratified and uneven terrains of wealth and influence. Arif Dirlik (1997) has famously read postcolonial theory, intimately linked to the poststructuralist turn in the United States, as the moment when postcolonial intellectuals arrived in the First World academy. In a later essay, Dirlik (2007) criticizes the culture of Theory as a culture of consumption that reflects a radical degradation of the political impulse, from the time when theory was enmeshed with radical politics until as late as the 1960s.

Rey Chow's provocative essay "European Theory in America," included in *The Age of the World Target* (2006), similarly situates the rise of poststructuralist theory in the United States by examining its historical conjuncture with the consolidation of area studies since the 1960s. The turn to self-referentiality and the deferral of meaning as promoted in this version of Theory coincided, for Chow, with the rise and consolidation of information-retrieval-oriented area studies, necessary for the rise and maintenance of the postwar empire that is the United States. Chow's concern is over the "epistemic scandal" (13) caused by the globalization of French Theory by American scholars in the medium of global English and applied to the discussions of the "wretched of the earth" (11). While we agree that this development has its scandalous aspects, we interpret that historical conjuncture as the manifestation of a double movement of the imperial consciousness. This imperial double movement is one of narcissism, often expressed as self-criticism (through Theory) occurring simultaneously with self-expansionism (through area studies). The interiorized "self-reflexive and (fashionably) mournful/melancholy postures" (13) of Theory are mirrored by exteriorized self-expansionism served by the information gathered by area studies scholars.

Thus, while some theorists may tend to drown in fashionable melancholia and mourning, area studies scholars are relegated to pragmatic and empirical research readily extracted for strategic purposes—this is the double movement of the imperial consciousness that is also in fact a highly effective division of labor: the theorists do theory, while the area studies "experts" do area. Wittingly or not, both groups ultimately serve the same purpose of furthering imperial agendas. But in the politics of knowledge within the university, theory has been deemed more sophisticated, and area studies is assumed to be uncritical, if not merely instrumentalist. This unambiguous binarism has been the cause of anguish for many theoretically minded scholars working in area studies who try to negotiate their own engagement with, and entry into, the temple of Theory. Recall that a similar interior-exterior mechanism was at work in earlier times as well: modernism as a literary practice of interiority can be understood partly as a practice of psychic displacement of colonial reality and a disavowal of colonial violence, as argued by Fredric Jameson, Raymond Williams, and others (Jameson 1990; Williams 1989). Poststructuralist theory, in its use in the United States, is equally inextricable from the cultural logic of the imperium; hence Chow's call, after Deleuze, to "restore words and things to their constitutive exteriority" (Deleuze 1988, 43; Chow 2006, 10, 23), or to put it differently, to expose the exteriority (imperial domination) that is the condition of possibility for interiority (poststructuralist theory).

If area studies was charged with the task of transforming the unknowable Third World into a knowable entity by turning it into the object of empirical analysis, the birth of ethnic studies in the United States was clearly an aftermath of the civil rights movements in the 1950s and 1960s, which were themselves inspired by the revolutionary movements across the Third World. One might argue that this revolutionary Third World is what area studies sought to contain by constructing a discourse of threat that is supposed to be based on hard-earned data, though some area studies scholars initially went into the field motivated by a more utopian Third Worldism.[3] The Title VI programs funded by the Department of Education, for instance, were aimed mainly to train students in "strategically important" languages, especially those spoken behind the supposed iron curtain of socialism. But it was the Third World and the civil rights movements in the United States that in turn formed a significant backdrop to the 1968 student protests in France and other radical movements around the globe. Fredric Jameson emphasized this in "Periodizing the 60s":

> It does not seem particularly controversial to mark the beginnings of what will come to be called the 60s in the Third World with the great movement of decolonization in British and French Africa. . . . Indeed, politically, a First World 60s owed much to Third-Worldism in terms of politicocultural models, as in a symbolic Maoism. . . . The new black politics and the civil rights movement . . . [were] also a movement of decolonization, and in any case the constant exchange and mutual influences between the American black movements and the various African and Caribbean ones are continuous and incalculable throughout this period. (Jameson 1988, 180)

What has since happened is by now a familiar story, comprising the Mao-
ist sixties in France, the younger generation's rejection of Sartre's imposing
influence, and the subsequent "linguistic turn" that heralded poststructuralism. Jameson marks this moment as the one when "philosophy" is replaced
by "theory" (1988, 193). The contemporary French philosopher Alain Badiou's (1999) call for a return to philosophy against what he calls "antiphi-
losophy" (read "Theory") makes sense only in this context. The disparaging
of Theory was widely shared by critics on the left, but as John McCumber
(2009) has pointed out in "Philosophy vs. Theory: Reshaping the Debate,"
the distinction between philosophy and Theory is far from conclusive.

One point that Eagleton's book makes clear and Jameson echoes is their
conflation of all that happened afterward as the same symptom of the depoliticization and neoliberalization brought forth by the unprecedented
expansion of capitalism. But contrary to Jameson's suggestion that the
post-1960s production of "new subjects of history"—decolonized peoples,
women, blacks, and other minorities—was endemic to the gradual loss of
class narrative in Theory, and hence part of a larger depoliticization process,
what we suggest is that they constitute anomalies or contradictions within
this process. Contrary to Eagleton's contention that Theory produced a cult
of the other, into which he throws ethnic studies, women's studies, and the
like—we argue that the otherness produced by Theory has never fully coincided with the new subjects of history as valorized and analyzed in ethnic
studies. Ethnic studies and Theory, though historically conjunctural, should
not be situated on the chain of equivalence that Jameson and Eagleton construct for the 1960s. In fact, during the heyday of Theory in the United
States, those who did Theory were largely disdainful of issues of race and
ethnicity, and it is ethnic studies that steadfastly held on to the category of
class and fought a valiant battle against the hegemony of Theory. The Marxist strain in the civil rights movements is something that cannot be so easily
dismissed; it left an indelible mark on the basic principles and ideals of
ethnic studies and its strategies for equality (Noblet 1993; Wieviorka 1998).
The otherness in and of ethnic studies is not at all the otherness in Theory
that neutralizes issues of class.

The otherness that is contained in Theory, we argue, has always been the
other in the self, the Eurocentric self quivering at the moment of encounter
with an abstract otherness, which may be a narcissistic exploration of the
unknowable within the self, a self-absorbed meditation on the ethical im-

plications of the self's unquestionable subjectivity, or the manifestation of a rebellion against Theory's fathers (such as Sartre or, broadly, the European philosophical tradition of universalism). The relationship between this other and the self tellingly replicates the structure of Lacanian extimacy, in which the other is "something strange to me, although it is at the heart of me" (Lacan 1992, 71). It is the Eurocentric unconscious that produces this other for itself, so that the "internal exclusion" (Balibar 2004, 43) of concrete others can remain unquestioned. For instance, in explaining that her intention in *Strangers to Ourselves* was to transfer Kant's "'cosmic' thinking to a more personal level" (130), Julia Kristeva (in an overview of her own contributions to French Theory) offers further interiorization of the other in the Lacanian vein. She explicitly conflates her psychoanalytic and therapeutic goals — to "restore the narcissism or the ideal ego" of the melancholic individual (2008, 129) — with what she sees as the current historical need to shore up national identity to solve social problems. She is interested in the *psychic* demand to restore pride as a primary means of addressing the concrete and urgent social issues of difference, immigration, and globalization that confront the European Union today. Although she insists on "the diversity of cultural models" as "the only guarantee for . . . humanity" (136), it is hard to see how a focus on interiority alone can achieve the goal of respectful diversity that we all share here.[4]

The capitalization of the word *Other* raised the term to a universal, theoretical category, detached from its use as a social, economic, and political category that actually *refers* to new subjects in history. The two recurring phrases in Derridean poststructuralism regarding otherness, "always already" (*toujours déjà*) and "to come" (à venir), denote the places where otherness is banished: to the always already existing structure, either yoked to a past from which there is no escape or linked to an uncertain future existing only as a promise (Lionnet and Shih 2005, 3). This is certainly not the otherness that can lead to daily indignities suffered as a result of structural racism or sexism by minority populations in the United States, which is the subject of ethnic studies. Neither is this the otherness suffered by minorities in France, so powerfully described in Alain Badiou's account of the frequent arrests to which his adopted son is subjected as a young black man in Paris (2006, 111–14). We have noted the hereness of the others as subjects of history in our previous work, *Minor Transnationalism*, and we insist further that "à venir" should more properly be understood as a future that has been ushered in by *concrete others* and is already upon us—a future that is finite. By recognizing the future that is here and the embodied differences that abstract otherness conceals, we want to acknowledge the distinct subjectivities of those who have been—and often continue to be—described as "people without history."

One has to note, however, that ethnic studies (and we include some early versions of Francophone studies in that designation) had clearly come under the influence of Theory by the mid-1980s and early 1990s. The transformation of the Korean American writer Theresa Hak-Kyung Cha's avant-garde text *Dictée* from being disparaged as irrelevant and irresponsible to community concerns to being celebrated as a classic in Asian American literary studies took just about one decade to complete from the late 1980s to the 1990s. The perception by a younger generation of scholars that the class-based paradigm of ethnic studies was less and less able to account for new and multifarious forms of citizenship and more variable forms of culture, coupled with the increasing institutionalization of ethnic studies, led to the awareness that ethnic studies scholars, especially in the humanities, must partake of the larger trends in Theory.

It is arguable that the two issues of *Critical Inquiry* from 1985 and 1986 gathered together in the volume *"Race," Writing, and Difference*, edited by Henry Louis Gates Jr. and K. Anthony Appiah (with essays by Houston Baker Jr., Mary Louise Pratt, Abdul Jan Mohamed, et al.), marked that moment for race studies, while *Black Literature and Literary Theory*, edited by Gates (with essays by Barbara Johnson, Wole Soyinka, Mary Helen Washington), first did so for African American literary studies in 1984.[5] The special issue of *Amerasia* titled "Thinking Theory in Asian American Studies," edited in 1995 by Michael Omi and Dana Takagi (with articles by Lisa Lowe, David Palumbo-Liu, Sau-ling Wong), did the same for Asian American studies, and the double special issue of *Yale French Studies* edited in 1993 by Françoise Lionnet and Ronnie Scharfman (with articles by Réda Bensmaïa, Maryse Condé, Abdelkebir Khatibi, and Mireille Rosello) indicated a similar turn for Francophone studies. In Chicano/a feminist studies, the collection *Making Face, Making Soul*, edited by Gloria Anzaldúa in 1990, opened the way for theoretically grounded discussions of identity. A comprehensive overview of ethnic literary studies in 1995 was provided by the collection *The Ethnic Canon*, edited by David Palumbo-Liu.

Throughout this process, dissident voices have arisen within ethnic studies: some were fundamentally antitheory and some argued for the re-conceptualization of Theory for specific uses. The poststructuralist celebration of the death of the subject did not work well for those clamoring for new subjectivities; the constant revalorization of the texts of "dead white male writers" since Plato by scholars such as Allan Bloom in *The Closing of the American Mind* and Harold Bloom in *The Western Canon* did not help expand the canon itself to include minority and women writers.[6] In a useful overview that contrasts sharply with the positions of Bloom and Bloom, Sharon Holland traces the debates on Theory in African American studies from Barbara Christian's critique of the race for theory to the work of Lindon Barrett, Hazel Carby, and Hortense Spillers; Holland emphasizes the imperative of gendered criticism "with both *theory* and *practice* in mind" (2000, 335).

But if ethnic studies scholars have often been placed on the defensive, tending to be reactive to Theory by developing their own theories of oppression and trauma, others have now come to compete for these theories by universalizing an originary wounding of the colonialist subject in support of a reactionary, nostalgic, and melancholic agenda, including, for example, that of anti-Castro Cubans in the United States and that of repatriated *pieds noirs* in France. The pieds noirs, while celebrating their French-Algerian heritage, continue to argue in favor of the recognition of the "positive" influence of colonialism (Stora 2007; Kimmelman 2009). In this logic, everyone is marginalized or oppressed by a different identity politics; everyone can be diasporic depending on how one defines diaspora; everyone suffers from melancholia; and everyone is hybrid, mixed, and has multiple subject positions. The particular experiences of being minoritized as the racial other were readily drowned out by the universal pathologizing of postmodern or fragmented subjectivity that Theory helped to inaugurate and rationalize. Furthermore, what is seriously overlooked in the use of the label *postmodern* is the phenomenon of cultural creolization, which predates it and exhibits patterns of creativity congruent with unpredictability, novelty, and parody, all associated with postmodern genres (Haring 2004; Lang 2000). Creolization, however, has not (yet?) carried the same kind of epistemological privilege that such patterns have acquired under the name of postmodernism.

The questions to ask at this crucial juncture are these: What do we make of the complex historical confluence of Theory, Third World liberation movements, the civil rights movements, the consolidation of area studies in the United States, and the emergence of ethnic studies in the same? How do we sort through the entanglements among these conjunctural formations, and what implications do these entanglements have for a different notion of theory with a lowercase *t*? What might this theory look like, where do we find it, and what might be its resources? This is not the Theory that foretells its death by melancholic abandon, pushing melancholia to the level of a universal pathology for any and all postmodern subjects. One form of melancholia is never the same as another, as each arises from distinct social, economic, political, and cultural situations (W. Brown 2002; Eng and Kazanjian 2002; Cheng 2001). To put it simply, the universalization of melancholia actually occludes the melancholia of racialized or sexualized subjects. The same can be said of any number of critical vocabularies regarding loss and trauma made current by Theory, which have led to forms of competitive victimology or "wars of memory" (Stora 2007). But as we insist here, more lucid articulations of these complex questions can emerge as a result of the relational (Glissant 1990), intersectional (Crenshaw 1989; V. Smith 1998), or multidirectional (Rothberg 2009) approaches that have been used productively by scholars whose theoretical focus encompasses broader sets of phenomena.

There is, then, quite a different story to tell about the age of theory in the American academy, one that neither keeps announcing its death nor universalizing its reach.

The Becoming Theory of the Minor

To begin with the task of trying to comprehend the nature of the entanglements of these intellectual and political formations, we may recall that the First World sixties in the United States, inspired by the Third World liberation movements, led to the creation of ethnic studies, in which the Marxist theory of class was inventively wedded to studies of race to the extent that race was often theorized *as* class. In France, by contrast, Marxism as theory gradually lost ground, when it was not outright repudiated. Marxism became more or less unspeakable, except for a few trenchant party Marxists such as Louis Althusser or the unapologetic but largely marginalized post-

Maoists such as Alain Badiou, who rose into prominence only after the death of Derrida, and primarily in California. It was only toward the end of his life that Derrida wrote *Specters of Marx*, as if finally to acknowledge the existence or influence of Marxism—albeit as a spectral one (Cheah 2003).

On historical grounds, the two epistemological moments coincide—ethnic studies and Theory—but perhaps they have been rightfully opposites of each other. The criticism we often heard, that ethnic studies was not "theoretically sophisticated," meaning it did not use enough Theory, turned out to be the consequence of ethnic studies' groundedness in the social, lacking the *universalizing* impulse that has arguably pushed Theory to the abyss of death. But ethnic studies and racially marked Francophone studies are not a symptom of Theory. While some leftist critics deplore what they consider to be the balkanization of the class-based collective by "smaller" units of analysis, such as gender, race, and ethnicity, they failed to see that ethnic studies is in fact largely responsible for keeping class analysis alive. If Marxist theorists such as Jameson and others continued to elaborate on Marxism in theory and offered important theoretical analyses of different stages of capitalism, it is ethnic studies that kept Marxism connected to the concrete social. The conservative charge against ethnic studies is perhaps better known and more prevalent: ethnic studies plays identity politics and destroys the universal foundations for commonalities among humans (though these commonalities privileged white-centrism and Eurocentrism). In this conservative case too, the charge has been that this trend only leads to fragmentation and balkanization.

Both camps, otherwise ideological opposites, are nonetheless complicit in their disparagement of ethnic studies, facilely connecting ethnic studies to Theory without tracing their divergent intellectual genealogies. They both charge identitarian struggles with the crimes committed not by ethnic studies or women's studies but, in the final analysis, by global capitalism and its liberal laissez-faire ideologies of relativism. One might say that this displacement may be either a symptom of the powerlessness of left critique in the face of the unprecedented triumph of contemporary capitalism or the sheer internalization of capitalist logic by the neoliberal conservatives.

The call for universalism thus seems to be coming from all directions these days: leftist,[7] neoliberal conservative, liberal humanist, and even from ethnic studies scholars who argue in favor of what might be termed a "post-difference ethics" or, in Paul Gilroy's term, a "strategic universalism" (2000, 95) beyond ethnic *ressentiment*. Our present moment, then, marks a new turn, perhaps to be named the new *universalist turn*, the political implications of which are not yet clear.

Disentangling the misidentification between the celebration of *différance* in Theory and the insistence on difference in ethnic studies therefore shows us an alternative genealogy of theory related to but also divergent from Theory, in the sense of the becoming minor of Theory and the becoming theory of the minor. This is probably the first entanglement between theory and Theory. Ethnic or Francophone studies predate the rise of Theory as a discipline, but as inherently interdisciplinary fields of study, their goals tend to be misrecognized and thus denied the status of theory. The same can readily be said of theorists of gender and sexuality in Francophone African or Southeast Asian studies, whose contribution is trivialized by those who privilege Theory (Nnaemeka 2004; Ha 2009). Chicana/o studies, native studies, African American studies, Latina/o studies, and Asian American studies have not called themselves "theory" *not* because their work always lacked theoretical rigor but because they focused on what they perceived to be more pressing priorities, above and beyond the need to label their methods and critical productions "theory."

The First World sixties in France were indebted not only to the revolutionary Third World, such as Maoism and anticolonial movements in Africa and the Caribbean, but also, reciprocally, to the civil rights movements in the United States.[8] It is well-known that Fanon's work has exerted direct influence on civil rights and black power ideologies (Turner and Alan 1978; Donadey, this volume; Young 2005). While the proponents of the linguistic turn in French thought suppressed the influence of Sartre and his explicit commitment to decolonization (which had been common among the intellectuals of his generation), it was Fanon who creatively used Sartrean phenomenology for the liberation of consciousness for the benefit of the colonized. This may be the second entanglement between Theory and theory, between the Americanized version of French poststructuralism and Francophone decolonial thought. As Lionnet has observed:

> If there is one singular convergence among French-speaking intellectuals who are read here [in the United States], and who have been influential in this country—from Albert Camus to Jacques Derrida, from Edmond

Jabès to Nathalie Sarraute, from Emmanuel Levinas to Marguerite Duras, from Julia Kristeva to Tzvetan Todorov, from Aimé Césaire to Maryse Condé, from Edouard Glissant to Abdelkebir Khatibi—it is their common experience of multiculturalism, of exile and displacement from either "la France coloniale" or Central Europe, and the fact that they are bilingual or multilingual, although they choose to write in French and their intellectual achievements are very much part of a certain cosmopolitan "Parisian" scene. (Lionnet 1998, 126)

If this list of theorists is not a typical one, it is because it clearly differs from the predominant American canon of French Theory, which would include perhaps only half of the theorists mentioned. If the predominant Theory in America can be described as the majority appropriation of Theory, then this list registers a minority orientation, a second becoming minor of Theory into theory. Indeed, what the works of the Francophone Césaire, Condé, Glissant, and Khatibi have in common is an attempt at the decolonization of the mind congruent with the agenda of ethnic studies.

In fact, the becoming minor of theory is consistent with the need to recuperate the radical roots of French thought, long sidestepped by two significant historical processes in France and the United States, respectively. First, French universalism, which assimilates within itself all forms of cultural diversity into a concept of Culture (or *culture générale*), hides geographic, racial, and other differences (Lionnet 2008). This is manifested in the refusal to articulate the immanence of intellectual life and the concrete geohistorical determinations of ideas. The constitutive significance of the event of the Algerian War to French thought is seldom given its due, when in fact the war was a formative experience for the major philosophers of the mid-twentieth century. Robert Young (1990), for instance, stresses that the historical roots of poststructuralism lie in the Algerian struggles of the fifties and sixties. It is well known that Derrida, Cixous, and Rancière were born in Algeria, but seldom is this information made explicitly relevant to their thought. Lyotard taught in Algeria between 1950 and 1952 and wrote sharp criticisms of the French colonial presence in his seldom-read political writings. Foucault taught in Tunisia, and his critique of the "ethnocentricity of reason" (Dosse 1998, 142) and rationalized war should also be understood alongside the rising tide of criticism against French colonialism in Algeria. The significance of the Vietnam War and the Chinese Cultural Revolution for this generation of intellectuals who were thereafter involved in May '68 was studied by historians, but not by the American heirs of those who profess to be experts in Theory. As a result, French thought became, in the United States, synonymous with depoliticized Theory.

This process of depoliticization was further enhanced by its travels in the American university system. Translated as fashionable Theory under the guises of psychoanalysis and poststructuralism, French thought became increasingly neutralized by a set of mutual misunderstandings between the producers of Theory and their readers. And here we come full circle to Jameson's and Eagleton's charge, which, in looking for what they consider to be the missing Marxian radicalism, actually undermines the radical roots already there. As previously stated, John McCumber (2009) has called for settling the debate between philosophy and theory by elucidating French thought's debt to German philosophy to understand the epistemological grounds of oppression and thereby resituating theory within philosophy. Not all Theory needs to be recuperated, of course, but McCumber's is an important reminder to think theory in geopolitical, historical, and genealogical terms, rather than as a network of transcendent and abstract ideas. That is, to think theory in Theory.

Thus, the radical writings of Césaire, Fanon, Khatibi, among others, while in dialogue with Hegelian, Nietzschean, and Sartrean thought, offered a set of theories that demand the undoing of the colonial structures of knowledge. In an eloquent passage from the essay "Pensée-autre" (Other Thinking/Thinking Otherwise) first published in 1977, Khatibi writes:

> When we enter into dialogue with Western thinkers of difference (such as Nietzsche, Heidegger, and among our close contemporaries, Maurice Blanchot and Jacques Derrida), we take into account not just their thinking style, but also their strategy and their lines of attack in order to press their thought into the service of our own struggles, which are of necessity about transforming the mind through a process of effective decolonization, a concrete thinking of difference. (Khatibi 1983, 20)

As a secular Muslim thinker, Khatibi insists on the kind of relational and dialogical thinking that can put the Western tradition in the service of its own disintegration and thus help achieve the decolonization of the mind. He discusses Western philosophers critical of the rationalist tradition from which they emerge, and chooses Islamic thinkers (e.g., Ibn Khaldûn) whose dialectical method engenders a critique of their own traditional practices. These two sets of thinkers are placed in confrontation and mutual critique, hence Khatibi's notion of "double critique" (43–111) that favors the margins.[9] Like Derrida, Khatibi is a thinker of the margin, but differently so: "A way of thinking that does not draw its inspiration from its own poverty is always elaborated with the object of dominating and humiliating; thought that is not *oriented to the minority, and marginal, fragmentary or incomplete* is ultimately directed upon ethnocide [*une pensée de l'ethnocide*]" (18), he declares. His approach thus helps us set aside différance (or endless deferral) and focus instead on the finite and concrete differences that matter: differences produced by colonialism and other structuring principles of inequality and minoritization (what Walter Mignolo calls "the colonial difference" [2000b, and this volume]).

To recognize the structuring principles of colonial inequality is to open the door to active involvement with social change and revolutionary struggles. It is about recognition and redistribution in a colonial context. Thus Fanon's involvement in the Algerian revolution and Césaire's early political commitment to the decolonization of the island colonies culminate in Glissant's complex understanding of the insidious nature of French domination in the Caribbean. In this regard, Fanon opposed "actional" to "reactional" thinking to escape from the circularity of dialectical negation, which remains dependent on the system that decolonizing or decolonial thinking is trying to undo (1967, 222; 2008, 197). In other words, decolonization requires a revolution in politics, thought, and language, all simultaneously, and it is much more than a reaction against colonialism. Rather, it is an act of self-assertion and self-creation. Thus Barnor Hesse, in this book, explores the meaning of the political in the wake of the democratic disavowal of black politics and self-affirmation since the Haitian Revolution. For him, race is a colonial category of governance that produces an idea of the political as constituted by and through the logic of creolization: modern democracy *as produced by* colonial entanglements. Hesse argues in favor of a redefinition of the traditional and gendered binaries of the private and the public in terms of a disavowed third term, the "subaltern sphere — the slaves, the colonized, the natives, the *racially segregated others*." To use race as a political and theoretical category, then, is to challenge Western

the women's movements of the mid-twentieth century in intersection with ethnic studies and Francophone postcolonial thought. Donadey reappropriates the category of the postcolonial from Anglocentric theorists, as she and Murdoch have done in *Postcolonial Theory and Francophone Literary Studies* (2005).

Simon Gikandi (2004) has argued in a different context that an intimate connection exists between poststructuralism and Anglophone postcolonial theory, noting, as an example, Bhabha's disavowal of Fanon's profound humanism. Indian intellectuals have largely dominated discussions on postcoloniality, focusing on questions of mimicry (Bhabha), derivativeness (Chatterjee), and the constraints of representation (Spivak 1988) at the expense of more transformative approaches. By emphasizing the difficulty of giving an account of oneself in the dominant and hegemonic language of the colonial power, their work has tended to generate a self-perpetuating and politically unproductive anxiety that could be said to be self-absorbed. This anxiety, in historical hindsight, is not unlike the melancholia of the First World theorists that we noted earlier. The anxiety of early Anglophone postcolonial theory would fall, for us, under the rubric of reactional theorizing, rather than actional theorizing, as privileged by Fanon. However, the intersection between postcolonial theory (Anglophone and otherwise) and Theory should not be debilitating, as we have tried to show. Dipesh Chakrabarty's provincialization of Europe, Ashis Nandy's India, which is not solipsistically defined in terms of the West, and Spivak's own trenchant criticism of the neocolonial production of knowledge (1993) can all show us a way out of the impasse of anxiety.

Takeuchi Yoshimi, a midcentury Japanese scholar of Chinese literature, wrote an influential essay called "Asia as Method" (Hōhō toshite no Ajia) in 1961, the insights of which have never been taken into account in the discussions of the social and intellectual movements of the global 1960s. A critic of Japanese imperialism, which he saw as mimicking European imperialism, Takeuchi made the important observation that Japanese thinkers willingly adopt Western thought to the extent of self-colonization. He saw in modern Chinese writers, especially Lu Xun, a truly resistant spirit to colonial knowledge, and used Lu Xun as an inspiration to propose "Asia as method." Instead of Asia being the content to be researched with Western methods, here Asia becomes the method with which to study the West. If different realities mandate different analytics, then Asia as a different reality offers different analytics, not so much to propose alternatives as to "further elevate those universal values that the West has produced," as Takeuchi puts it (2005, 165).

The reverse of Asia as method—"the West as method"—has actually been more common all across Asia. The predominant intellectual paradigm for many Asian intellectuals throughout the twentieth century has been Western. These Asian intellectuals used the West as method to evaluate the universal values that Asia itself has produced, because Asian universals as such also need to be critiqued for the way they were translated into hegemonic practices in Asia. What we have, then, is a nonessentialist conception of method, or theory in a different name. If minor formations become method and theory, then new analytics will be brought to the foreground to creolize the universalisms we live with today, doing so from the bottom up and from the inside out. It is this process of becoming theory of the minor that we are also calling creolization.

As Pheng Cheah demonstrates, postcolonial theory is itself a creolized theory. However, he argues, Fanon's transformative transposition of Freud's theory of trauma can and should be critiqued to arrive at a concrete understanding of the paradigm of power as both more than a question of mental dynamics and not just a matter of *external* imposition. Cheah invokes the Derridean concept of "autoimmunity" to conceptualize the excesses of capital flows that led to the Asian financial crisis in 1997 (and, indeed, to today's catastrophic economic situation), and he is echoed by Liz Constable's expansion of Kelly Oliver's analysis of the tension between the psychic and the social and her focus on the political economy of the structures of affect in the lives of postcolonial Algerians. In her efforts to rethink psychoanalytical concepts from a minoritized perspective, Constable highlights the relational and transcolonial (Lionnet and Shih 2005, 11, 17), rather than merely postcolonial dimensions of unmourned loss. She thus produces a lucid example of a vernacular and creolized transposition of these concepts.

Does such a wide-ranging approach to creolization leave us vulnerable to charges of overgeneralization? We address this in the next section to highlight the epistemological challenges posed by the goal of achieving a truly democratic understanding of intellectual, scholarly, and political work in a planetary context.

Creolizations

In his landmark study of 1992, *Des îles, des hommes, des langues: Essai sur la créolisation linguistique et culturelle*, the eminent French linguist Robert Chaudenson cautions against overgeneralization of the concept of creolization. He explains the etymology of the word *creole* and theorizes the sophisticated process of linguistic creolization as it developed in diverse French colonial environments. He maintains the importance of discriminating among geographically specific uses of the terms *creole* and *creolization* but also underlines some basic commonalities. *Creole* was originally used to describe children born to European settlers in the New World and in the island colonies of the Indian Ocean and in the Caribbean basin. The word derives from the Spanish *criollo* and the Portuguese *crioulo* (or its older form *creoulo*). By the first half of the eighteenth century, the French word *créole* was used to refer to blacks, whites, and mulattoes born in the Caribbean, Louisiana, or the Mascarenes, although the semantics evolved toward slightly different racial meanings in New Orleans as opposed to western Louisiana, or in Mauritius versus Réunion or Haiti. While in contemporary Mauritius the term is used to refer primarily to nonwhites, in Réunion and in the Antilles, by contrast, it still refers to whites as well as blacks and mulattoes (Chaudenson 2001, 5–8). This instability is a function of historically specific dynamics that militate against any easy universalization of the concept.[13]

There are many different creole languages. Their typology is complex, and linguists continue to disagree on the genesis of these vernaculars, although it is understood that most are European-language based. But all French-based creoles, for example, are not the same. In different locales, the word *creole* refers to different ethnic groups as well as to the combination of different language systems (European, African, South Asian, Carib) that came together in the contact zones to constitute a lingua franca forged in the crucible of colonization. Creolization in the most general sense refers to the results of a history of contact and to the subsequent process of indigenization or nativization of European settlers. It underscores racial and cultural mixing due to colonization, slavery, and migration. But *créolie, creolité* (creoleness), and *créolisation* have also been appropriated to widely differing ideological ends: either to register a range of divisive identitarian and linguistic categories that emphasize social and ethnic cleavages or to promote forms of "ecumenicity" aimed at transcending the exact same cleavages (Lionnet 1993). An "ethics of vigilance" (Enwezor et al. 2003; Ramassamy 2003) is thus crucial when discussing those diverse processes. Anxiety toward generalizing the concept of creolization beyond its context-specific uses has been well articulated by Stephen Palmié in 2006, in a long review essay, "Creolization and Its Discontents." Palmié gives an account of how the concept has gathered, in recent years, general purchase within the fields of archaeology and cultural anthropology. He is strongly suspicious of the "metaphorics" of creolization and spends the larger part of his essay on the need to remain specific and regionalist. Because creolization is a historically, contextually, and regionally specific concept, one should use it as theoretical or cultural metaphor with great prudence.

These cautionary stances notwithstanding, we want to point out that all life stories of theoretical concepts do begin as regional concepts; they are all first historically and contextually specific before they become widely disseminated, applied, or assumed to be universal. It is, on the one hand, as Palmié notes, a matter of "conceptual politics" that certain concepts can overcome their particularity while others are not able to or not given a chance to. On the other hand, what is also at issue is the degree of pretentiousness that we attribute to a given theory. Our hunch is that without being Theory with a capital T, theory can engage with the objects of one's analysis in multiple ways and to different levels of intensity. When objects of analysis are not simple instances and illustrations of theory and are not made to conform to theory, theory as such performs a very different function. Aihwa Ong and Stephen Collier propose the practice of midrange theorizing that is empirically based and theorizes and revises itself on the go; Arif Dirlik (after Mao) emphasizes theory's need to confront concrete reality at all times, so that theory itself is open to "different interpretations against the test of different realities" (2007, 15); Radhakrishnan (after Said) talks about theory's capacity to build connections and find common ground, and notes theory's need to be rooted in immanence with a promise of transcendence or "transitivity" (2003, viii; 178); the art historian Nicolas Bourriaud (after Althusser) develops a theory of relational aesthetics based on the "materialism of encounter" (indebted to Heidegger's "The Origin of the Work of Art") where each particular artwork is a "proposal to live in a shared world" linking individuals in social forms that are material and historical (2002, 18–22). We can easily be reminded of similar calls for theory coming from various positions that do not necessarily see eye to eye with each other but share the same overall objective: the search for a theory that is simultaneously rooted in changing material and historical processes while promising a certain transitivity to that which is emergent.

In proposing the creolization of theory, we have a similar intention here. To begin with, the distinction between *créolité* and *créolisation* as made by Édouard Glissant and others is informative: creoleness refers to a state; creolization refers to a process. Creoleness is a state and a condition in which the constituent elements may become hardened and reified, thus erecting "multilingualism or multiethnicity into a dogma or model" (Chanda 2000). By contrast, creolization is an open-ended process that can be happening in different parts of the world. Indeed, it has been happening everywhere: Latin America, the Caribbean, the Indian Ocean, Southeast Asia, and the new Europe. As Lee Haring puts it: "When acculturation, transculturation, mixing, and hybridization occur with enough intensity, they become the norm" (2003, 21). The ways in which concepts such as "Creole" and "cosmopolitan" can overlap *and* diverge will need to be further studied if we are to give creolization its full conceptual range, as Lionnet has pointed out (Lionnet 2009; Lionnet and Spear, forthcoming).

Earlier processes of creolization emerged from violent encounters that were colonial and imperial; today, the dark side of globalization is a contemporary manifestation of similar dynamics. In the interview reprinted in this book, Glissant relates contemporary creolization to globalization and what he calls the *tout-monde*. But precisely because processes of creolization are thoroughly unpredictable, we must stress that the *chaos-monde* of creolization needs to be rigorously delineated historically and geographically. Dominique Chancé's useful summary of the received meanings of creolization, and her critique of the utopian slippages to which the concept can give rise, can serve here as conclusive reminders of the complexity of the issues raised in this introduction.

Unmoored uses of the concept of creolization can take it in the direction of merely playful bricolage or transculturalism. Without an anchor in history, creolization can become too pliable, like any other concept that might too easily be decontextualized, such as hybridity, mixture, bricolage, and transculturation.[14] What we insist on, along with Stuart Hall or Françoise Vergès, is that the strength of the concept arises directly from its historical specificity. As a process that registers the history of slavery, plantation culture, colonization, settlement, forced migration, and most recently the uneven global circulation of labor, creolization describes the encounter among peoples in a highly stratified terrain. So it is not just any transculturation but "forced transculturation." As Hall notes:

> Creolization is, as it were, forced transculturation under the circumstances peculiar to transportation, slavery, and colonization. Of course, both terms describe societies where different cultures are forced to establish reciprocal relationships of some kind. But, in creolization, the process of "fusion" occurs in circumstances of massive disparities of power and the exercise of a brutal cultural dominance and incorporation between the different cultural elements. (Hall 2003a, 186)

It is not the kind of bricolage that celebrates just any form of mixture or postmodern pastiche (Haring 2003, 2004) but a bricolage that is a tactical response to a situation of "domination and conflict" (Vergès 2003a, 84). This conception of creolization militates against the neutralization and obfuscation of power dynamics. Hall continues:

> Creolization *always* entails inequality, hierarchization, issues of domination and subalternity, mastery and servitude, control and resistance. Questions of *power*, as well as issues of *entanglement*, are always at stake. (Hall 2003b, 31)

Hall highlights issues of power and entanglement, much as Glissant does repeatedly in all his oeuvre, invoking the *point d'intrication* (commonly translated as "entanglement" [1989, 26]) that is the moment of encounter between power and its other and between cultures. These terms—*power* and *entanglement*—refer to the crucial dynamics that our own use of *creolization* is meant to index.

By using the expression "the creolization of theory," we want to stress three complementary meanings of the process this expression describes—*creolization as theory*, *creolized theory*, and *creolization of theory*—all born of encounter and entanglement in uneven terrains. We emphasize the need for theory precisely because we believe in the transformative potential of a theory that can change the form of our entanglement with and in the world. Simone de Beauvoir's existential insight that if a theory is convincing, it changes our relationship to the world and colors our experience of it, is highly relevant here.[15] For Beauvoir, theory has a direct and immediate impact on her relationship to others; it is not a self-contained, intransitive activity but something that "colors" our experience of the world, destabilizing and unsettling received perceptions. Reading Beauvoir literally here, a "convincing" theory for our times is indeed one that takes color into account, one that acknowledges the racial structuring of the world, one that enables us to question previous assumptions and to challenge the existing cultural or philosophical doxa that passes for Theory. European philosophy presupposes that the activity of thought is colorblind and unmoored from determinations of immanence, but Beauvoir's insight helps us see how creolization as theory is rooted in the world of immanence. In this sense, theory is what forces us to engage with abstractions in a way that takes us outside of our comfortable or common-sense view of reality and its representations while also making clear that these abstractions arise from the uneven terrains of existence in a world marked by dissymmetry.

By virtue of that fact, theory is primarily a distancing mechanism, but we can speak of two forms of distancing here: distancing as a grand gesture of generalization that is in fact based on a myopic understanding of the world, and distancing as a necessary mechanism that propels us outside of our own subjective mode of being and our disciplinary comfort zones. The coupling of theory with the idea of its possible creolization raises questions about conceptual purity, the clear and distinct ideas that Descartes called "first principles" and that Glissant militates against in his insistence on the notion of opacity (2000, 111–20, 189–94; Lionnet 2008). That is why creolization as theory can undermine the tired opposing arguments about the usefulness (or not) of theory, and the relevance of methodologies that remain divorced from the existential realities of gender, race, class, and sexuality. The death of theory as articulated by scholars on both the left and the right reveals their need to defend the status quo of dialectical thinking, an approach that always excludes the remainders produced by colonialism. Their argument is one that has made strange bedfellows of both idealists and materialists, those who defend a conservative view of the "literary" and those who are faithful to radical Marxism, both apparently arguing for a return to more "authentic" or grounded methodologies (even if the exact nature of those methodologies puts one side at odds with the other). What is glaringly absent from this intimate debate between the aforementioned bedfellows is the difference that color makes. Race as a structuring principle of the world is intimately connected not only to social relations but also to epistemological formations; it is a way of living and looking at the world; it is theory (Shih 2008).

The difference that geography makes can be gleaned clearly from the different knowledge systems in the world, which suggests to us the crucial task of decolonizing epistemology. A major consequence of colonialism, whether oceanic, settler, or continental, is what Boaventura de Sousa Santos calls "epistemicide" (2005, xix). Racialized, epistemicide is performed by what Mignolo calls, in a milder language, "epistemic racism" (this volume). Arguing for "global cognitive justice," Santos poses the power differential between the global North and the global South in the realm of knowledge as that between Northern epistemologies and Southern epistemologies. Sandra Harding's (1998) contention that all science is "ethnoscience," including Western science with universalistic pretensions, is aimed to achieve the same kind of decolonization of knowledge in the field of science studies. The question of indigenous knowledge, now gathering momentum as the "IK Movement" around the world, foregrounds how something that may be called "settler epistemology" has papered over different, nontextual, ways of knowing the world with respect to philosophy, language, ecology, biodiversity, and other such all-encompassing issues.[16] Different pedagogies have thus emerged in the last few decades, such as Paulo Freire's well-known *Pedagogy of the Oppressed* in 1968 and the more recent *Methodologies of the Oppressed* by Chela Sandoval, as well as Sandy Grande's *Red Pedagogy* and Linda Tuhiwai Smith's *Decolonizing Methodologies*. Calling them methodologies and pedagogies underscores their practical engagement with social realities, but they are in fact also theories of knowledge.

The argument for epistemological diversity and democracy is not an argument for epistemological relativism. Santos cautions that relativism is premised on an "absence of criteria for hierarchies of validity among different forms of knowledge" and is therefore not a tenable position (2005, xi). History has shown, time and time again, how structures of knowledge have been made hierarchical, privileging a perspective that is misconstrued as

universal, especially in fields such as science and philosophy. Besides recognizing those other vast epistemological resources from a nonrelativistic
viewpoint, the goal here is also to foreground the knowledge produced as a
result of colonial and other encounters.

When we say *creolization as theory*, we are thus referring to encounters
as situations that produce the possibility of a theory or a method that can
itself be conceptualized as creolization. But this is not to idealize all encounters. Heidegger's later concept of *Dasein*, produced in dialogue with Japanese translations of Chinese Taoist philosophy, is an example of intellectual
conversation in the mode of a "republic of ideas" between two powerful
philosophical traditions. Heidegger never clearly acknowledged his philosophical debt to Asian conceptualizations of being, especially the ones derived from his direct exchanges with philosophers of the Kyoto school such
as Kuki Shuzo. In a similar vein, poststructuralist thinkers such as Derrida
or Lyotard never engaged with Arabic thought and language, although their
interest in Algerian politics and culture is very much a part of the development of theories of deconstruction.

By contrast, Takeuchi's critique of Japanese mimeticism of the West by
means of Chinese literature is born of the shame of Japanese imperialism in
Asia, a perceived epistemological subjugation of the Japanese to the West,
and the American occupation of Japan after World War II. Takeuchi studied
the Chinese language with humility and conviction in the early twentieth
century when Japan had already gone through a century of cultural movements against Chinese influence (since the Meiji Restoration) and reposi-
tioned itself as superior to China and thus destined to conquer it. Not that
dominant Chinese epistemologies were not oppressive vis-à-vis their internal others within China, but that at this historical moment, using China to
critique the West was a strong form of Asian self-critique.

Leo Ching, in this book, argues that Takeuchi's Lu Xun, however, remains
a romantic one, when we consider the context of Japanese colonialism in
Taiwan and Japanese philosophy's complicity with it. While the other philosophers of the Kyoto school such as Kōyama and Kōsaka criticized Eurocentrism with profound conviction, their theories reveal a "thinly disguised
justification" for continuing Japanese aggression in Asia, all the while de-
ploying the language of Hegelian metaphysics. The difference that matters
here is the one between two different imperialisms, Western and Japanese,

and this "imperial difference" (Mignolo's term) elides the lived realities of colonialism in Taiwan. Through this elision, Taiwan can never be considered the site of theory. The crucial question, therefore, is not "Why does Taiwan not produce theory?" The issue is about suppressed local histories and subaltern knowledges, and about the geopolitics of knowledge in a global context. Hence Ching's theoretical movement is a lateral one, from Taiwan literature to decolonial thought in Latin America and vice versa, creating a conversation between two forms of subaltern knowledge emanating from two different geopolitical locations—what we have termed "minor transnational" encounters (Lionnet and Shih 2005).

Mignolo provides a conceptual formula to help us think through such geopolitics of knowledge by transforming the Cartesian dogma of "I think therefore I am" to "I am where I think." Drawing from the Colombian Santiago Castro-Gómez, the Argentine Rodolfo Kusch, the Jamaican Sylvia Wynter, and the Algerian Malik Bennabi, Mignolo argues for the imperative to recognize the intimate connection among biography ("I am"), geography ("where"), and knowledge ("I think"). This procedure exposes the pretensions to universality of Western thought and activates a process of epistemic democratization, which is also a movement toward "pluriversality." He lays bare how epistemic difference between the colonizer (as *humanitas*) and the colonized (as *anthropos*) has been constructed, and how decolonial thinking has directly and consistently challenged such epistemic racism. This is why Mignolo notes that the paradoxical consequence of global colonial thinking is the simultaneous rise of decolonial thought all across the world.

Decolonial thinking has existed alongside movements of peoples from formerly colonized and other subaltern countries to the metropoles of Europe. The rights of these relocated subjects are the objects of Balibar's reflection on the "gigantic inequality" in the global circulation and mobility of persons. Perceived as external to the polity to which they are forced to migrate for reasons of economic survival, such persons are no longer merely strangers but the enemy in the new Europe. Balibar calls for a renewal of the *droit de cité* (right to belong) from a "cosmopolitical" perspective to eliminate the border that reinforces radically unequal constructions of the exterior and interior elements that are constitutive of the nation. Hence his reconceptualization of a "diasporic citizenship," the implications of which are to be carefully distinguished from unmoored or depoliticized concepts of diaspora. This new vision of inclusive citizenship partakes of the kind of pluralization and democratization of thinking in the field of knowledge that Mignolo and others discuss.

Similarly, Fatima El-Tayeb and Ping-hui Liao analyze the contributions of second-generation migrants to the public polity and to democratic plurality. El Tayeb analyzes the impossible positions of immigrants and second-generation citizens of color and offers methodological challenges to the colorblind political ideologies of the European Union. She blames Eurocentric and gender-neutral theories for their inability to offer satisfactory accounts of these positions, and proposes instead a queer critique that can destabilize categories and thus allow her more thoroughly to think through questions of race and citizenship. Ping-hui Liao, on the other hand, focuses on the cultural politics of creolization in the work of the Chinese American playwright David Henry Hwang to suggest that second-generation culture-writing by Hwang can operate outside the Hegelian dialectic, much like Fanon's "actional" thinking discussed earlier. Hwang attempts to move beyond "ethnic style" and engenders a mode of collaboration with Philip Glass that shows mutual entanglement and reciprocal enrichment in a cosmopolitan process of creolization.

When we use the expression *creolized theory*, we want to register the epistemological entanglement between the knowledge systems of colonizer and colonized, between Theory and theory. Entanglement is an existential condition with a long history, one that takes many different forms in the continuous process of creolization. Creolized theory is not simply a reactive epistemological position against colonialism but one that is open to creolization conceived (as we have suggested all along) as a dynamic, never-ending, and ongoing phenomenon that begins in the plantation economies of the New World (with their violent encounters that nonetheless gave rise to productive forms of contact, the *mises en relation* theorized by Glissant) that continues to take new forms in the contemporary world, leading to unknown and unforeseeable results. In today's world of financial meltdowns and immense power differentials exacerbated by globalization, people from all areas of the planet are experiencing something akin to the "shock of space and time" of early plantation cultures (Gallagher 2002). Creolization as we understand it registers both the violence of past and present colonialisms and the epistemological transformations wrought by new encounters. As Françoise Vergès puts it:

There is something in the process and practices of creolization that can teach other groups and individuals who are caught in the maelstrom of globalization today. . . . There are strategies that have emerged . . . strategies of resistance, of inventiveness, of creativity in the arts, music, and even in the political discourse that would give, or rather allow comparisons, or transfers of tools . . . exchange rather than hegemonization. (Vergès 2003b, 209)

If many have resisted or are resisting the perceived hegemony of certain theories that get applied indiscriminately to a minoritized or creole content, our goal is to develop a critical language that assumes creolization as the ground of theory. Creolized theory is open to vernacular grammars, methods, and lexicons in the originary sense of creolization as a linguistic phenomenon, but also in the sense that it is a living practice that precedes yet calls for theorization while resisting ossification. Creolized theory enables unexpected comparisons and the use of different analytical tools. It can thus make Theory more pliable, less rigid, substituting exchange and communication for hegemonization. If creolization seeks to express the polycentricity of theory and the diversity of "encounters that are never fixed but constantly reworked and reconfigured" (Enwezor et al. 2003, 16), then it seems to us ever more urgent to attempt theory in the many idioms and languages that are congruent with our diverse orientations as transnational producers of knowledge.

The contributors to this book rigorously think through the intellectual, disciplinary, and ethical consequences of the optical shifts generated by our efforts to reconfigure the order of knowledge in and out of the academy. We have grouped the book's chapters in two parts, followed by a pair of appendixes. We have purposely discussed each chapter in relation to the theoretical points raised at various stages of our argument in this introduction in order to underscore the very practice of intellectual exchange and intersectional thinking that motivates our theoretical project.

Part I, "Creolizing Methodologies," brings together political theory (Hesse), political economy (Cheah), psychoanalysis (Cheah, Constable), feminism and ethnic studies (Donadey), gender and film (Constable), and literature and music (Liao) to flesh out the promise of the double meaning of the title. Depending on whether one understands *creolizing* to be a verb or an adjective, one can infer, on the one hand, that each contributor is en-

tially in the Spanish, Portuguese, and French American colonies, *creole*, in its different versions, specified Europeans born in the colony as distinct from the metropole; Europeans whose European culture was compromised and curiously shaped by the cross-cultural environment of the colony. Underlying this was an informal distinction between pure Europeans and impure Europeans. Second, *creole* by the eighteenth century came to describe colonized people born in the colonies, partial descendants of slaves, whose African ancestry was mixed with European slave owners, and whose European culture and lighter pigmentation were born of colonial life. At the same time, the term also began to define the cultural and linguistic differences negotiated by the enslaved between black people born in the colony and those imported directly from Africa. It marked shifting and at times unreliable cultural distinctions between light-skinned creoles and dark-skinned creoles, as well as contested yet permeable Europeanized frontiers with the African cultural presence. Third, by the late eighteenth century and the early nineteenth, *creole* became heavily associated with particular language forms. Derived from historically combining European and African languages, culturally different vocabularies and syntactical structures, it emerged as a pragmatic means of communication between masters and slaves. Subsequently it became increasingly associated with the colonized populations and their descendants, often signifying a blurred distinction between Caribbean and European vocabularies, as well as sharp conflicts between African and European speech rhythms and comparative idioms of meaning (Glissant 1989; Dayan 1995; Chaudenson 2001; Enwezor et al. 2003).

What we can see in this historical schema of transculturation, in the movement from cultures to bodies to languages, is a logic of creolization that implicates each in the relations of European colonialities. It involves colonial imaginaries of autonomous, pure Europeanness seeking but failing to avoid contamination by representations from impure non-Europeanness, which in turn try to either assimilate Europeanness or to become extricated from it. There are also at work here antagonisms and accommodations between different claims to linguistic, cultural, and political representation that imbricate the dominant and the subordinate in the same transcultural relations. Conceptually we must also allow for mutual exchanges that influence and mediate the relation between colonizers and colonized, despite the historically European colonizing tendency to deny the dimension of cultural interdependency. Although the European colonial hegemony insisted on remaining dominant, and representative, while declaring the insignificance, marginalization, or nonexistence of a relation with the colonized other, this too is part of the logic of creolization. As is the colonized, non-European other's involvement in redefining and unsettling the dominating culture while articulating alternative cultural forms as a basis of its agency.

Each of these imbrications is as much the logic of creolization as the conventional separation of social forms (e.g., cultures, bodies, languages) into creolized and noncreolized identities. Particularly when read against the modern histories of the Americas, these still-legible colonial gestations remind us that creolization also describes the outcomes of intimate relations and discrepant fusions between formerly geographically disparate cultures; variously European and hegemonic, as well as variously American, African, Asian, and subaltern (cf. Hall 2003a; Lowe 2005). Yet it is from these historically modern conditions of European coloniality that the contemporary Western imaginary of the political has managed to extract itself as if racially unmarked, culturally immaculate, and unquestionably ever present. If creolization emerges from the vocabularies and grammars, sonics and oralities, representations and performativities, ruptured and transformed from the colonialities of European modernity, is it really possible to understand the political outside these entanglements?

Creolized Entanglements

Writing about creolization in the early modern French Caribbean colony, Doris Garraway (2005) cautions against defining it transparently as the result of cultural flows between already ethnically and racially constituted groups. Instead she offers a paradigmatic view of creolization as cultural transformation, "productive of new ways of thinking, knowing and imagining that diverge from colonialist epistemologies and exclusionary identity formations based in fixed notions of race, language and nation" (Garraway 2005, 18). Noticeably this approach does not obscure the relation between creolization and coloniality that is the restive condition of divergences from such dominant discourses and the basis of new trajectories of representation. It also begins to question the apparent self-evident qualities of ethnicity and race in the colonial setting.

Creolization in this sense, as Stuart Hall suggests, constitutes ethnicity and race as "issues of domination and subalterneity, mastery and servitude, control and resistance," because questions of "power, as well as issues of entanglement, are always at stake" (Hall 2003a, 31). This enables us to think about how creolization might be productive of the political, marking its Western status as fraught with the kinds of negotiations, antagonisms, and incommensurabilities that connect modernity's Europe with other parts of the world. Initially taking place through the formation of new colonial economies and polities, it can be seen to emerge from the relations associated with discrepant forms of identification and racial regulation, culturally extending throughout the colony, between the metropole and colony, and within the metropole itself.

At the outset it needs to be emphasized that what primarily entangles the coloniality of creolization with the political is race. It is the constituting of race that produces the antagonistic distinctions and relational identities of European coloniality. Within the frame of creolization, therefore, it is important to understand the anatomy of race as a political institution in terms of colonial lineage rather than biological ancestry. This is what is suggested by Eric Wolf's (1982) observations on the emergence and circulation of the categories "Indian" and "Negro" throughout the Americas from the sixteenth century onward. Wolf suggests these ostensibly racial categories were distinctive because they did not refer to preexisting ethnicities, biological differences, or even cultural self-representations emanating from the marked populations themselves. Rather, in the case of the Indians, the designation referred to the conquered, and in the case of the Negroes it referred to the enslaved.

This recalls the colonial designs of early modern European transatlantic polities and their institutionalization as racial taxonomic states (Stoler 2002). The attributions "Negro" and "Indian" were constructed as raciality in three constitutive and imbricated ways: first, populations associated with enforced and exploitable labor; second, respective subordinate and regulated locations within colonial governance; and third, the imposed debasements of non-European otherness in the same colonial process that sedimented the relationality of race. Against the idea of biologically induced racial categories (emphasizing self-evident differences between Europeans, Indians, and Negroes), this suggests that race could never have been procured as an ontological datum outside the creolizing frame of coloniality. Race was

constituted as a colonial category of governance. Arising from the administration of colonial antagonisms, negotiations, and incommensurabilities,
it inscribed the governmental imprimatur of a hegemonic Europe over a
subaltern non-Europe. Race was the colonial sedimentation of the political. Understanding its profound significance, however, requires coming to
terms with how the imaginaries of liberalism, democracy, and this practice
and conceptualization of race were fused, that is, creolized, in the institutions of, and resistances to, European expansionism, the conquests of the
Americas, and the Atlantic enslavement of Africans (cf. Mignolo 2000b).

Perhaps we should also consider the West as always already creolized by
virtue of its modernity and coloniality. Édouard Glissant (1989) suggests as
much in his account of creolization as the irreducibility of any cross-cultural
phenomena in which the content of, and differences between, ostensibly
distinctive yet now related cultures were not distinguishable in that way
before colonial contact. So, for example, despite the proprietarily cultural
claims for the political meanings of democracy usually advanced as the exclusive (racial) preserve of western Europe and the United States, it might
be argued that even by the late eighteenth century, the emergent modern
discourse of the political was colonially framed and antagonistically cross-
cultural. Its constitutional ideas of citizenship, equality, and national sovereignty were overdetermined by the American (1776) and French (1789)
revolutions against European monarchism and the Haitian (1791) revolution
against European colonialism. This series of revolutions therefore becomes
radically unthinkable outside the consequences of the relations between different cultural entanglements (European, African, American), in each colonial site of revolution, especially their various racial implications for the
representation of democracy and democratic representation. The political
is thus no longer conceivable as a "language of a single origin, but rather a
cross-cultural language" (Glissant 1989, 127).

To claim the creolization of emergent modern democracy implies that
it was shaped and inscribed by the cultural differences and racial entanglements emanating from metropole-colony configurations produced in political relation with each other. Creolization questions the idea of racial exclu-
sivity in the Western origins of the modernity of the political; it also signifies
the illusion of a pure democratic imaginary in the formations of subjects,
discourses, and institutions, since none of these have been "spared the cross-

cultural process" (Glissant 1989, 140). But this does not mean creolization erases the formation of distinct cultural or political entities; rather, it simply affirms the implications of diverse colonial relationality as part of the continual process of modern entity formation (Glissant 1989), including modern democracy. At the same time, it highlights the problem of how to reconcile this with contemporary political theory's approach to conceptualizing the meaning of the political, which has routinely colonized it as unitarily European, American, and Western.

Colonizing the Political

In recent years, a number of primarily European philosophers and political theorists have begun to discuss the meaning of the political and its relation to the question of politics in efforts to recast its meaning in the changing social contortions of Western polities.[2] In the interrogation of both politics and the political as different concepts, new insights about the changing complexity of contemporary Western social and cultural forms are emerging. Some of these suggest that Western societies are undergoing deep processes of depoliticization in which the economics of consumer choices are replacing the politics of ideological alternatives (cf. Touraine 2000). While others argue that social and political theory itself is increasingly succumbing to an antipolitical vision that refuses to acknowledge the antagonistic dimension constitutive of the political (cf. Mouffe 2005, 2).

At stake in these discussions are ideas underpinning the restoration of politics (the ontic) as a socially meaningful, creative, disruptive, liberating activity and the recognition of the political (the ontological) as constituting the institutional field and therefore regulating the horizon of conflictual social relationships (cf. Rancière 1999; Laclau 2005). In some ways, these discussions echo earlier twentieth-century criticisms from Heidegger, Schmitt, Weber, and Arendt of liberalism's reduction of the political to the directives of Western technology and administration. In this tradition of critique, technology dispenses with the affective and collective dimensions of politics, substituting economic calculations and rational individualism for social mobilization and social change. It establishes itself "as an overly quantitative and abstract force that eradicates the concrete and qualitative particularities of human existence" (McCormick 1999, 18). Contemporary critiques of technological solutions to pervasive social questions indict the global ascendancy of neoliberalism and its corresponding evisceration of social institutions and social solidarities. The contention of neoliberalism appears to be that the social good is enhanced through extending the range and frequency of market transactions, and consequently it reinforces the recruitment of social relations to the sovereignty of the market (Harvey 2005), also producing as its effects the meaninglessness of politics, emptying it of beliefs, ideologies, and social values (Agamben 2000).

For political theorists, however, it is not only the hegemony of neoliberalism and its sedimented forms of depoliticization that are in question. At the intersection between these conceptual reformulations of the political and politics are various constructions of the people and democracy. Whether the people are phrased in terms of the "people/multitude" (Hardt and Negri 2000), "democracy/populism" (Laclau 2005), or "arithmetical equality" and "geometrical equality" (Rancière 1999),[3] each construction also invokes democracy as a compromised egalitarian space, bringing critical attention to bear on unremittingly contested relations between *demos* and *ethnos*, homogeneity and heterogeneity, inclusion and exclusion.

Such invocations of the political seem to suggest contemporary discussions are in dialogue with the ghost of Carl Schmitt, the conservative and sometime fascist thinker of the early twentieth century, whose work as a political theorist and philosopher of jurisprudence is attracting increasing attention in critical theory, most notably in the influential recent work of Giorgio Agamben (2000, 1998). Schmitt's *The Concept of the Political*, first published in 1932, has become a significant point of departure for rethinking the idea of the political. It addresses a concern with what is seen as the elimination of decidedly political questions in preoccupations with economic or ethical concerns under the auspices of liberalism in Western political and social theory. For Chantal Mouffe (2005), this "post-political vision" is "fraught with political dangers." It replays deep-seated social antagonisms in a "moral register." Assuming the desirability of consensus and reconciliation, where social alternatives should always be at stake, it usurps and extinguishes the agonism of a pluralist democracy. This ignores "the affective dimension mobilized by collective identifications," while continuing to imagine that such passions are "bound to disappear with the advance of liberalism and the progress of rationality" (Mouffe 2005, 1–6). One of the inspirations for Mouffe's critique of liberalism and its disavowal of the pluralistic predicate of democracy is clearly Schmitt's concept of the political, which embodies and assembles a national, civil, or social distinction between friend and enemy (Schmitt 1932/1996, 26). There is, however, more to the concept of the political that can be read from Schmitt's formulations than has so far been embraced by radical democratic theorists.

Although Schmitt also argues that the "concept of the state presupposes the concept of the political" (1932/1996, 19), this does not mean the political is reducible to the state. Rather, it suggests that the antagonisms constituted by the friend-enemy distinction arise within the horizon of the state, which, given its monopolization of power and representations of national unity, is obliged to regulate and order conflicts within a paradigm of order, coexistence, and pacification. The political in the form of the friend-enemy distinction can occur or irrupt anywhere across the social field, between states, between states and nonstate actors, between nonstate actors. What is at stake in tying the political to the friend-enemy distinction is the "ever present possibility of conflict" (32). This means that people organized as distinctive collectivities, with particular interests, ideals, or ways of life, in their preparedness if necessary to go to war (based on the mutual recognition of friends and enemies), are constitutively opposed to each other's power or representation and institute the political as a relation of antagonism. Unlike the Hobbesian idea of the state of nature characterized by the war of all against all, where the political is associated with the spatial embodiment of the regulatory state, Schmitt emphasizes its ubiquitous relationality. In other words, the political does not comprise a designated "sphere of objects" but is a "public relationship between people" capable of irrupting into the friend-enemy distinction "from any sphere of human life" (Bockenforde 1998, 38).

This does not mean that Schmitt's invocation of war actually has to take place; it is not as in Clausewitz's famous observation that "war is the continuation of politics by other means"; rather, war is the ultimate referral in the enactment of the political, creating a "specifically political behavior" (Schmitt 1932/1996, 34). Nevertheless, when reading Schmitt, the figure of prospective war needs to be understood conceptually as having three tiers, each associated with a distinctive specification of the political, and the second and third tiers involving a potentially greater escalation of antagonism than the one before it. The first is the civil war within European nation-states, the second the national war between European nation-states, and the third the colonial war between European nation-empires and their non-European others. The idea of an escalated third tier is also suggested by Schmitt's (2004) later work in the early 1960s, *The Theory of the Partisan*, which radically reformulates his concept of the political, giving it a less European parochial and more global meaning. It refines the significance of the friend-enemy distinction to include the partisan in civil wars, especially anticolonial wars against the prevailing state power; notably, it is the European template of colonial sovereignty that for Schmitt prevails conceptually in these hegemonic state forms. Consequently we can read the third tier of prospective war as revealing the colonial and racial ambiguities of the political as an institutionalized antagonism in the constitution of Europeanness and non-Europeanness across the globe.

In delineating the history of such antagonisms, we should recall that virtually all European colonies were conquered violently (Pagden 1995), some involving versions of ethnic cleansing (e.g., the United States and Australia), laying the basis for what has been described as "genocidal democracies" (Mann 2005). The first substantial victims of modernity's industrialization of mass warfare and its new military technologies were non-Europeans and nonwhites in the colonies. Not only was the "armaments gap the cutting edge of colonialism," but in its official narratives, "military conquest was given the normative gloss of spreading civilized behavior" (Lawrence 1997). By the late nineteenth century, the so-called lesser races were increasingly deemed in European and American colonial discourses as either objects for extermination or candidates for extinction (Lindqvist 1997; Brantlinger 2003), being conceived neither as political subjects nor as agents of history. During the early decades of the twentieth century, "after numerous colonial wars," most of the territories that made up the Americas, Africa, Asia, and the Pacific were regulated by European empires, resulting in the assimilation of "non-European peoples into a system of law," fundamentally derived from "European thought" and colonial experiences (Anghie 2005, 32–33).

This denouement, though constitutive of a *jus publicum Europaeum* (Schmitt 1932/1996) or a "Eurocentric world order" (Schmitt 2003), is mostly excised from contemporary critical commentary on the meaning of the political. Yet it is remarkable that a serious engagement with a reactionary yet radical thinker like Schmitt does reveal an understanding (albeit in the form of endorsement) of a colonial world that affects and is affected by Western thought. Consider, for example, Schmitt's characterization of the political as "the most intense and extreme antagonism," which occurs almost incidentally in the context of his brief remarks on "the thousand year struggle between Christians and Moslems." He posits this as an exemplary case of the friend-enemy distinction: it explicitly straddles the divide between European and non-European, about which Schmitt is emphatic, observing that never "did it occur to a Christian to surrender rather than defend Europe out of love toward the Saracens or Turks" (1932/1996, 29).

Almost surreptitiously, Schmitt's most penetrating clarification of the "political enemy" arrives in the specter of the nonwhite, non-European, non-Christian, who is "the other, the stranger," and for whom "it is sufficient for his nature that he is in a specifically intense way, existentially something different and alien so that in the extreme case, conflicts with him are possible" (27). What are we to make of this sudden intrusion of the non-European into a European political discourse? Jacques Derrida suggests insightfully that Schmitt's commitment to the idea of defending Europe against its non-European invader announces the limit of the political as previously formulated by him. It is no longer a description of a political war but a "combat with the political at stake, a struggle for politics." The non-European, nonwhite, non-Christian is not simply the political enemy but, in its radical alienness, becomes the enemy of the political itself (Derrida 2005a, 89).

What this entangled distinction between the political enemy and the enemy of the political signifies is the willed inhabitation of Western historical and cultural idioms, which insist on "the tradition of the juridical and political called European" (Derrida 2005a, 89). Consequently foreclosed are other non-European claims to politics, which can only be represented as the potential for antagonism by distinguishing between the friend of the political and the enemy of the political. As we shall see, it is this particular relation of European coloniality that symbolizes modern Western entanglements of creolization. It is particularly evident where the political is implied as coextensive with democracy and the democracy is accountable to the populism in calculating racial majority versus racial minority (cf. Asad 2003).

At the same time, it is also evident in liberalism, the "symbolic framework" of democracy (Mouffe 2005), insofar as liberalism has been colonially "articulated to 'Europeanism,' that is to say, to a defence of the European way of life and ideological values as representing 'civilization'" (Laclau 1979, 179). Anything outside this designation of "civilization" is not only proscribed but pathologized as fanatical or criminal and hence apolitical (cf. Fanon 1963; Sayyid 2003). In these terms, where the non-European, nonwhite other is conceived as the enemy of the political, the creolization of the political also reveals itself in three distinct modes of subject formation as otherness. First, the political assimilation of the nonwhite non-European to Western institutional regulations as racial subjects of governance or what is commonly known as race relations, particularly given their dissociation from international relations (Hesse and Sayyid 2006). Second, their interpellations as postcolonial subjects by the prescriptions and constraints of colorblind liberal-democratic polities symbolically, though not materially, denuded of racism (cf. Brown et al. 2003). Third, their subjectifications as proscribed otherness, those whose activities and representations are seen as questioning the revered meaning of the political, who are consequently barred institutionally and theoretically from the political, not only as people without history but also as people without politics. It is these racial inscriptions of coloniality that contemporary reformulations of the political have neglected to address; despite their apparent seduction by the promise of democracy and insistent protean ideas of the people, they disavow creolization in the Western embodiment of the political.

Embodying the Democratic

The colonial and racial asymmetries of Western democracy are now regularly exorcised by political narratives in which democracy's attainment and inheritance are enunciated as the cultural superiority of Western polities. Democracy often seems to be conflated with the idea of a political regime in which only there is it possible to be "truly human" (Sayyid 2005). In embodying this universal figuration, the discrepancies accruing from its racial forms of dehumanization are overlooked because it is assumed that outside Western humanism, "everything else is either cultural accretion or a deviation from that norm" (Sayyid 2005, 38). Such analyses fail to consider what the political might signify if we resist exculpating the histories of Western democratic nations compromised by their liberal and colonial inscriptions in a series of racial regimes (Mills 1997; Goldberg 2002; Winant 2001).[4] That Western democratic regimes in the postcolonial era remain entangled in racially representing nonwhites either as epigones aspiring toward Western civilization or as recidivists constitutionally estranged from it suggests at the least that the persistence of coloniality inside liberalism needs to be grasped as part of what frames the embodiment of the political. Where this ontology is foreclosed by contemporary political and social theory, its corresponding concealment of an imperial culture in the racially embodied polity valorizes the unmarked routinization of white rule (cf. Said 1993; Tully 1995), disguised or ventriloquized as democracy.

The contemporary resources of Western liberal and radical democratic theory routinely avoid addressing the colonial and racial as constitutive of Western polities. Yet the irony remains that our endeavors can be assisted by thinking of these issues deconstructively through the conservative and fascist Schmitt, whose work on the immersion of the political in a Eurocentric world order is invaluable, though generally overlooked (see Schmitt 2003, 2004). Schmitt was very much aware of the colonial dimensions of the West's institution of the political as liberal democracy, as well as the extent to which it had secured the international legitimacy of its law and politics in a world order based on the unequal relations between European colonizers and colonized non-Europeans. The significance of this is explicitly acknowledged in Schmitt's contention that "a democracy—because inequality always belongs to equality—can exclude one part of those governed without ceasing to be a democracy" (Schmitt 1985). Disrupting the conventions of liberal political theory whose concept of "regime space" is invariably the nation-state,[5] Schmitt's critique of democracy incorporates the colonial territoriality of "nation-empires" (Hesse and Sayyid 2006), singling out for special comment the British Empire, whose proclamations of universal suffrage during the 1930s did not extend to its colonized inhabitants:

> Colonies, protectorates, mandates, interventions, treaties, and similar forms of dependence make it possible today for a democracy to govern a heterogeneous population without making them citizens, making them dependent upon a democratic state and at the same time held apart from the state. That is the political and constitutional meaning of the nice formula "the colonies are foreign in public law, but domestic in international law." (Schmitt 1985, 10)

Traditionally the conceptual influences of the colonial, the racial, and the non-European in Western political theory and theories of international law seem to have been strangely disavowed. Though central to shaping the constitution of canonical Western discourses on sovereignty, freedom, property, and democracy, their formative impact is rarely the subject of intellectual excavation (Springborg 1992; Mehta 1999; Anghie 2005). This leaves a problem for contemporary historical accounts of the political, namely, how to explain the Western performative script of governing non-European and non-white populations through the imbricated rule of liberalism-democracy *and* colonialism-imperialism while formally representing these aspects of unity in governance as if they were constitutionally separate and incommensurable. It illuminates what Bonnie Honig describes as "the displacement of politics in political theory" (1993, 1–17). Occurring where a valorized politics is overly identified with the "juridical, administrative, or regulative tasks of stabilizing moral and political subjects," it therefore eliminates from its institutional vision "dissonance, resistance, conflict or struggle," while the displacement of the disruptive pathologized politics marks it as having no "political genealogy, function or significance."

But this also reveals the "imperfect closure" of the instituted regulative space, exposing its susceptibility to being "haunted," if not "destabilized," by the disruptive politics whose incidence continues to be proscribed by the closures of the political (Honig 1993). Such displacements, however, are not only theoretical and strategic, as Honig implies, but also social and structural. In other words, if there are disruptive (black) politics threatening the liberal institution of the (democratic) political, this can only be because that disruption is constitutive. This is because the political is already "dislocated" (cf. Laclau 1990; Sumic 2004) by the historical formations (colonial and racial) that it tries to conceal through displacement (e.g. race relations, minority communities), but which return as the repressed.

Opening up this theorization of the political requires our thinking together the distinctions between friend and enemy, and between friend of the political and enemy of the political, from the terrain of colonial excess and racial otherness, trying to understand the binary spaces in which the liberal and the colonial, the democratic and the racial, form entangled articulations. From this dialogical perspective, which resembles "border thinking" (Mignolo 2000b), the institution of the political is suffused by two logics of colonial formation conventionally disavowed though not entirely displaced by the democratic embodiment of the political.[6] The first is a Western and Eurocentric logic. This describes not only the potential antagonisms within and between Western states but also between the Eurocentric world order and the world of the others regulated by that order. Hence the political can find its incarnation in the discrepant imbrications of metropole and colony, racial segregation, racial majority and minorities, West and non-West, and the global North-South divide.

Second, the political has a universalist and racialized logic. It is a historical site of antagonisms because of various relations, tensions, and meanings constitutively implicated in the West's holding the liberal-democratic and colonial-imperial worlds both together under racial governance and apart in universalist representations. In effect facing both ways at once, espousing civilization and exploitation, humanitarianism and genocide, democracy and ethnic cleansing (Césaire 1955/1972; Bhabha 1994; Mann 2005). Within these logics of the political, although the figures of the West, Europe, and America are taken to democratically embody it, the historicity of that embodiment cannot be conceived as absent from its colonial inheritances, nor from the enduring entanglements of democracy's unacknowledged creolization.

Creolized Democracy

Despite its absence from Western canonical discussions of the political, democracy, and modernity, particularly in those textual spaces where the American and French revolutions are considered primary conceptual resources, the impact and meaning of the Haitian revolution remains profound. Yet somehow this has eluded the intellectual understanding of many Western political historians and political theorists (Trouillot 1997; Fischer 2004; Scott 2004).

Even if we credit the contemporary convergence between the idea of the political and the meaning of democracy, discussions of democracy seem to invent a historicity internal to the West devoid of racial-colonial constitution and dislocation. Political theorists might be able to agree minimally that democracy involves the management of power relations to minimize domination (Shapiro 2003), which includes "respecting the basic equality of all citizens," particularly "in their orientation toward the common needs and concerns of the people themselves" (Keenan 2003). But the suspicion remains that rhetorically democracy is a metaphor for valorized forms of government deemed only available from the political history of the West (Sayyid 2005).

For example, Claude Lefort in an influential thesis associates the democratic revolution with creating the conditions in which the "locus of power becomes an empty place," where monarchy is no longer seen to *embody* the right of rule and the "corporeality of the social," in that sense, becomes "dissolved" (Lefort 1988). In this context, an empty place of power can be occupied by any*body*, opening up the space for the people, the demos. However, Ernesto Laclau suggests one significant difficulty with this argument is that thinking of "emptiness" as merely a "structural location" rather than also a "type of identity" underestimates the ways in which a regime like modern democracy is sustained by the "symbolic framework of society";[7] for example, liberalism clearly places "symbolic limits" on "who can occupy the place of power." Describing this as a "contingent historical articulation," Laclau rightly argues that not only do forms of democracy exist outside the liberal symbolic framework, but a plurality of symbolic frameworks make the designation of democracy possible (Laclau 2005).

The importance of this also lies in what Laclau does not consider: that the hegemonic logic at work in the institution of liberalism as a symbolic framework for democracy is also constituted in terms of the regime space, the imperial territoriality of sovereignty. For both the American and French revolutions, the regime space was not simply the emerging nation-state but the nation-empire, whether this is understood as the regime space of citizens, slaves, and indigenous peoples, or metropole and colony. The symbolic framework for modern democracy was not liberalism alone; it was indivisibly liberalism-colonialism. This means that conceptually we can only think in terms of the *partial* emptiness of the locus of power insofar as the political subjectivity that becomes signified as the demos is contoured to assume a European colonial-racial embodiment, not the symbolism of the European monarch's body but the white European's (masculine) body, across the nation-empire. Unlike the once-vaunted "mixed regime" (i.e., monarchy, aristocracy, democracy) of classical antiquity (Springborg 2001), the representative regime of Western modernity emerged straddling

lution, more than the American one, provided a model for changes for the free colored and eventually for the slaves in the other colonies" (202). But as we have seen, thinking these revolutions in sequence does not tell the whole early modern democratic story. The Haitian revolution provided a unique model of anticolonialism that interrogated racial inequalities and demonstrated the potency of autonomous black political action, inspiring enslaved and colonized black populations throughout the Americas (Hunt 1988; Sheller 2001). The embryonic democratic discourse was creolized across three distinct political spaces and entangled in the simultaneity of liberal republicanism, colonialist independence, and black (antislavery) emancipation. This may suggest that the *origin* of the democratic imaginary is less important than the shifting, combined, and contested meanings it acquires within the entangled process of its creolization. However, as we recognize the significance of the Haitian revolution to the democratic imaginary, we should be mindful of its importance in constitutionally underwriting and therefore signifying a modern incarnation of black politics under the duress of the Western-formulated political.

Symptom: Black Politics

Perhaps what the Haitian revolution demonstrates more than anything is that modern black politics begins symptomatically with the West's repression of its antislavery and anti-racial-domination movements.[9] Nevertheless, though the symptom as the signifier of what returns as the repressed requires consideration, here it is the constitutive function of the symptom that has the greater importance (Žižek 1989). In relation to the putative universalism of Western democracy, black politics symptomatically redirects our attention to a "certain fissure, an asymmetry, a certain 'pathological' imbalance which belies the universalism" of the West. Now if that pathological imbalance is understood as coloniality-raciality, then black politics as its symptom exposes it as constitutive of Western universalism. Black politics points not merely to the "imperfect realization" of "universal principles" but also to itself as the symptom that bears the subversion of the universal foundation productive of those principles. It is symptomatic of a racial dislocation that is necessary for the liberal democratic West to "achieve its closure, its accomplished form" (Žižek 1989, 21–23). This is why it is important not to see in the idea of symptom some notional black political content hidden by the Western democratic form, but to see it instead as the trace of what gives rise to that democratic form in the first place. The concern is more with the revelation of the political affirmed in the disavowal of its creolization, not simply with what is disavowed as such. It is how disavowal (contrary to its force) is aligned with the creolized genesis of the political, which needs to be explained.

C. L. R James and W. E. B. Du Bois begin to address this alignment during the 1930s when they variously explore the relation between black politics and the political in modernity. For example, James's *A History of Negro Revolt* (1938) provided compelling historical and analytical coherence to the transnational and transcontinental struggles for emancipation undertaken by enslaved and colonized peoples of African descent in the modern world. It marked an attempt to define black politics as a distinctive and constitutive arena of modern politics, not simply describing the enslaved and colonized as conscripted by modernity but also depicting them as its architects (cf. Scott 2004). James elaborated a diasporic formation of black politics:

> The history of the Negro in his relation to European civilization falls into two divisions, the Negro in Africa and the Negro in America and the West Indies. Up to the "eighties" of the last century [i.e., the nineteenth] only one tenth of Africa was in the hands of Europeans. Until that time, therefore it is the attempt of the Negro in the Western World to free himself from his burdens which has significance in western history. In the last quarter of the nineteenth century, European civilization turned again to Africa, this time not for slaves to work the plantations of America, but for actual control of territory and population. Today the position of Africans in Africa is one of the major problems of contemporary politics. An attempt is made here to give some account and analysis of Negro revolts through the centuries; in the days of slavery, in Africa during the last half century, and in America and the West Indies today. (James 1938, 7)

In the analyses that follow, James's displacement of Western representations of incommensurability between the politics of the African Diaspora (which includes Africa) and modern politics, while retaining a focus on the colonial relation between the two, points to how we might further conceptualize the creolization of the political. James defies the Western uncertainties, if not incomprehension, that have traditionally surrounded the politics and aesthetics of the "black radical tradition" (Robinson 1983; Moten 2003), its cosmopolitanism and transnationality (Nwankwo 2005; Hanchard 2006). His intervention asks us to consider its diasporic signs, emphasizing the philosophically repressed Western formations in which they were gestated, namely, colonial entanglements conventionally dissociated from modern politics.

James's own reflections on contemporary politics invoke colonial historicity in the institution of the political. Though not fully appreciating the governmental dimensions constitutive of race, he nevertheless recognizes the distinction between European and non-European as the colonial characterization of modernity. In this sense, we can understand James to be interrogating the construction of the political alongside the disavowal of the colonial-racial institution of modernity, something usually eclipsed by the political and social theory that readily confines the plantation, the colony, and the racially segregated to obscurity or aberration. That this kind of creolized exposition is not considered part of the founding of contemporary political thought, yet once exposed cannot be expelled from it, is precisely the theoretical challenge represented by black politics.

A History of Negro Revolt is quite rightly read as the analytical context for James's more celebrated *Black Jacobins*, also published in the same year. In that juxtaposition we can clearly see the importance to black politics of renarrating the historicity of colonial-racial formations in the contemporary meaning of political. The impulse to a political renarration of history toward the present, because the creolized political present is not represented in the history of the past, recalls what Glissant (1989) describes as the "quarrel with history," and bears a strong family resemblance to "genealogy," understood as a history of a problematic present (Foucault 1977, 1980). Genealogy begins with a questioning of formations in the present that until problematized seem beyond questioning and in the act of questioning appear to have little relation to prevailing historical accounts of the past, obliging a counterhistory of what makes particular formations present as they are. Michel Foucault suggests that if we seek antecedents to this present in terms of its questioning, what is "found at the historical beginning of things is not the inviolable identity of their origin; it is the dissension of other things," in a word, "disparity" (Foucault 1977, 142).

It is precisely the questioning of disparity in the conception of political origins, through renarration, that W. E. B. Du Bois initiated in *Black Reconstruction in America* (1935). There he interrogated the failure of official American political historiography to account for the extent to which the labor of black people in the United States had provided the "founding stone of a new economic system in the nineteenth century" so important for the development of the modern world (Du Bois 1935/1962, 15). His critical historical examinations of the post–Civil War period in the United States demonstrated how black workers played a highly significant role in the reconstruction of the Southern states both economically through labor and politically through participation in administration and government. Although the impact of their role could be depicted as the "widening and strengthening" of "human democracy," as a political phenomenon it was generally erased by white American historians. Their "blind spot" and "propaganda of history" were responsible for the systematic conceptual exclusion of the role and influence of black people from the social construction and reconstruction of the United States (Du Bois 1935/1962).

We should not overlook how readily the theoretical and historical disavowal of black politics begins with erasing the significance of black people's struggles to overcome slavery, particularly in "an attempt to enter democracy" (Du Bois 1935/1962, 715). Du Bois suggests the displacement of black politics from political theory and the institutions of the political is motivated by the desire to avoid any disruption to racialized textual and governmental arrangements that privileged what is normatively attributed to Europeanness and whiteness.

Because the politics of the former slaves presaged an insistence that democracy be transformed by the eradication of racial governance and its expansion through black self-representation, it suggested there was something constitutively problematic with Western liberal democracy. In Du Bois's renarration of the present, the regime of democracy-race and its liberal-colonial symbolic framework is retrieved from erasure, enabling the quarrel with history to be refigured as a genealogy of creolization with black politics represented as its symptom. Here what might be described as a "repressed truth" (Žižek 1989) emerges symptomatically where black politics becomes the truth of the colonial-racial dimensions of social relations. This suggests the political is coterminous with the repressed colonial history of the liberal-democratic West, whose public sphere resists symbolization of the colonial-racial West.

If we interpret the diasporic meaning of black politics through the idea of the symptom, it can be read as a mobilized, subaltern challenge to the Western public sphere because it encounters itself there as radical, racial otherness and is represented as the pathology of destabilization and dislocation. In engaging this meaning of black politics in modernity, it is important to acknowledge how struggles over black representation and the initialization of black agency are deeply inscribed in the symptomatic practices of what I want to call *circumvention*. This emerges as an irruptive opening in a racially disciplinary political space, incarnating the possibilities of revising, opposing, and changing the representational structures of the racial regime. Provisionally it involves a constrained racialized reversal, turning subordination into insubordination; but it also comprises a series of strategic interventions calculated to disrupt the legitimacy of racialized governance.

Circumvention is concerned with creating spaces of interrogation and narration, embodying historically and metaphorically the "slaves' representation and reversal of the master's attempt to transform a human being into a commodity" (Gates 1988, 128). It is the constitutive antislavery logic of black politics. Not only seeking to overturn the hegemony of white normativity in the rule of the political, it restructures the narration of its past in the exculpated present. In effect, circumvention produces an alternative "signifying frame" that provides the creolization of the political with its "symbolic place and meaning" (Žižek 1989). Consequently black politics, in taking this form of working through the symptom, induces the symbolization of "long-forgotten traumatic events" (Žižek 1989), procreated from the contemporary West's colonial ancestry of race. Symptomatically black, it condenses and mobilizes a history and critique of the liberal-democratic public sphere foreclosed by the Western socio-discursive order of its genesis. Black politics is the symptom of creolization repressed in the modern institution and representation of the political as well as its interpretation.

How might social and political theory begin to treat seriously the creolization of the political? One approach would be to consider the historical development of modern Western societies as entangled in the complex construction of three expressive spheres: the public, the private, and the subaltern.[10] The familiar public and private dimensions of the European and American white metropolis are not usually recognized as having formed an expressive unity of civilization in relation to the governance and regulation of the uncivilized non-European colonies or nonwhite populations of a subaltern sphere. Consequently, sparse attention has been devoted to examining how the color line, international relations, and race relations were both produced and reproduced through this creolization of the political. In turning attention this way, we should note that the civility of a pronounced public sphere and a secluded private sphere, despite their apparent gendered opposition, owed its Western hegemonic meaning to a regulatory civilization, resourced by and defined against a subaltern sphere—the slaves, the colonized, the natives, the racially segregated others. Creolization might therefore be described as the incidence of raciality-coloniality in the institution of the political *and* its entanglements with the public-private and subaltern aspects of those Western formations.

Symptomatically, the meaning of black politics is contained in the irruptive challenge to the disavowal of these creolized entanglements. Its immanence as circumvention and therefore agency unravels liberal democratic specifications of the political that deny the colonial-racial entanglements of the people as demos. If the Western polity and Western political theory continue to sustain racial hegemony by erasing evidence of their colonial formations and their indebtedness to white normativity, then creolization cannot but evoke the political.

Notes

My thanks to Tonya Bibbs, Shu-mei Shih, and especially S. Sayyid for extremely helpful commentary.

1 The meaning of the political will be developed throughout the chapter. At this stage, it can be understood as referring to the antagonisms and incommensurabilities revealed in social formations marked by relations of regulation, law, authority, and power. This would include antagonisms and incommensurabilities within and between governments, civil societies, nations, communities, and identities. A fuller version of this argument is developed in Hesse (forthcoming,).

2 A text that is an important recent catalyst in these discussions is Lacoue-Labarthe and Nancy 1997. Their concern with the retreat or withdrawal of the meaning of the political from philosophical discussion also suggested such a potential discussion was particularly constrained. The process through which the political was disap-

pearing was also distorting the residues of its appearance and therefore had to be thought in a new way. Lacoue-Labarthe and Nancy's distinction "politics/the political" is used to rethink the difference in meaning and relation between two things. First, the social interventions of constituted people, politics, and second, what can be established philosophically or theoretically as the principle of sovereignty in the instituted social field, that is, the political.

3 Broadly, the critical focus that unites these thinkers, despite their very different concerns, is on the discrepancies between the social formation of the people and the political representation of the people in democratic discourses, particularly where the former produces a social excess that is politically excluded by the latter.

4 These studies enable us to think of a racial regime as a distinctly modern phenomenon in the mainstream of Western political culture rather than at its extremes. It suggests that the idea of racial stratification and its regulation, particularly in terms of white supremacy or European coloniality, has historically defined the institution of the modern Western state.

5 It is important to recognize that modern political theory has traditionally assumed the figure of Western regimes operating in a neatly divided Westphalian order consisting of territorially bounded, sovereign national monarchies or nation-states, whose political, legal, and economic forms were similarly territorialized. This figure of the Western state completely eclipses the institutionality of their national colonial forms as if the regime-space did not also include, was indeed constituted by, an imperial territoriality. This is what I mean by "nation-empire" (Hesse and Sayyid 2006). For a different conception of regime space that stresses space in terms of democratic and governmental capacities, see Tilly 2006.

6 "Border thinking" emanates from the colonial difference that underwrites dialogic situations in which a "fractured enunciation is enacted from the subaltern perspective as a response to the hegemonic discourse." In this context, it brings together and erases the borders between "knowing about and knowing from" colonial difference (Mignolo 2000b, x, 310).

7 The distinction between (democratic) regimes and their (liberal) symbolic frameworks has been developed by Mouffe (2005).

8 Tilly's (2006, 21, 61) procedural definition of democratization seems applicable here. He defines it as the "extent to which persons subject to the government's authority have broad equal rights to influence governmental affairs and receive protection from arbitrary governmental action." More importantly, he argues that democratization "always occurs in part as a result of contention and always generates extensive contention." It is important to see the critique of Western democracy's representational insulation from its colonial-racial dimensions as part of the contentiousness that also undermines the claims to equality of its racially subordinate subjects who mobilize critiques of its colonial-racist practices.

9 The concept of the symptom used in this section is drawn from Slavoj Žižek's (1989) formulation of Lacanian psychoanalysis.

10 The importance of challenging the Aristotelian inheritance in the liberal political gendered distinction between public and private was an important task of (white) feminist political theory in the democratic expansion of the public sphere and opposition to the private sphere's naturalization of masculine domination (see Shanley and Pateman 1991).

TWO

POSTSLAVERY AND POSTCOLONIAL
REPRESENTATIONS
Comparative Approaches

Anne Donadey

The evolution of any field of study always generates its share of anxiety, especially in an increasingly minoritized context such as the humanities in the higher-education system in the United States. When the civil rights, feminist, and decolonization struggles of the 1950s to 1970s began to infiltrate academic curricula in the 1970s, and when works by writers of color became integrated into the curriculum in the 1990s, this new configuration unsettled the centrality of the "dead white male" canon, resulting in the bitter so-called culture wars of the 1990s. In parallel, the interdisciplinary insights of a generation of postwar, posthumanist French thinkers began to influence various disciplines in the United States in the humanities and even the social sciences in the 1970s, rising to prominence in the 1980s and also generating bitter feuds about the dominance of critical theory and what some felt was an unwarranted "linguistic turn" in the 1990s. As even the most posthumanist writers such as Jacques Derrida began to move toward autobiography and other modes of writing, including a rising concern for ethical issues and social engagement, however, the dominance of Continental theory began to wane in the late 1990s, leading to current pronouncements about the presumed death of theory.

As this book seeks to demonstrate, theory, rather than having died, has shifted into spaces that, because they are not the expected ones of Western postmodernism, render theory perhaps invisible to the eye that is not accustomed to looking for it elsewhere. Theory has become creolized, morphing into a minoritized production of discourse and method, especially in the fields of postcolonial and ethnic studies. What have arguably been the two major sea changes in humanities studies in the United States during the last forty years—the opening of the curriculum to ethnic, women's, postcolonial, and sexuality studies and the prominence of French theory—have now come together in what Lionnet and Shih call the creolization of theory.

The creolization of theory is, of course, not a new phenomenon; Lionnet and other scholars have demonstrated that major postmodern theoretical concepts were anticipated by similar insights in the literary and autobiographical works of African American, American Indian, Latino, and postcolonial writers. Further, researchers have also shown that French theorists were influenced by the decolonization movements of the 1950s and 1960s in general and the Algerian context in particular.[1] In the late 1980s, Barbara Christian opposed what she saw as a hermetic and obfuscating Continental theory to African American dynamic and illuminating "theorizing." This book endeavors to show that theory and theorizing are no longer opposed and have now come together in productive ways. Although, as Shu-mei Shih bemoans, ethnic studies is often dropped from the equation in the debates over the death of theory, this chapter makes a case for the centrality of postcolonial, Francophone, feminist, and ethnic studies in the new configuration of creolized theory. More specifically, I seek to demonstrate the need for carefully theorized comparative explorations of postcolonial and U.S. ethnic literature.[2]

Like several scholars currently developing transnational frameworks, I call for more in-depth engagement between academic fields of study that are fluidly connected but often kept arbitrarily separate due to disciplinary or linguistic constraints. The stakes are high: as Chela Sandoval (2000) argues in *Methodology of the Oppressed*, it is crucial to map out "permeable boundar[ies]" (130), points of intersection and divergence between cognate but separate fields that are all motivated by what she calls "an ethically *democratic imperative*" lest we be faced with constantly having to reinvent the wheel (112). In an ethical, decolonial comparative project, no field of study should be subsumed under another. Each field can valuably learn from the other, while at the same time maintaining its own specificity, using a model of overlapping frameworks rather than one of assimilation. Ella Shohat makes a similar call for more intersections between area studies and transnational feminist studies. Like Sandoval, Shohat warns that "we should especially pay attention to the ways universities erect disciplinary borders and maintain conceptual boundaries that continue to reproduce the discursive, overlapping quarantine of interconnected fields of inquiry" (2002, 69). Similarly, in their anthology *Minor Transnationalism*, Lionnet and Shih (2005) develop productive intersections between ethnic studies and area studies, including postcolonial, Francophone, and feminist issues. In particular, they seek to "examine the relationships among different margins" (2) and focus on "minor-to-minor networks" (8).

I offer an example of such a situated project by bringing to light parallels between African American and postcolonial Algerian fictional working through of history by women writers. This chapter will demonstrate clear similarities of concern between Octavia E. Butler's *Kindred* and Assia Djebar's *La femme sans sépulture* (The Unburied Woman). I address various ways in which Butler and Djebar confront the contemporary legacy of traumatic national pasts. *Kindred* (1979) uses the time-travel device to send its narrator, Dana Franklin, a modern-day African American woman, back to the antebellum South. Butler puts Dana in the impossible quandary of having to save the life of Rufus Weylin, the white slaveholder who will grow up to rape and impregnate Alice Greenwood, Dana's female ancestor, to ensure Dana's very existence in the present. In *La femme sans sépulture* (2002), Djebar rewrites the life of real-life *mujahida* (freedom fighter) Zoulikha Oudai, who was a central figure of anticolonial resistance in Djebar's region during the Algerian war of liberation in the mid-1950s. Zoulikha was tortured and killed by the French, and her body was never recovered. Although the topics and time frames of both books are clearly very different, both stage a causal relationship between the events of the past and their influence on the present. In the first part of this chapter, I present theoretical, historical, and literary grounds for this comparative project. I then focus on Butler's and Djebar's fictional rewritings of history in the last section.

I should make it clear that I am not trying to appropriate *Kindred* to the postcolonial or *La femme sans sépulture* to a U.S. corpus. Rather, I am interested in highlighting the strong parallels and intersections between African American and postcolonial literatures that are worth investigating in more detail. In responding to the current push toward internationalizing the academic curriculum, we must be careful not to circumvent ethnic studies frameworks and should avoid imposing postcolonial or transnational approaches onto literature written by people of color in the United States. The comparison I wish to pursue between Djebar's and Butler's works inscribes itself explicitly against such attempts to bypass serious inquiry into racial issues in the United States today. As Mae Henderson notes in her cautionary words about black cultural studies, it is crucial not to let conceptual frameworks "not grounded in African American history and culture" occlude the important (and often similar) work previously done in fields such as African American studies (1996, 63). It is important that postcolonial or transnational studies not become the new overarching theoretical frameworks subsuming and appropriating work done in African American studies, thus paradoxically recolonizing it (see M. Henderson 1996, 63; Lubiano 1996, 76; Mostern 2000; DuCille 1994; Shohat 1998, 41–42).

In particular, it is clear that black feminist and—to use Sandoval's formulation, which is more precise than "feminist of color"—"U.S. Third World feminist" theorizations of intersectional perspectives articulating the interlocking nature of race, gender, class, and other factors have had a major influence on postcolonial and Francophone studies (see D. King 1988; V. Smith 1998; Crenshaw 1989; McClintock 1995; Sharpe 2003; Trinh 1989; Lionnet 1989). The paradigm shift that intersectional perspectives initiated in feminist and ethnic studies (away from a monist model based on gender or race to a multiple model taking the articulations of various factors into account) opened the way for postcolonial and Francophone scholars to explore the intersections of gender, colonialism, and race. For Valerie Smith, "black feminism provides strategies of reading simultaneity" (1998, xv). Such reading strategies are as useful in a postcolonial context as they are in a postslavery one. Rather than seeking to conflate postcolonial and U.S. ethnic frameworks, a process that Kalpana Seshadri-Crooks rightly criticizes (2000, 4–5), I agree with Shu-mei Shih that "postcolonial studies is more politically productive for the local terrain when *in dialogue with* ethnic studies" (2004, 29n9; italics mine). In this chapter, I provide an example of such a dialogue in comparative ethnic and postcolonial studies, a dialogue that was ushered in and made possible by the insights of black feminists and U.S. Third World feminists.[3]

It is relatively unproblematic to highlight parallels and intersections between ethnic literature in the United States and postcolonial studies when focusing on African American, sub-Saharan African, and Caribbean literature given the existence of the black Atlantic as a historical reality and a theorized concept referring to the circulation of bodies, intellectuals, and ideas between Africa, the Caribbean, the United States, and Europe. While Paul Gilroy primarily focused his attention on a male, modernist, Anglophone corpus, there is clearly room to expand his generative concept to include postcolonial, Francophone, female black Atlantic writers. It should be remembered that a few years before Gilroy, Vèvè Clark had proposed just such a broad framework of "diaspora literacy" for understanding contemporary Francophone female Caribbean literature. It may seem more of a challenge to compare African American and Algerian literature. Although most Algerians are not black, I argue that Algeria does have a certain intellectual and political connection to the black Atlantic, if only because of the influence of the decolonization theorist Frantz Fanon. Born in the French Caribbean colony of Martinique, Fanon studied in France, participated in the Algerian war of liberation, and died in the United States. His theoretical writings, which were informed by his transnational experiences in the Caribbean, France, and Algeria, were highly influential in the 1970s among the Black Panthers. As one of the major precursors of the field of postcolonial studies and a theorist of racism, Fanon is therefore a fitting figure to conjure up at the beginning of a comparison between the works of an African American and an Algerian writer.

Other theoretical connections can be made. Ashraf Rushdy, writing about the African American literary tradition, and I, writing about women writers from Algeria, both independently argued that one of the characteristics of African American and of postcolonial literature, respectively, is their palimpsestic nature, which we characterized slightly differently. Rushdy defined "palimpsest narratives" as fiction in which a contemporary African American character "is forced to adopt a bitemporal perspective that shows the continuity and discontinuities from the period of slavery" (2001, 5). In these narratives, "the present is always written against a background where the past is erased but still legible" (8), and it is represented through family relationships. Whereas African American palimpsest narratives return to the specific site of trauma that was the experience of slavery (99), postcolonial writers often return to their own sites of trauma, which usually have to do with the periods of colonization, decolonization, or postindependence. Inspired by Lionnet's redefinitions of postcolonial *métissage* in *Autobiographical Voices*, I argued in *Recasting Postcolonialism* that postcolonial writers feel the necessity of rewriting the past because the dominant versions of history have left gaps and misrepresentations. These writers thus overwrite the palimpsest of historiography, filling out its blanks and responding to its misrepresentations through fiction. Rushdy used Butler's *Kindred* as one of the texts proving the existence of African American palimpsest narratives. One of the authors on whose works I based my understanding of postcolonial rewritings of the historical palimpsest is Assia Djebar. To demonstrate some of the parallels between African American and postcolonial use of the palimpsest narrative, I provide a comparative analysis of Butler's *Kindred* and Djebar's *La femme sans sépulture*.

Before doing so, I highlight the historical parallels between the two contexts. Blacks were enslaved in many parts of what was to become the United States for almost 250 years, between 1619 and 1865. Algerians were colonized by the French for over 130 years, between 1830 and 1962. In both cases, their living conditions were atrocious and their status second-class; it took a war to end both slavery and colonization. These wars were experienced as civil wars that have left marks on the consciousness of black and white American, French, and Algerian people today (Stora 1991; Donadey 2001, 1–18). Benjamin Stora, a historian of the Algerian war, offers intriguing parallels between colonial Algeria and the antebellum South, thus providing historical support for this comparison. Stora demonstrates that French colonials in Algeria had explicitly developed a southern, Confederate imaginary (1999, 21; 2003, 8). Although it appears that for both the French colonials and Stora himself there is a certain melding of antebellum South (the plantation system, the Algerian war seen in parallel to the Civil War) and U.S. frontier ideology (Manifest Destiny, French colonists as pioneers conquering a new frontier), Stora convincingly argues that the colonial imaginary of French Algeria did reflect a sense of identification with the slaveholding South and the Native-destroying West (1999, 14–27; 2003, 8–11). It makes sense, then, that postcolonial reworkings of a historical past in Algeria would evince parallels with postslavery reworkings of a historical past in the United States, as they are responding to intersecting discourses and practices.

Since the Civil Rights Act of 1964 and the Voting Rights Act of 1965 changed the country from a "racial dictatorship" into a racial "hegemony," the United States has sought to present itself as a "racial democracy" (Omi and Winant 1994, 65–69). One of the consequences of this has been that dominant discourses constantly seek to erase both the country's violent past and the continuing impact of that past on the present. As a corrective, African American writers strive to remember a history of slavery that is never fully fleshed out in dominant versions of the American[4] past. There is also a long history of French amnesia with respect to its colonial past in general and to the Algerian war of liberation in particular (Stora 1991; Donadey 2001, 1–18). Although successive Algerian governments set up the war of liberation from the French as the nation's foundational event, that official history has also silenced certain aspects of the war, especially with respect to the exact nature of the participation of women. Because of the gaps and silences of official history (whether U.S., French, or Algerian), writers turn to fiction as a privileged way to make what Adrienne Rich calls "educated guesses" about that violent past, putting flesh on the skeleton of history (1986, 148; see also Lionnet 1989, 4–5). Writers seek to redress the gaps and misrepresentations of dominant history through fiction because fiction, more than history, is able to do what Djebar (1978) has called "rekindl[ing] the vividness of the past" so that it will cease to be a ghostly presence haunting the nation's collective consciousness (Morrison 1989, 11).

Since the 1970s, we have also witnessed a rethinking of the status of history and narrative, which has highlighted the ideological underpinnings of dominant history and blurred the strict line between history and fiction (White 1973). Although this rethinking is often attributed to the ascendancy of a postmodern paradigm, the anticolonial, civil rights, and feminist movements of the 1950s to the 1970s were instrumental in criticizing the role that history was being made to play as "advertisement for the state" (Janet Koenig, quoted in Rich 1986, 141). This rethinking of the status of history as narrative legitimated the project of rewriting history through fiction, especially when dominant history was clearly partial and in need of correction. This has been equally true in the U.S. and the Algerian contexts, and *Kindred* and *La femme sans sépulture* are excellent examples of the use of fiction to rewrite the blanks of history.

Both texts fit the description of historiographic metafiction proposed by Linda Hutcheon (1988, 113–18; see Mitchell 2002, 11). Going beyond the mimetic, realist aspect of the traditional novel, both works problematize the question of representation and truth from the standpoint of marginalized groups. Both texts "install and then blur the line between fiction and history"

(Hutcheon 1988, 113). *La femme sans sépulture* opens up questions about the status of fictional biography as an intervention into historiographic debates. In the "Avertissement" (Note to the Reader), Djebar explicitly problematizes the question of representation and truth: her book is a *roman* (novel) that includes "fidélité historique" (historical accuracy) and "approche documentaire" (a documentary approach) as well as the work of "imagination." Such an appeal to "liberté romanesque" (novelistic freedom) serves to enhance an inner "vérité" (truth) about Zoulikha (9).[5] Similarly, what Toni Morrison says about her own works also applies to Butler's *Kindred*: it is "a kind of literary archeology" in which only through "the imaginative act" may one "yield up a kind of a truth"; such an "imaginative act is bound up with memory" (Morrison 1990, 302, 305). A few years before Hutcheon proposed her definition of historiographic metafiction, Sandra Govan had already begun to highlight the ways in which *Kindred* "renovate[d] the historical novel" (1986, 79) in terms similar to Hutcheon's.[6] Both *Kindred* and *La femme sans sépulture* function as what Pierre Nora calls *lieux de mémoire* (realms of memory) and what Toni Morrison calls "sites of memory" (see Mitchell 2002, 17). The critic Clarisse Zimra similarly points out that Morrison and Djebar (and I would add Butler) take on "the ethical imperative of inventing a past that would otherwise disappear" (Zimra 2003, 60).

There are differences as well as similarities between Butler and Djebar. Butler was based in the Los Angeles area for most of her life and wrote in her native language, English. Djebar, born and raised in Algeria, lived most of her adult life between Algeria and France. She has been living in the United States since the mid-1990s and is currently a professor at New York University. She writes in a French that is inflected by the flow, rhythms, and vocabulary of Arabic (Donadey 2000a). Both are well-known writers, but in quite different genres. Butler began writing in the 1970s and is primarily known for her stunning science fiction novels and short stories. *Kindred* is her only book not to fit in that category, although her last few works may be seen as more futuristic dystopia than science fiction. Djebar, Algeria's best-known woman writer, has been publishing since the late 1950s, during the decolonization of her country from the French. She is about ten years older than Butler. Her intricate novels and short stories focus on rewriting a history of struggle against colonization and women's oppression. Similarly, all of Butler's works, especially *Kindred*, are clearly about rewriting African

American history (Govan 1986, 79). Her inspiration for futuristic tales such as the Xenogenesis trilogy has its roots in the slavery past. Neither author has shied from the label feminist, and both stage the necessity as well as the extreme difficulty of female solidarity in oppressive situations.

Both authors are known for their series of texts: the Patternist, Xenogenesis, and Parable series for Butler; the Algerian Quartet for Djebar. Both have garnered high critical praise and literary prizes for their oeuvres, which are taught in university classes and are the subjects of numerous academic studies. Djebar has recently received the most prestigious honor bestowed on intellectuals writing in French, being elected to the Académie Française (a body of illustrious writers) in June 2005. Although Djebar's book was published twenty-three years after Butler's, Djebar began writing about Zoulikha Oudai's story in the early 1980s and dedicated her feature film *La nouba des femmes du Mont Chenoua* (1978) in part to her. Both books focus on a female protagonist, although male figures are clearly more important in *Kindred* than in *La femme sans sépulture* (a consistent feature of African American womanist perspectives). Both address themselves to a multiple audience (black and white Americans in the case of Butler, Algerian and French people in the case of Djebar). Finally, it should be mentioned that Butler has never addressed the Algerian situation, and Djebar has never attended to the U.S. context. Butler actually seemed to be quite unaware of the problems with her glorification of space colonialism as a new kind of Manifest Destiny (which is especially evident in the Parable series, but which Thelma Shinn Richard does not discuss in her essay on Butler's postcolonial perspective). Likewise, Djebar does not make a place for black women in her vision of transnational, transethnic female solidarity (Donadey 2001, 108).

Kindred is about the centrality of slavery in American history and its contemporary consequences (140); in other words, its main concern is the influence of the past on the present. The novel can be fruitfully read as a national allegory, and Dana and her white husband Kevin as representative Americans.[7] This interpretation is supported by the symbolism of several dates in the text, the most obvious of which is July 4, 1976, the last time Dana is sent back to the past (*Kindred*, 243; Crossley 1988, xix). Lest we miss it, the symbolism of the date is highlighted several times (*Kindred*, 64, 243; see Rushdy 2001, 108; Kubitschek 1991, 28). Other dates in the narrative serve as more subtle reminders of the history of the United States. For example, the time of

Dana's third travel to the past is 1819, another bicentennial that is much less remembered than that of the founding of the nation. Many history books note that in 1619, the first enslaved Africans were brought to Jamestown, Virginia (we are rarely reminded that Africans landed in Virginia at least a year before the Pilgrims at Plymouth Rock). The fact that white Americans need to face the beginning of this history too is represented by the fact that the only time in the narrative that Kevin accompanies Dana to the past is on that very date. Finally, Dana returns to the present for the penultimate time on June 19, 1976 (*Kindred*, 243). June 19 may be a reference to Juneteenth, the celebration of the end of slavery. This celebration, which began in Texas on June 19, 1865, is considered to be African American Emancipation Day.[8] In addition, that Dana and Kevin's last name is Franklin is relevant to an interpretation of *Kindred* as national allegory, since Benjamin Franklin was part of the nation's foundation (Kubitschek 1991, 42), as well as of its history of slavery. Once the owner of two slaves, whom he eventually freed, Franklin favored the education of former slaves and signed a petition to Congress calling for the abolition of slavery in 1790.[9]

One may also ask why Butler would choose California and Maryland as the two main sites for her narrative. California only became a U.S. state in 1850 and was not a slave state. As for Maryland, many Americans now think of it as part of the North or the East (depending on their geographic location), rather than as a former slave state. One allegorical interpretation is that all Americans, from California to Maryland, coast to coast, black and white, need to revisit the past to move forward into the future. By choosing states that cannot easily be identified today as North-Yankee or South-Rebel, Butler is intimating that the entire country is implicated in the need to confront the history of slavery. In particular, racism should not just be seen as something other regions can easily eschew responsibility for by blaming it only on the Deep South (Mitchell 2002, 45).[10]

As representative Americans, Dana and Kevin are unprepared for an encounter with the harshness of their history. When they are finally reunited in the past after Kevin has been marooned there for five years, they hardly recognize each other at first because the wounds and marks of history have inscribed themselves on both of their bodies, especially on Dana's (Paulin 1997, 189). Interpreted in light of the national allegory, these multiple wounds imply that this necessary and unavoidable return to the past will be painful for both blacks and whites, although more so for blacks, and that whites will need to metaphorically return to the past for a longer period to understand what was done and the present consequences. Butler is intimating that all Americans must account for a history of slavery if we are to create a viable future for this country, and that although inevitable, this process will not be painless (Kubitschek 1991, 41–42; Mitchell 2002, 59). Dana's loss of an arm and Kevin's and Dana's various scars, physical and psychic, symbolize the parts of themselves they left in the past. As Lisa Long says in almost Djebarian language, "the loss of Dana's arm reflects the intransigence of history" (2002, 474). Dana and Kevin's marriage represents the intertwined histories and symbiotic relationship between blacks and whites in the United States. As Angelyn Mitchell (2002) puts it, Dana and Kevin's "interracial relationship can be read as a metaphor for how America may be healed" (60); Butler "emphasizes the necessity of integrated collective engagement and coalition building across the color line as a way of solving some of our contemporary race problems" (62).[11]

Neither book is neatly packaged with an easy closure. At the end of *Kindred*, not all of our (or Dana's) questions are answered (Crossley 1988, xi). Readers and characters alike are left wondering about a number of things, such as what exactly happened in the past to Kevin and to some of the enslaved characters, and what will happen to Dana and Kevin's relationship. These gaps and silences reflect the fact that part of the history is irretrievable. Similarly, Djebar is not seeking to replace the silences of history with a univocal commemoration of women's participation in the war of independence. She avoids such fixed monumentalization in *La femme sans sépulture* through the use of a sometimes destabilizing polyphony of women's voices. Whereas in *Kindred* it is the interracial couple that carries the weight of the national allegory, in *La femme sans sépulture* it is the relationships among women that are privileged in the retelling of the construction of the Algerian nation and its projection into the future; however, the couple does have its importance in Djebar's narrative as well, as does female solidarity in Butler's.

Djebar's narrative focuses on the ghostly presence-absence of the disappeared freedom fighter Zoulikha, whose disembodied voice paradoxically highlights her own embodiment and the geography of her body. As Butler integrates time travel in her novel, making Dana appear like an ageless ghost to the nineteenth-century characters in whose time she mysteriously appears from time to time (*Kindred*, 23–24, 30, 130, 133), so Djebar includes the dead woman's first-person monologues in a decidedly antirealist move. Djebar is interested in Zoulikha for many reasons besides her being a freedom fighter and war martyr: she was "la première fille musulmane diplômée de la région" (the first Muslim girl with a school degree in the region) in 1930 (*La femme*, 18, also 166), chose the men she wanted to marry (18, 138–39), asked for a divorce twice (19–20, 140–43), moved to the city by herself to work (169), had a female relative raise her daughter (169), and was unique in not wearing a veil or a headscarf as a young woman in the city (19). She was not afraid to call colonists, female (22–23) and male (19–20), on their racism or to criticize the injustices of the colonial system in front of French people, who nicknamed her "l'anarchiste" (the anarchist) (19). She donned the veil again later on (21, 70, 173) and died a martyr at forty-two (213). That Zoulikha was able to make many choices that were not normally accepted for women in the early twentieth century makes her the perfect Djebarian heroine (Regaïeg 2004, 77). As Djebar has said in an interview, "A travers Zoulikha, ses vies multiples . . . tous les schémas classiques sont bouleversés" (Zoulikha and her many lives . . . deeply disrupt all the usual patterns) (Armel 2002, 102). The insistence on Zoulikha's headstrongness from an early age establishes a trajectory connecting her earlier protofeminism to her later nationalist engagement (*La femme* 74, 89). In a contemporary postcolonial context in which feminism is often presented as inimical to nationalism, Maghrebian authors like Djebar and Fatima Mernissi have been clear about drawing out the articulations between the two (Donadey 2000b). Zoulikha's nationalist engagement is woman centered, since it involves a network of city women helping the *mujahidin*. Through the figure of Zoulikha, Djebar rewrites Algerian historiography by giving a positive place to feminism alongside nationalism.

The text draws out the integral parallels between feminist and nationalist engagement in Zoulikha's third monologue (166–71). It details Zoulikha's pleasure at walking outdoors wearing French clothing (167–68, 171) and being "la Mauresque qui travaillait dehors et qui sortait sans voile!" (the Moorish woman who worked outside the home and went out unveiled) (170). In contrast, people in her village had been shocked and commented that she was "déguisée" (in disguise) (i.e., according to them, it was not natural for her to be dressed in European clothing [166–69]). In an inversion of this naturalization of the veil for Algerian women, Zoulikha did not feel that wearing European clothing was wearing a disguise. Instead, it is her war militant garb (that of a traditional peasant woman) that is repeatedly described as being a disguise (74, 116, 118, 148, 154–55, 165, 195).[12] Similarly, in *Kindred*, Dana's normal twentieth-century attire, pants, causes her to be repeatedly read as a man in the nineteenth century.

Zoulikha's donning the veil again is explained in her third monologue, which brings up echoes of Fanon's comments about the "dynamisme historique du voile" (historical dynamism of the veil) (47). Zoulikha's relationship with her third husband was based on equality, communication, and respect, and because of that, she no longer felt that she must transgress (173). Unlike everyone else around her, he was able to see her beyond multiple overdeterminations: "je ne lui paraissais ni déguisée, ni enfermée, ni maquillée" (I did not appear to him as being disguised, enclosed, or made-up) (173). At that point, the veil loses its overdetermination, which explains why Zoulikha is able to wear it for the first time (Bacholle-Boskovic 2003, 83). Once again, she makes the choice herself. The description of her relationship with her husband (173–74) is perhaps the most positive description of male-female relationships ever written by Djebar (or in Maghrebian fiction generally). Both spouses are united by nationalist fervor as well as a deep, abiding love for each other (173–74). In *La femme sans sépulture*, Djebar foregrounds a representative, respected Algerian woman whose feminist and nationalist engagement went hand in hand, and who was able to negotiate and partially transcend both Algerian and Western overdeterminations of the veil.

Toni Morrison's concept of "rememory," as described by Rushdy, is helpful to understand Zoulikha's presence-absence in the streets and memories of her city: "Individual experiences of suffering continue to exist at the site where the suffering happened" (Rushdy 2001, 6). The narrator-author, as well as Zoulikha's daughters Hania and Mina, looks for traces of Zoulikha's presence in the landscape (*La femme*, 58–60, 86). *La femme sans sépulture* is an answer to Hania's repeated question, "Où trouver le corps de ma mère?" (Where shall I find my mother's body?) (60). Zoulikha's life is evoked in fragmentary ways through the testimony of several generations of women, as her own voice and memory paradoxically crisscross the city, years after her death. This is not a seamless narrative, not a seamless memory; it is a broken memory, but one that persists. It is not a matter of re-creating a totalizing, mythologizing narrative of Zoulikha the heroine but a matter of rewriting her story by paying attention to the parts of the story that remain alive in others' memories.

Several of the testifying women express a fear of speaking too easily about Zoulikha in a way that would congeal her memory instead of keeping it alive. There are two modes of speaking about the past, then, and one of them paradoxically silences the past further. Such is the official, commemorative approach, which would serve only to "se débarrasser ainsi de son souvenir" (rid ourselves of her memory) (51), that is, to bury dead heroes (84, 210). This approach would make the heroine into a "statue" (207). Djebar is criticizing the way in which official Algerian commemoration served to fix memory into a rigid interpretation of the past, which Zoulikha and the other narrators in the novel reject (see Norindr 1999). The other mode of remembering the past is one that opens a space for the expression of emotions connected to the past (*La femme*, 48–49) and therefore keeps Zoulikha's memory alive by allowing those who loved her to convey in what ways she is still alive for them (84). This second stance is one that approaches its subject with "respect" (51). In such an approach to retelling history, one must relive the past by becoming immersed in it (74). This process is staged narratively in *Kindred*. Rememory is an active process of reconstitution that involves passing on the story in such a way that it becomes real, embodied, lived through the storyteller's mediation (*La femme* 148, 151–52).

It is not a question of giving Zoulikha a proper burial, and Djebar should not be seen as a modern-day Antigone (this in spite of the many references to theater and tragedy in general, and echoes of *Antigone* in particular, in *La femme sans sépulture*).[13] Indeed, Zoulikha's voice, viewing burial as a betrayal, expresses regrets that a worshiping *mujahid* buried her body (210–11). This may be read allegorically as a way of highlighting the potential for burying the past involved in creating memorials. As Michael O'Riley rightly notes, Djebar is criticizing "the obsession of recuperation" and "the possessive act of burial that engenders claims to History and its ghosts" (O'Riley 2004, 75, 84n14). What is at stake for Djebar is the imperative of letting voices circulate rather than burying them. Zoulikha's engagement in the mountains is described by her voice in terms of a "renaissance" (rebirth)

(*La femme*, 176) due to being outside, free, a common feminist trope in Djebar's work (199). Until the bitter end, Zoulikha remains a figure in motion, which for Djebar expresses liberation. Ali's song at the end of Djebar's film *La nouba*, which briefly mentioned Zoulikha's life and death, already made this clear: "Zoulikha vivante s'asseoit parmi les monts / Elle bondit comme les chevaux et les coursiers" (Zoulikha still lives in the mountains / she leaps like a mare). In Djebar's rewriting, Zoulikha's voice will forever circulate outside as a troublesome witness.

Ultimately, both novels can be read as anamnesis, a collective remembering of the past across generations to suggest a possible collective healing and national reconciliation that must pass through the repressed of culture and history in all of its violence.[14] Both narratives reflect back on an important anniversary, the bicentennial of the United States and the fortieth anniversary of the end of the Algerian war, respectively (Mitchell 2002, 44; Horváth 2004, 39). *Kindred* brilliantly shows not only how the past impacts the present in myriad ways but also how the future can be molded and reoriented through our painful engagement with the past (Rushdy 2001, 7; Mitchell 2002, 17, 43–44, 59). In a very real sense, then, what will happen to Dana and Kevin's relationship in the future is up to us, residents in the United States today, no matter how closely entangled with the history of slavery we feel we are.[15]

Postcolonial and postslavery anamnesis differs somewhat from its Platonic counterpart. For Plato, anamnesis is a maieutic process of recalling forgotten knowledge through which the individual soul becomes whole again. Postcolonial and ethnic writers in the United States focus on anamnesis as a process that is collective rather than individual and always yields fragmentary rather than complete knowledge (Lionnet 1989, 118). The healing process involved in postcolonial and postslavery anamnesis always includes a lack of closure and a lingering sense of loss, symbolized in *Kindred* by Dana's loss of an arm. Djebar's metaphor for this process of anamnesis in *La femme* is an ancient mosaic representing Ulysses and the sirens, which are figured as three "femmes-oiseaux" (bird women) ready to take flight (106). The three bird women are doubled in the narrative, which includes the generation of the mothers (Zoulikha, Lla Lbia, Zohra) and that of the daughters (the narrator-author, Hania, Mina). The mosaic is symbolic of the desire of contemporary women to fly away, like Zoulikha (108–9). Later,

Djebar imagines that "Zoulikha l'héroïne flotte inexorablement, comme un oiseau aux larges ailes transparentes et diaprées, dans la mémoire de chaque femme d'ici. . . . La mémoire de Césarée, déployée en mosaïques: couleurs pâlies, mais présence ineffacée, même si nous la ressortons brisée, émiettée, de chacune de nos ruines" (Zoulikha the heroine inexorably hovers over the memory of each woman here, like a bird with outstretched, translucent and shimmering wings. . . . The memory of Césarée deploys itself as a mosaic with fading colors but indelible presence, even though we extract it from each of our ruins in shattered, crumbling form) (128–29). Zoulikha's voice is compared to the mermaids' song and the listening narrator to Ulysses (214). As Michael O'Riley notes, "The mosaic constitutes a *mise en abyme* of the text and of the author-narrator's relationship to its depiction of colonial history" (2004, 78). The form of Djebar's narrative is akin to a mosaic; each voice is like a piece of ceramic that reconstitutes a portion of the story of Zoulikha. In the mosaic as in the text, "L'une des trois femmes-oiseaux," like Zoulikha, "a un corps à demi-effacé. Mais les couleurs, elles, persistent" (One of the three bird women's body is half erased. But in spite of this, the colors remain) (108–9; see also O'Riley 2004, 78–80). As the women's voices come together, they provide a historical fresco, but parts of it remain under erasure. That Zoulikha is explicitly compared to Jesus several times in the narrative, and that parallels are made between her body's disappearance and Jesus's resurrection, also draw on the religious meaning of anamnesis: the collective recollection of Jesus's incarnation, life, death, and resurrection (16, 63, 66, 202–3, 215; see also Bacholle-Boskovic 2003, 87–88). Since Jesus is considered a prophet in Islam, Zoulikha is thus figured as a new, female prophet. The collective telling and retelling of events in her life, martyr-dom, and death become a liturgical event providing release and healing, as is made clear in chapter 9 (150–57).

In this context of feminist rewriting, the reason why Djebar chooses to use both names for her city, Césarée and Cherchell, acquires metaphorical meaning: for a Francophone reader, the name Césarée recalls the word for C-section, *césarienne*, and the name Cherchell may recall the word *chercher* (to look for, to search). Hania's condition as a lethargic woman who no longer has her period and is described as being "habitée" (inhabited) could be interpreted to mean that Hania is metaphorically pregnant with her mother (62, 85). The narrator may then be seen as a delivering midwife. This interpretation is supported by the use of the metaphor "O langes du souvenir!" (Oh, to be wrapped in the swaddling clothes of memory!) to refer to the process by which Hania remembers her mother's story for the narrator (88). As opposed to a commemoration that would be a deathly shroud covering Zoulikha, here anamnesis is a life-affirming process in which memory is alive (swaddling clothes). This version of anamnesis as *maieusis* returns us to the Socratic method and to Platonic anamnesis (see Lionnet 1989, 87).[16] A similar process is at work in *Kindred*, since Dana must ensure the birth of her ancestor Hagar, serving as her metaphorical midwife by watching over Hagar's mother Alice and father Rufus until Hagar is born. After Alice is raped by Rufus, escapes with her husband Isaac, and is brought back half-dead to the Weylin plantation as Rufus's newly purchased slave, she reverts to childhood for a time, both physically and mentally, and Dana has to care for her as she would a child. The roles are reversed: the descendant acts as her ancestor's mother and helps her regain her past knowledge and functions (153–58). Djebar and Butler thus present us with a complex feminist "reappropriation of the best form of ancient Socratic *maieusis*" and a postcolonial or postslavery version of Platonic anamnesis (Lionnet 1989, 196).[17]

For the critic Dominique Fisher, anamnesis involves "donner corps dans l'écrit aux refoulés de l'histoire, aux voix sans écriture" (bodying forth the repressed of history and unwritten voices through writing) in a writing that "devient apte à saisir le mouvement des corps" (becomes able to grasp the movement of bodies), a definition that is fully relevant to both texts under study (Fisher 2003, 118, 121). It is only at the end of *La femme sans sépulture* that Djebar can bring up the more recent postcolonial violence in Algeria, which she compares to that of the Algerian war (218) and which she refuses to forget (219). The rememory of Zoulikha is linked to that of "d'autres Zoulikha" (other Zoulikhas), anonymous women who were killed during the recent violence, whose memories Djebar feels the need to honor as well (219). Finally, she ends with an homage to her father, buried in that same city of Césarée (220). The anamnesis of Zoulikha opens up onto a national anamnesis for all the people (especially women) who died violently in Algeria, as well as onto a personal anamnesis for the beloved father, the one who once took young Djebar toward the French language, holding her hand (Djebar 1985, 11). The book's circular structure brings us back, not just to its beginning, but to the beginning of Djebar's fictional meditation on Algerian history, *L'Amour, la fantasia*, and beyond it to her own beginnings as a feminist thanks to the education provided by the father. It also takes us forward, making parallels between the violence of the past and that of the present in Algeria.

The push for anamnesis in both *La femme sans sépulture* and *Kindred* should not be read as a utopian gesture. As Mireille Rosello seems to fear, national reconciliation need not mean an easy resolution that covers over power differences (2005, 130). What Butler and Djebar seem to have in mind is the working through of historical divisions through the active, honest, and painful involvement of all parties. That neither book allows for an easy closure indicates that anamnesis will be an ongoing process that may never resolve divisions fully but will open up a necessary, if difficult, dialogue.

I hope that this brief examination of the parallels between Octavia Butler's *Kindred* and Assia Djebar's *La femme sans sépulture* has suggested some possible productive feminist intersections between African American and ethnic studies and postcolonial and Francophone studies. Christine Mac-Leod's comment that Toni Morrison's *Beloved* figures "one of the most urgent items on the contemporary postcolonial agenda—the need to find ways of being responsible to one's own history without remaining trapped by it" (1997, 65) clearly resonates in the context of both *Kindred* and *La femme sans sépulture*. Both texts enact similar tactics to represent the historical unrepresentable through fiction and to work feminist, womanist, and postcolonial interventions into the construction of the nation. As such, they bring us closer to understanding some of the similarities and differences between representations of postslavery and postcolonial conditions, opening up new possibilities for creolized theorizing.

Notes

Parts of this chapter were previously published in *Research in African Literatures* 39, no. 3 (fall 2008): 65–81, under the title "African American and Francophone Postcolonial Memory: Octavia Butler's *Kindred* and Assia Djebar's *La femme sans sépulture*."

1 Although poststructuralism is often presented as a discourse having influenced major postcolonial theorists and writers (Bhabha by Lacan, the Moroccan Abdelkebir Khatibi by Derrida, the U. S.-based Algerian critic Reda Bensmaia by Barthes, etc.), some critics have sought to reverse such a Eurocentric history of criticism by

pointing out several related arguments. Lionnet and Robert Young, among others, suggest that it was the experience of decolonization, that is, the loss of the French empire and of French centrality, as well as the personal experience of being in the colonies before or during decolonization, that led "Parisian" intellectuals such as Cixous, Derrida, Duras, Foucault, Lyotard, and others to ponder a condition of fragmentation, split subjectivity, excentricity, and uncertainty (Young 1990, 1; Lionnet 1998a, 121; 1998b, 13; 1995, 169; Lionnet and Shih 2005, 3). In this sense, the postmodern is dependent on the postcolonial rather than the reverse. Such a condition, described by Lyotard as postmodern, was nothing new to colonized people, who may be said to have been experiencing the so-called postmodern condition for centuries. As Rey Chow argues, "Postmodernism . . . is only a belated articulation of what the West's 'others' have lived all along" (1992, 103) (see also Bhabha and Comaroff 2002, 21; Lubiano 1991, 156; Mitchell 2002, 11; Sandoval 2000, 7–9, 27, 33–35). For Young, "postmodernism can best be defined as European culture's awareness that it is no longer the unquestioned and dominant centre of the world" (1990, 19). Postmodernism, then, becomes a European symptom of decolonization, the Western side of postcolonialism. The "belatedness" of the postcolonial—of which much has been made—is thus paradoxically accompanied by an anticipatory aspect.

2 I use the terms *ethnic literature* and *ethnic studies* provisionally to refer to the literary, critical, and theoretical production relating to people of color in the United States. I realize that the term *ethnic*, like the terms *minority*, *multicultural*, and *people of color*, is highly problematic. I am particularly aware that the term is inadequate given the continuing colonial situation of Native peoples in the United States. I also recognize that ethnic studies is an umbrella term that covers diverse areas of study. As Mae Henderson points out, it was the establishment of African American studies programs that paved the way for "feminist studies, ethnic studies, postcolonial studies, gay and lesbian studies, and cultural studies" (1996, 66). I retain the term that many university departments that focus on comparative African American, Latino, Asian American, and American Indian studies use to name themselves. I use the term *ethnic studies* when making a broad-based argument about these four fields of inquiry together, but it is important to remember that issues of importance to each field are incommensurable. When discussing black history, literature, and politics specifically, I refer to black or African American studies. Although my argument here focuses on specific intersections between postcolonial and African American studies, the same argument can be (and has been) extended to postcolonial and Latino, Asian American, and indigenous studies (see Shih 2004; Byrd 2002; Shohat and Stam 1994; Donadey 2007).

3 See MacLeod 1997 for a generally persuasive, if occasionally problematic, call for comparative approaches between African American and postcolonial studies. See also edited volumes by Singh and Schmidt (2000) and C. Richard King (2000) for careful considerations of postcoloniality and the United States. For a compelling argument taking Gilroy's *Black Atlantic* as a point of convergence between postcolo-

nial and African American studies, see Gruesser 2005. For a somewhat problematic positioning of Butler's works as postcolonial, see Richard 2005/2006.

4 "American" properly refers to the two continents rather than a specific nation within these continents.

5 All translations from the French are my own.

6 On how *Kindred* rewrites slave narratives, see Crossley 1988; Govan 1986; Levecq 2000; and Maida 1991. For an argument about genre mixing in *Kindred* and a detailed analysis of the ways in which the text is and is not historiographic metafiction, see Turner 2003.

7 While I disagree with Fredric Jameson when he claims that all Third World texts should primarily be read as national allegories, it does occasionally happen that interpreting a text as a national allegory is valid, whether it be a Third or First World text, as is the case here. For a detailed critique of Jameson, see Ahmad, who notes that African American literature "is replete with national allegories" (1992, 24). For a cogent critique of the national allegory model, see Shih 2004, 20–22.

8 "Juneteenth.com World Wide Celebration!" Juneteenth.com.

9 "Citizen Ben," PBS.org (http://www.pbs.org/benfranklin/l3_citizen_abolitionist .html).

10 Levecq also notes that Frederick Douglass was born and lived for a while in Maryland; Crossley and Levecq both discuss how Butler uses Douglass's narrative as an intertext (*Kindred*, 72, 140; Crossley 1988, xx; Levecq 2000, 543). Finally, the Mason-Dixon Line, which, in the early part of the nineteenth century, became the dividing line between the North and the South, marked the border between Pennsylvania (a free state), Maryland, and Delaware (both slave states) (see "Geography: The Mason-Dixon Line," About.com [http://geography.about.com/library/weekly/ aa041999.htm]; Ampadu 2004–5, 73).

11 On the subversive aspect of Dana and Kevin's marriage as a "narrative of consensual interracial desire," see Foster 2007, 148.

12 There are many echoes and revisions of Fanon's landmark essay "L'Algérie se dévoile" (Algeria Unveiled) in *La femme sans sépulture*. The scene in which Zoulikha follows a *mudjahid* to cross a French checkpoint recalls Fanon's similar descriptions, as well as Gillo Pontecorvo's visual rendering of Fanon's text in *The Battle of Algiers*, and is described as a silent film (*La femme*, 154). The main reversal is that whereas in Fanon's "L'Algérie" the women carry the weapons for the "real" male militants, here the young man is Zoulikha's guide, and he carries the basket containing nationalist flags for the *female* militant (Fanon 1959/1965, 37, 40–41; Djebar, *La femme*, 154–56). Another reversal of Fanon occurs toward the end of the narrative, when Zoulikha's youngest daughter, Mina, describes traveling alone to join her mother in the mountains at age twelve, dressed up in a veil for the first time to look older than she is, feeling disoriented by the small angle of vision afforded by the veil (190). Fanon had described a similar disorientation experienced by Algerian female militants walking outside, unveiled, for the first time (42).

13 Rosello makes the same argument (2005, 158). I believe that Horváth misses this point when she claims that "par les moyens de la littérature, Djebar crée le tombeau imaginaire de Zoulikha" (through literature, Djebar creates Zoulikha's imaginary grave) (2004, 43–44). Mireille Calle-Gruber's (2005, 79) interpretation is similar to Horváth's. In contrast, Beïda Chikhi insightfully notes that Djebar "dérange les morts que d'autres ont rangés, ouvre les tombeaux que d'autres ont scellés" (disturbs the dead whom others had packed away and opens up tombs that others had sealed) (1997, 227).

14 Rushdy refers to rememory as "magical anamnesis" (2001, 6). See also Mitchell 2002, 21; and Regaïeg 2004, 91. An early formulation of anamnesis in the African American and Francophone postcolonial contexts can be found in Lionnet 1989, 118, 222–23.

15 *Kindred* was published about thirty years ago (a twenty-five-year edition came out in 2004), but it remains relevant to the present situation in the United States, which shows how much ground the nation still needs to cover to deal with its tradition of racism. One weakness of the book is that it presents the United States in black-and-white terms only (there is only one brief allusion to Americans Indians). Given that the multicultural makeup of the country in general and of California in particular increasingly includes Latinos and Asians, among others, *Kindred*'s view of race relations in black-and-white terms is the only way in which the book has aged. It clearly reflects the influence of 1960s and 1970s race relations paradigms, which had already begun to change by the late 1970s, especially in California.

16 Muriel Walker discusses another use of the term *langes* by Djebar in *Vaste est la prison*. Walker notes that the term is used unexpectedly in a context of death, "les langes de l'amour mort" (the swaddling clothes of a dead love) (Djebar 1995, 11). In the broader context of all of Djebar's work, then, the life-affirming aspect of anamnesis is always in danger of being "mort-né" (stillborn) (Walker 2008, 52–53); the seesaw motion between love and fantasia remains more than ever at the heart of Djebar's writing.

17 I thank Louisa MacKenzie for her suggestion that I make clearer the connections and disconnections between Platonic and postcolonial and postslavery anamnesis.

THREE

CRISES OF MONEY

Pheng Cheah

I n its main accepted usage, the noun *Creole* refers to a member of a European settler society, European in race or blood, but born in a colony. A Creole is therefore by nature of origin distinguished both from someone born in Europe and from the indigenous inhabitants of a colonized society. As an adjective, however, *creole* can refer to the attributes or characteristics that pertain to this segment of a settler society, especially in the domain of language. *Creolize*, the verb formed from the adjective, can therefore suggest the active process of the genesis of a new form of culture from colonial population flows, as the result of the transformation of European cultural forms as they are transposed in another space beyond their established frames of reference.

Despite its self-proclaimed radicality, the tacit frame of reference of critical theory regardless of how it is defined remains firmly in the North Atlantic. For at least two decades, it has been the task of postcolonial theory, loosely termed, to remind critical theory of its Eurocentric limits and to point to different forms of theorization that may arise in colonial and postcolonial space. Postcolonial theory then can be considered as the creolization of theory insofar as it seeks, broadly speaking, to examine how philosophical ideals and critical concepts are transformed when they are activated in spaces with social and political histories that are different from the North Atlantic. The question, however, is whether or not postcolonial theory itself is attentive enough to the ever-changing present, whether contemporary globalization leads to another transformation of the key concepts of postcolonial theory.

Indeed, in their academic blockbuster of 2000, *Empire*, Michael Hardt and Antonio Negri make the polemical argument that postcolonial theory leads to a dead end because it remains obsessed with the modern form of domination associated with colonialism that is no longer the primary mode of power operating in contemporary globalization (138–46). There is some truth to this claim regardless of the relative merits and weaknesses of their own account of the postmodern sovereignty they call "empire." The origins of postcolonial theory and cultural critique in the discipline of literary studies have meant that their analyses of oppression, domination, and exploitation have taken as their fundamental paradigm the experience of nineteenth-century European territorial imperialism and colonialism. Hence, if we consider the critique of Orientalist discourse or representational systems (Said), the racist stereotypes of colonial discourse, or even the epistemic violence of colonial subject formation through the civilizing processes of colonial law and education (Spivak), these different variations of postcolonial cultural critique are bound by a common understanding of power that emphasizes its "mentalist" or "imagistic" and "imaginative" character, whether this is understood in terms of the role of myth, ideology, or discursive norms that are imposed on the colonized subject at the moment of its constitution.

The psychoanalytic concept of trauma has the benefit of extending this analytical grid to cover forms of injury and suffering beyond the processes of consciousness or, as we now say too glibly, "the subject." It can give intelligibility to forms of hurt that are registered or encrypted through psychical processes outside the order of conscious experience, perception, and representation. Nevertheless the question that remains to be explored is whether forms of power in contemporary globalization can adequately be understood as primarily *psychical* in their functioning.

In this chapter, I examine the creolization of the psychoanalytic concept of trauma as it becomes transposed in colonial space in the writings of Frantz Fanon. I outline some of the central presuppositions of Fanon's application of the concept of trauma to the critique of colonialism. I then consider how Fanon's creolization of the concept of trauma into an analytical principle for understanding colonial power and oppression must itself be radically questioned in contemporary globalization. The second section of the chapter proceeds by testing these presuppositions through an examination of a series of events in Asia that on the surface seem to lend themselves perfectly to the vocabulary of trauma: the financial crises that afflicted East and Southeast Asia that were triggered by the assault on the Thai baht by currency speculators, on May 14–15, 1997. I then conclude with a brief indication of some future directions for postcolonial cultural critique.

Let me place two caveats at the threshold. First, I am not questioning the usefulness of trauma as a category of clinical practice or meta-psychological theory. I am only concerned with the limits of that concept as it has been taken up in postcolonial cultural critique for understanding the operations of power in the contemporary world. Second, a comprehensive discussion of the causes and devastating consequences of the Asian financial crisis is beyond the scope of this chapter, and, indeed, beyond my abilities. When we practice cultural critique, the best we can do is to offer a grid of intelligibility for understanding a concrete situation in a certain political interest. There is an enormous body of political-economic analysis concerned with the financial crisis. I have no disciplinary expertise in political economy, but I can learn from this literature and use it to reevaluate and tinker with the basic presuppositions of postcolonial theory so that it can be less hubristic and more in touch with postindustrial global capitalism. Such a process of transformative transposition is in principle open-ended. A critic must always stop within the limits of what he or she believes to be "the current conjuncture." But that *coupure* is as determined as it is arbitrary. No theoretical analysis can be interminable.

Trauma in Postcolonial Cultural Critique:
Fanon's Creolization of Freud on Trauma

The concept of trauma originates from the etiology of neurosis. In its earliest formulation by Freud in his collaborative work with Josef Breuer, trauma originates in the affect of fright that accompanies an accidental event or physical injury. When such a distressing affect is not adequately processed by the affected subject by means of responsive action, adequate representation, or verbalization (abreaction), it is converted into a repressed memory. The memory of the affect then becomes a psychical trauma and the cause behind the formation of various kinds of neurotic symptoms. In Freud's words, "a trauma would have to be defined as an accretion of excitation in the nervous system, which the latter has been unable to dispose of adequately by motor reaction" ("Extracts," 137). "Any impression which the nervous system has difficulty in disposing of by means of associative thinking or of motor reaction becomes a psychical trauma" (154). It is important to emphasize that the trauma is not the mere physical event but the memory of the psychical affect the event induces. In cases of trauma, the repressed memory of the affect becomes lodged or encrypted within the psyche and continues to act long after the passing of the physical event.[1] As Breuer and Freud put it, "The psychical trauma—or more precisely the memory of the trauma—acts [*wirkt*] like a foreign body which long after its entry must continue to be regarded as an agent that is still operative [*gegenwärtig wirkendes Agens*]" ("VM," 85; 6). The psychical trauma thus functions like a parasite that will continually weaken its host or, better yet, a spirit whose continuing effectivity will repeatedly undermine the self-control of the living body it has possessed.

For present purposes, two features of Freud's early understanding of trauma are important. First, even before his formulation of the concept of libido or sexual energy, Freud suggested in his individual case studies that trauma should be analyzed in terms of quantified excitations (*Erregungen*) that impinge on the nervous system and leave a residue or trace because they have not been discharged either through abreaction or thought activity: "We regard hysterical symptoms as the effects and residues of excitations which have impacted on [*beeinflußt*] the nervous system as traumas. It is impossible any longer at this point to avoid introducing the idea of quantities (even though not measurable ones). We must regard the process as though a sum of excitation impinging on the nervous system is transformed into chronic symptoms in so far as it has not been employed for external action in proportion to its amount" ("Frau Emmy," 141; 86). These accumulating excitations are transformed or converted into chronic somatic symptoms, and where the transformation is incomplete, "some part at least of the affect that accompanies the trauma persists [*verbleibt*] in consciousness as a component of the subject's state of feeling [*Stimmung*]" (142; 86–87). Second, Freud argues that trauma involves a radical decentering of the ego that causes it to cede the autonomy of its intentional actions. The psychical trauma occurs because the ego expels an idea that is in contradiction with itself, which it does by repressing it into the unconscious.

The traumatic moment proper, then, is the one at which the contradiction forces itself upon the ego [*der Widerspruch sich dem Ich aufdrängt*] and at which the latter decides on the expulsion [*Verweisung*] of the contradictory idea [*Vorstellung*]. That idea is not annihilated by an expulsion of this kind, but merely repressed into the unconscious. When this process occurs for the first time there comes into being a nucleus and centre of crystallization for the formation [*Bildung*] of a psychical group divorced from the ego—a group around which everything which would imply an acceptance of the contradictory idea subsequently collects. The splitting of consciousness in these cases of acquired hysteria is accordingly a deliberate and intentional one, at least often introduced by a volitional act. The actual outcome is something other than what the subject [*das Individuum*] intended: he wanted to do away with [*aufheben*] an idea, as though it had never appeared, but all he succeeds in doing is to isolate it psychically. ("Miß Lucy R.," 182; 123)

In this intentional act of repression, the ego unwittingly undermines its own autonomy by splitting itself. It creates or forms a psychical abscess that is divorced from itself, and this abscess can be filled with other memories and associations that are linked to the contradictory idea it seeks to banish. The contradictory idea therefore becomes an other within the self that has a life of its own. We should therefore understand trauma as a form of radical heteronomy where the trace or mnemic residue of something that originates from outside the subject (the accident or physical injury) takes shape within the very inside of the subject as an alterity or otherness, an alien power that undermines its self-control.

This means that trauma is always already a matter of domination (*Herrschaft*) and power (*Macht*). It concerns domination of an a priori kind, domination that precedes any historical form of social or political domination, because it is always about the security and self-mastery—one might even say the sovereignty—of the ego, the protection of an interiority from anything that impacts on or falls on this inside from the outside. The more elaborate account of trauma in *Beyond the Pleasure Principle* (1940) emphasizes once again its psychical character. It is not "direct damage to the molecular structure or even to the histological structure of the elements of the nervous system" but concerns effects produced on the mental apparatus, "the organ of the mind [*Seelenorgan*] by the breach in the shield against stimuli [*Reizschutzes*] and by the problems that follow in its train."[2] What is important here is not just the excitation caused by the external stimulus but the ability of the mental apparatus to protect itself against such excitations through anticipation and defense mechanisms such as libidinal cathexes that can bind excitations. Trauma occurs when the ego's capacity for security is compromised, when the protective shield it erects against the outside world is penetrated. This is the first step of the ego's loss of self-mastery, when its system of defense begins to break down. "We describe as 'traumatic' any excitations from outside which are powerful [*stark*] enough to break through the protective shield. . . . The concept of trauma necessarily implies a connection of this kind with a breach in an otherwise efficacious barrier against stimuli [*wirksame Reizabhaltung*]. Such an event as an external trauma is bound to provoke a disturbance on a large scale in the functioning of the organism's energy and to set in motion every possible defensive means [*Abwehrmittel*]" (JL, 29; 301).

Precisely because trauma is the breakdown of the psychical security system, it is connected to fright (*Schreck*) instead of mere fear (*Furcht*) or anxiety (*Angst*).[3] Fright refers to a state of encountering danger without any prior preparation because such danger, like the pure event, comes upon one completely by surprise. The mental apparatus is here completely vulnerable because its defenses are not up. In contradistinction, anxiety, which is a state of expecting danger or preparing for it, can never lead to traumatic neurosis because "it protects its subject against fright and so against fright-neuroses" (JL, 10; 282). Indeed, preparedness for anxiety and the hypercathexis of the receptive system that accompanies it "represents the ultimate line of defense of the shield against stimuli [*die letzte Linie des Reizschutzes darstellt*]" (JL, 32; 303).[4]

We cannot simply say that the vocabulary of security and protection and the imagery of a defensive position in war that permeates Freud's distinction between "systems that are unprepared and systems that are well prepared through being hypercathected" are merely metaphorical (JL, 32, 303). It may very well be that the phenomenon of security that is a crucial theme in the political philosophy of Hobbes, Spinoza, Rousseau, and Locke, among many others, is merely the *projection* or extension of the security of the mental apparatus—its defensive or protective mechanisms in relation to stimuli—in the realm of social-anthropological existence.[5] One can understand psychical security as a pre-positive form of security that precedes any historical form of social or political security and the loss of self-mastery and autonomy in traumatic neuroses as a form of pre-positive domination by another that can function as an opening and foothold for social and political domination. In other words, the security of an individual psyche's interiority in its interaction with the external world and its management of internal excitations is the basis for historical forms of sociality and political community. Conversely, psychical insecurity or trauma is also the basis for violence and domination qua the determinate negation of community and belonging. This is a theme that is radicalized in Lacan's theory of aggressivity as an original tendency of the ego's paranoiac structure (see Lacan 1977).

Let us now turn to consider how Frantz Fanon deploys the concept of trauma for the political critique of colonial racist violence. In *Black Skin, White Masks*, the concept is modified in two related ways even as its governing motif, the protection of interiority, remains intact. On the one hand, Fanon finds Freud's concept of trauma illuminating because it locates the origins of neuroses in specific psychical traumas or pathogenic experiences (*Erlebnisse*) back to which symptoms can be traced through psychoanalytic treatment.[6] On the other hand, Fanon suggests that psychoanalysis is only of limited usefulness for the analysis of colonial racism because its primary focus is on the individual. "Freud insisted that the individual factor be taken into account through psychoanalysis. He substituted for a phylogenetic theory the ontogenetic perspective. It will be seen that the black man's alienation is not an individual question. Beside phylogeny and ontogeny stands sociogeny" (BSWM, 11). "For the black man . . . historical and economic realities come into the picture" (BSWM, 161n25). The psychical trauma caused by colonial racism therefore involves a twofold deformation of the classical concept of trauma. First, the traumatic experience of colonial racism (as emblematized by identity-fixing racial slurs or appellations such as "dirty nigger" or "look, a Negro," or racist images that circulate in popular culture) is registered by an individual who experiences it not as a unique individual but as a member of a larger group, the colonized black man. Second, the weakness or impotence of the individual's mental apparatus, its lack of preparation and inability to bind trauma-related excitations through hypercathexis, is caused by material sociopolitical circumstances, namely, the context of colonial domination, in which the black man is always already constituted as an inadequate or injured subject. In other words, the excessive excitation and the resulting trauma are induced not by an isolated accidental event or unexpected injury but by the formative impact of the social context of colonial domination on individual consciousness, especially the extreme exploitation, deprivation, and immiseration brought about by colonial violence and the decimation of traditional values and binding communal norms. In Fanon's words, "The arrival of the white man in Madagascar shattered not only [the Malagasy's] horizons but its psychological mechanisms. . . . An island like Madagascar, invaded overnight by 'pioneers of civilization,' even if those pioneers conducted themselves as well as they knew how, suffered the loss of its basic structure. . . . The landing of the white man on Madagascar inflicted injury without measure. The consequences of that irruption of Europeans onto Madagascar were not psychological alone, since, as every authority has observed, there are inner relationships between consciousness and the social context" (*BSWM*, 97).

We can call this kind of incessant quotidian trauma that characterizes colonialism "structural" or "systemic" trauma because its unceasing or continuous character arises from the oppressive processes of a structure or system that is imposed on a subject, which is forced to inhabit that structure or system.[7] The three terms Fanon deploys for the analysis of colonial trauma are "the collective unconscious," "collective catharsis," and the "historico-racial" or "racial-epidermal schema." In Fanon's reconstruction, the Jungian postulate of a collective unconscious refers to the immoral impulses and shameful desires of a civilization or society as a collective subject that have been repressed. If this collective unconscious is territorially situated in terms of a specific civilization, then in the European collective unconscious, the principle of evil is projected onto African people (*BSWM*, 190). With the onset of colonialism, the European collective unconscious and all its archetypes are imposed on the African, who therefore identifies with the white man and European civilization and repudiates his blackness as a signifier of evil and immorality.[8] But because the black man in colonial society is repeatedly reminded of, and is compelled to recognize, his blackness, this ambiguity of being and repudiating blackness cannot be repressed. Instead it must be endured and suffered in daily conscious existence. This is an important component of the systemic character of colonial trauma. In Fanon's words, "the negro lives an ambiguity that is extraordinarily neurotic. . . . [He] recognizes that he is living an error" (BSWM, 192). Unlike "normal" trauma, if one can say that, colonial trauma is not hidden, forgotten, or repressed.[9] Instead, colonial trauma has subjugated the black person's very consciousness and colonized every facet of his daily existence such that he consciously lives and suffers his entire body as an open sore.

This radical or hyperbolic neurosis is exacerbated by the fact that collective catharsis is not possible for the black person. Collective catharsis refers to a channel or outlet that enables the release of collective aggressive forces that have accumulated in children (BSWM, 145). Comic books and adventure stories are cultural forms of media or mediation that enable catharsis through the child's identification with the protagonist, whose aggressive behavior is directed at the villain. But since the villain is always figured as black, and the black child identifies with the white protagonist and adopts his attitude and truths, the black child develops the same self-destructive and suicidal consciousness found in the systemic trauma of the black adult. Here, as in the case of the collective unconscious, the systematic circulation of colonial-racist cultural images, significations, and representations is the structural cause of quotidian suffering and victimage.

Indeed, such images and representations are part of the mechanism of individuation of the black person. They actively fabricate his individual body in all its sensuous corporeality by creating a "historico-racial schema," a "corporeal malediction" that obstructs the formation of a genuine corporeal schema through which a genuine, autonomous dialectical relation between body and world can take place (BSWM, 111). In Fanon's poignant words, "the white man . . . had woven me out of a thousand details, anecdotes, stories" (BSWM, 111). Here too, the entire body of the black person, or more precisely, its image, is the immediate, real cause of traumatic suffering: "I took myself far off from my own presence, far indeed, and made myself an object. What else could it be for me but an amputation, an excision, a hemorrhage that spattered my whole body with black blood?" (BSWM, 112).

The trauma associated with the colonial experience thus stretches the classical psychoanalytic concept in at least three ways. First, it is a systemic form of trauma that is incessant or planned. Instead of being generated by an isolated event of injury, the trauma issues from social, political, and economic structures. Second, the traumatic cause (blackness) is not repressed or forgotten. It is patently and obviously part of the realm of conscious perception and is openly recognized. Third, since the traumatic cause is not repressed, the subordination of the ego to the trauma as an alterity is not intermittent or partial. The black man is completely dominated by the other, that is, the white man's image of the black body. These three traits of colonial trauma indicate that it is not amenable to a merely therapeutic resolution. In the colonial situation, the verbalization of trauma does not lead to the better management of excitations. Instead, the verbal recognition by the black person that he is black is a further deepening and exacerbation of the trauma. It depletes and eviscerates the subject further.

Indeed, Fanon goes a step further. He distinguishes mere psychical trauma from the real struggle for life under colonialism and characterizes the educative native intelligentsia's quest for psychical disalienation as almost self-indulgent in comparison with the plantation laborer's or dockworker's struggle for survival. "For the Negro who works on a sugar plantation in Le Robert, there is only one solution: to fight. He will embark on this struggle, and he will pursue it, not as the result of a Marxist or idealistic analysis but quite simply because he cannot conceive of life otherwise than in the form of a battle against exploitation, misery, and hunger" (BSWM, 224). Hence the only complete resolution to colonial trauma is the formation of a collective political subject (the radical popular nation) that will destroy through revolutionary action the material conditions that caused the trauma in the first place. In a passage from *The Wretched of the Earth* that echoes Marx's eschatological argument that the proletarian revolution is imperative not only for individuals "to achieve self-activity [*Selbstbetätigung*], but, also, merely to safeguard their very existence," Fanon suggests that the imperative behind anticolonial revolution is the dignity of sheer corporeal survival (Marx and Engels 1932/1970, 57; 92). "For a colonized people, the most essential value, because it is the most meaningful, is first and foremost the land: the land, which must provide bread and, naturally, dignity. But this dignity has nothing to do with 'human' dignity. The colonized subject has never heard of such an ideal. All he has ever seen on his land is that he can be arrested, beaten, and starved with impunity; and no sermonizer on morals, no priest has ever stepped in to bear the blows in his place or share his bread" (Fanon 2004, 9).

At the same time, however, Fanon's insistence on the dignity of sheer life as the necessary outcome of his analysis of colonial trauma leaves the governing motif of the classical concept of trauma intact. For whether it is a matter of mere corporeal survival or being able to lead an emotionally healthy, bearable, and less unhappy life, what is always at stake is the *security* of the living self, the organism's ability to protect itself from physical or psychical distress that comes from the outside.[10] The ultimate aim of Fanon's explication is to remove the various external impositions that have led to the evisceration of black consciousness: the collective unconscious, the racial-epidermal schema, the various processes of unconscious socialization of the black person as an individual, but most important, the social, political, and economic conditions of European colonialism. *Black Skin, White Masks* is intended to be a mirror that enables the black person to recognize himself as a universal human being so that he can be returned to the path of a normal or undistorted dialectical relation to the world.[11] The important point here is that this involves the constitution of a strong consciousness that can master and bind the physical and psychical excitations impacting on it. Fanon's project is essentially one of helping the subject regain its self-mastery, power, or sovereignty so that it can return to an autonomous, normal path of development, one free of any heteronomy or subordination to an other. The fundamental principle or value governing Fanon's project thus remains that of security: the reconsolidation and strengthening of an interior so that it can withstand or regulate any breaching from the outside, so that it can stem any excessive exposure to alterity. (Colonial) political domination or subjugation is traumatic because it causes the erosion and loss of the colonized subject's psychical self-mastery. Conversely, political and economic sovereignty or self-determination is the necessary condition for black consciousness to regain its self-mastery and health.

Miracle and Crash: The Power of Global Financialization in Asia

That Fanon analyzes colonial racist violence in terms of the psychoanalytic concept of trauma suggests a special affinity between the understanding of power implied by the idea of trauma and the workings of colonial power. In both cases, power is understood in terms of the security and defensive capacity of an interiority. The subject's loss of power is figured as subjugation and domination by another, and its restoration or reconsolidation is figured as the regaining of independence and self-mastery. The necessary counter-part of physical violence or coercion by the sovereign imperial power is a form of mental or psychical oppression: subject constitution through ideol-ogy, myth, or discourse. Fanon's work is exemplary because he fuses psycho-analytic and political registers. His solution to colonial trauma is revolution-ary decolonization and the restoration of sovereignty for the people.

Because postcolonial cultural critique originates from the analysis of colonialism, it subscribes to the same understanding of power as some-thing that is imposed from the outside on a subject, although postcolonial critique and the analysis of colonialism may differ on the nature of resis-tance. Because postcolonial cultural critique is a subfield of literary studies, it focuses on the mental or psychical modality of power. To take the most obvious example, in *Orientalism*, Edward Said characterized Orientalist dis-course as the imposition of a system of representation on the conscious-ness of peoples in the East through the historical project of colonialism, even to the point that a mythical collective mentality has been fabricated for those peoples. Similarly, Gayatri Spivak's seminal essay "Can the Subaltern Speak?" is concerned with the muting of the subaltern's voice and interests (epistemic violence) by an array of ideologically fabricated subjects such as the colonial subject or the colonized indigenous elite, and the postcolonial or Third World subject as native informant.[12]

It may, however, be anachronistic for us to assume that the impact of contemporary globalization on postcolonial societies can be understood through the colonial-sovereign paradigm of power. Much contemporary social-scientific literature on "the African tragedy" certainly suggests that the exercise of geopolitical power in the contemporary era remains the same. Neocolonialism gives the lie to the assumption that decolonization is the regaining of self-mastery by the various collective national subjects of Africa. The various neocolonial states in the African continent are internally weak and lack popular support. Run by indigenous nonproductive compra-dor bourgeois elites who have grown fat from theft capitalism, these states rule by military oppression that cannot in many cases effectively control the ethnic and tribal conflicts that are tearing apart several African countries. Generally speaking, these African states remain satellites of the former colo-nial powers as well as the newer neocolonial power, the United States, and the path of development of African countries is imposed on them by these external powers and by international agencies such as the World Bank and the IMF. As evidenced by Achille Mbembe's prodigious body of work, the violent consequences that follow from the continuing underdevelopment of Africa readily lend themselves to be read under the sign of trauma.[13]

But Africa is perhaps not the best example of the impact of globalization on postcolonial nations. It can be argued that the very "underdevelopment" of Africa indicates its lack of integration within the circuit of global capitalist accumulation, or at least its extremely minimal or partial integration as the supplier of raw materials and as the remnants of an *effete* international division of labor that is not yet or not even industrial.[14] This structural stagnation makes the African situation especially intelligible through the grid of colonial power. However, if we shift our glance to the hyperdeveloping Asia of the 1990s, it would seem that contemporary globalization operates according to an entirely different dynamic of power. Hyperdeveloping Asia lies at the other end of the spectrum in terms of its highly accelerated integration into the circuits of globalization. If it is the case that globalization involves the ascendancy of a new modality and logics—or, better yet, physiology of power—then the analytical categories of postcolonial theory, which originate from the analysis of colonial power, necessarily lose their explanatory force. Since the concept of trauma is underwritten by a similar paradigm of power, its pertinence to an analysis of power in the contemporary postcolonial world also becomes questionable.[15]

This is not to say that sovereign power no longer exists. But it finds itself sustained by a more diffuse form of power with which it is sometimes in a conflictual relationship. Nor am I suggesting that Africa and East Asia should be situated within a unilinear quasi-developmental history in which their stages of development correspond to different stages of power. I am suggesting that globalization involves multiple modalities of power that need to be situated in relation to each other and that a given modality of power can be more pronounced or ascendant in a given location depending on its position in a given conjuncture of global capitalism.

We commonly equate the weakening of state sovereignty with economic globalization. But the transnationalization of political economy was only possible because its initial formation was conditioned by the rise of certain technologies that were detachable from the territorial state. These are the technologies associated with commercial and monetary flows. Thus, writing about the "two great ensembles of political knowledge" that gave shape to "the reason of state"—namely, the diplomatic-military technology of inter-state alliances and militarization and the technology of policing—Foucault points to a third mediating technology: "At the junction point of these two great technologies, and as a shared instrument, one must place commerce and monetary circulation between states: enrichment through commerce offers the possibility of increasing the population, the manpower, produc-tion, and export, and of endowing oneself with large, powerful armies" (Foucault 1997, 69). The constitutive nature of money as a technology of biopower that Foucault points to is in stark contrast to Marx's understand-ing of money as a phantom and a prosthetic monster that epitomizes the alienated, inverted world of inhuman capital, as exemplified by his reading of Shakespeare's *Timon of Athens*. Much African literature beautifully the-matizes this view of money and glittering objects of consumption as prod-ucts of alienation, for example, Ngugi wa Thiong'o's *Devil on the Cross*, or Ayi Kwei Armah's *The Beautyful Ones Are Not Yet Born*. Money as alienation is continuous with the ideologico-discursive modality of sovereign power that obsesses postcolonial theory. I contend that financial globalization puts this view of power into question by reinscribing it within a more complex web of powers, and this requires us to rethink the key analytical concepts of postcolonial theory.

To this end, I turn now to consider the Asian financial crisis of 1997. It is an illuminating test case because on its face, it is so easily characterized in terms of trauma. Here, then, is a very summary and dry description. The Asian financial crisis refers to a series of linked events that was set off by the assault on the Thai baht by currency speculators on May 14–15, 1997. The falling currency triggered investor panic, leading to a crashing stock market and falling property prices. As the result of a "contagion" or "domino" effect, the pattern was repeated with some variations in countries throughout the region, some of which were generally perceived to have much stronger eco-nomic fundamentals than Thailand, for instance, Malaysia and South Korea. By the end of 1997, the Asian crisis was full-blown. The region financed its high growth through huge private foreign debt, much of it in the form of short-term portfolio investment. With rising herdlike panic among foreign fund managers, the direction of these short-term capital inflows was re-versed, leading to a severe liquidity crunch that caused local corporations to collapse and massive unemployment even as inflation grew as a result of the devalued local currencies. The combined effect was a drastic deterioration of living standards, especially for the millions of poor people, and this suffering escalated into social and political upheaval such as the downfall of the Suharto government, the destabilization of Mahathir's regime, and riots, destruction, and death.

In popular and academic literature alike, the financial crisis has been portrayed through extended metaphors of security and warfare: pillage, invasion and attack, battle and defense, the onslaught of the enclosed interior core of an organism. Later, when this invasion is in a temporary lull, the attacked economies and countries are figured as being under siege or being held hostage, and even later, when the invasion has done its worst, as suffering in a meltdown, collapse, and crisis that will have long aftershocks.

> What began as a debt crisis has become a fully-fledged development crisis. . . . Many millions of poor people are at risk, and many millions of people who were confident of middle-class status feel robbed of their lifetime savings and security. It is not a humanitarian tragedy on the scale of North Korea, but the loss of security and productivity is a tragedy nonetheless, almost as cruel as war. (Wade and Veneroso 1998a, 4)

> This manipulation of market forces by powerful actors constitutes a form of financial and economic warfare. . . . In the late 20th century, the outright "conquest of nations," meaning the control over productive assets, labour, natural resources and institutions, can be carried out in an impersonal fashion. . . . "Financial warfare" also applies to complex speculative instruments, including the gamut of derivative trade forward foreign exchange transactions, currency options, hedge funds, index funds etc. Speculative instruments have been used with the ultimate purpose of capturing financial wealth and acquiring control over productive assets. (Chossudovsky 1998, 41–42)

Such imagery, when taken together with the argument about the emergence of a new international financial architecture that ties together the capital-liberalizing agendas of the IMF, WTO, and OECD, strongly suggests that the countries and national economies affected by the crisis, and even the region as a whole, can be considered as collective subjects that have experienced breaches of their protective shields as a result of being traversed by flows of finance capital that they cannot tolerate or master. Insofar as their interiority has been rendered vulnerable, such collective subjects can therefore be seen as undergoing a systemic trauma associated with global financialization, much like the systemic trauma of colonialism, which in turn causes trauma in their individual members whose lives have indelibly been scarred by the crisis. Indeed, the accumulation of massive short-term cross-border debts that can flow out without warning is described in terms of an intolerable buildup of energy that cannot be mastered or controlled by available defense mechanisms such as capital controls or foreign exchange reserves. As Jeffrey Sachs puts it:

> What we've experienced is a financial panic. The banks were pouring money into Asia up to mid-1997. Since then, they have been abruptly taking money out. That kind of change of direction leads to the kind of crisis we're seeing, with collapsing exchange rates, destabilized equity markets and economies going into free fall. . . . Whenever there's a lot of short-term debt around, it's possible for capital movements to be self-fulfilling. If you predict doom and the short-term capital flows out and there are not enough foreign exchange reserves to cover the outflow, doom will occur. From a national policy point of view, the lesson is don't allow short-term cross-border debt to build up to such high levels that you become vulnerable to a self-fulfilling outflow of capital.[16]

Robert Wade and Frank Veneroso make an identical argument: "Whatever the balance between 'real' and 'financial' causes of the crisis, the capital account opening that they [East Asian countries] undertook mostly in the 1990s is centrally implicated. Capital account liberalization first allowed large and uncoordinated inflows and then torrential outflows in the second half of 1997 and on into 1998. . . . No nation can survive such a whipsaw without great disruption, especially when weakly institutionalized political structures are unable to support a negotiated sharing of the burden" (1998b, 20–21).

But things are considerably more complicated if we remember that global capital flows do not merely breach the interior core of the economies of Asian nations. They are crucial to their prodigious growth and development and can thus be said to constitute the very foundation of these economies in such a manner that the distinction of an inside from an outside no longer holds. This is the distinctive feature of contemporary globalization.

It brings about the constitutive exposure of nation-states qua collective subjects. Such exposure is constitutive because it is not imposed on nation-states but is instead something they actively will and desire in their attempt to develop and increase their power, if one can impute a collective political will at the level of state agency. A World Bank article aptly figures capital flows as the lifeblood of economic growth and advises that only greater liberalization of capital flows can help East Asia to recover.

> Capital flows are the lifeblood of economic growth, and the region's capital hemorrhage must be staunched and reversed. Restoration of capital flows is a high priority. This would help relieve the compression of private consumption that comes with the massive swing to a current account surplus. Restoring capital flows can only be done by reactivating the economies and providing a context that will restore investor confidence. . . . Only by restoring capital flows can East Asia resume growth, and only by resuming growth can it reverse the massive income losses that have imperiled the livelihoods of so many people in such a short time. (World Bank 1998a, 335–36)

But if the lifeblood of the body comes from outside it, if the body can maintain its strength and power only by means of transfusion even in normal or nonemergency situations, then the self-recursivity of the organism is always already compromised, and its survival is always already heteronomous. It is in this sense that financial globalization involves a new physiology of power where even life itself or mere survival requires the nation-state, conceived as a living body, to open itself up to an other. This new physiology of power brings into the sharpest relief what can be called "originary technicity": the necessary supplementation of natural organic life by *techne* in general. The national body survives, grows, and becomes powerful only by exposing itself without return, that is to say, by compromising and contaminating itself. Indeed, even maintaining the circulation of blood requires a country to create an infrastructure that can potentially damage it because this will open it to the outside even more. This is the real meaning of structural adjustment: "The countries are doing their part to restore confidence. They have enacted structural reforms, opened their markets wider to foreign direct investment, and protected the creditworthiness of their economies by assuming financial system liabilities" (World Bank 1998a, 336).

We should not assume that the structural adjustment policies prescribed as a cure to the financial crisis are merely ideological reflections of the interests of OECD countries. In a sense, structural adjustment only takes financial globalization's physiology of power to its natural conclusion. This physiology of power predates the financial crisis and is its condition of possibility. This new form of power has two main components. First, the huge buildup of capital in developed countries, partly due to the huge current account surplus in Japan in the 1990s, created an excess of liquidity in the world system that spilled over into financial asset markets. Much of this money ended up in the hands of financial institutions in the United States, Japan, and Europe. Banks, pension funds, and international institutional investors who were flush with liquidity invested heavily in the U.S. stock market, leading to the long equity boom, and also scoured the world looking for avenues of speculative investment in "emerging markets" that would yield quick and high returns.[17] Second, most developing countries actively liberalized their financial markets to benefit from this unprecedented degree of access to international finance. This welcoming of finance capital by East and Southeast Asian states merely continued the active role they had played in the preceding decades in attracting foreign capital to fuel the impressive development and economic growth that is now known as the East Asian economic miracle. This kind of state that assumes a widened and authoritative role in governing market forces to achieve rapid industrialization is called the developmental state in social scientific literature (Wade 2004). Singapore is probably the best example of the complicity between the developmental state and neoliberal global capital. Unlike Hong Kong, South Korea, and Taiwan, Singaporean economic success and its achievement of being Asia's most "postindustrial" society and most advanced welfare state "has not been built by state influence or subsidies to domestic capital, but rather by the state's alliance with transnational (TNC) capital. In Singapore about 70% of the economy (and about 80% of manufacturing industry) is foreign owned" (J. Henderson 1993, 212).

This means that the very condition of high economic growth—namely, constitutive exposure to capital flows—is, at one and the same time, also the condition of crisis. As Western and Japanese banks and investment houses pump more and more capital into these countries on the assumption that this prodigious growth will continue, it also makes these countries more and more vulnerable in the event of a massive withdrawal of capital.

Much academic literature has insisted on the important need to distinguish between capital inflows before and during the 1990s. The earlier flows, it is argued, were mainly flows of foreign direct investment (FDI) and long-term capital that were carefully coordinated, supervised, and monitored by the developmental state and generated "real" productive economic activities. In contradistinction, the later flows, which occurred after Asian governments undertook radical financial deregulation encouraged by the IMF, the OECD, and Western governments, are flows of short-term, speculative capital that occur via unsupervised loans between private companies and foreign lenders. They are mainly portfolio investments, capital that is channeled into unproductive avenues such as equity and real estate markets, and it is the failure of regulating this kind of "bad," "unproductive," hot, or mobile capital inflow for which greedy local companies clamored that is the cause of the financial crisis.[18] Different variations on this essentially moralistic classification of capital flows into the real and the virtual, the productive and the speculative, have distributed the blame and responsibility for the financial crisis in slightly different ways. For instance, it has been argued that "unfettered financial liberalization" centered on "stock market development and portfolio capital inflows [is] unlikely to help developing countries in achieving speedier industrialization and faster long-term economic growth" and, indeed, may have a highly negative impact because it is a highly volatile form of casino capitalism (Singh and Weisse 1998, 618; J. Henderson 1993, 214). It has also been suggested that there are internal weaknesses in the real economies of many Asian nations that provided a strong foothold for casino capitalism, for instance, the significant role of overseas Chinese business networks in East Asian hyperdevelopment that had a predilection for real-estate development, and property and stock market speculation and were not subjected to investment discipline by the Thai, Malaysian, and Indonesian states. It is argued that "the relative absence of an institutional capacity and competence capable of influencing the sectoral trajectory of inward and domestic investment flows" is due to the lack of interest among the "blatant and largely rent-seeking" political elites, and a lack of political will to establish regulatory institutions (J. Henderson 1999, 337–38, 343). These internal factors have prevented the construction of effective developmental states such as those found in Taiwan and Singapore, thereby compounding tendencies toward the formation of weak and unsound national economies that are structurally vulnerable to the outflow of "highly mobile" "impatient" casino capital and the resulting financial crisis.

Such analytical distinctions between so-called good and bad forms of capital flows are no doubt important. They logically lead to sound arguments about the necessity of closing or at least heavily regulating capital accounts.[19] But in my humble opinion, such erudite economic studies presuppose a regulatory model of nation-state power that is no longer entirely feasible even if it seems normatively attractive. In financial globalization, the sovereign nation-state finds itself inscribed within and sustained by a different physiology of power. Any opening of the nation-state to free-market structures—and this is inevitable in the current conjuncture—implies an a priori vulnerability to the speculative disequilibriums and retrogression associated with international capital markets. Indeed, his championing of capital controls notwithstanding, Robert Wade is forced to admit that "once an economy adopts a regime of free capital movements, it can sustain market-steering arrangements of the 'Asian political economy' kind only with difficulty, as the Asian crisis shows," because free capital movements are regarded by financial powers such as the United States as a means of forcing emerging economies to adopt the entire panoply of free-market structures: "The U.S. national interest is to have the rest of the world play by American rules of both cross-border capital movement and domestic arrangements for finance, corporate governance, labour markets, and the like. Not only Wall Street but most of the bigger U.S. manufacturing and service companies want this broader agenda, for which the Wall Street free capital movement agenda is the most powerful instrument" (Wade and Veneroso 1998b, 36).

The older regulatory model of power is inadequate and utopian for three reasons. First, the expectation that the state should divert and discipline investment flows through a combination of capital controls and investor education presupposes the benevolence of political and economic elites whose very hegemony and economic power are premised on these massive inflows of speculative capital. These elites are not the victims of casino capitalism but its willing participants and active agents. Second, even when the corrupt or weak political will of the indigenous political and economic elite is denounced, it is still presupposed that the nation-people, especially the emergent middle class, is homogeneous, pure, and uncontaminated, and that one can discern a popular will whose interests are opposed to that of speculative capital. This is why the international and local media repeatedly portrayed the middle class as the victim of the financial crisis. But, in fact, this emergent middle class was also the beneficiary of stock and property speculation, feeding its frenzied consumption of expensive imports through speculative profits. Even today, the middle-class investor and the small-business proprietor and tradesman in Southeast Asia still dream of the glory days of the pre-1997 stock market boom. They have also been spectralized by the neoliberal free-market spirit of the owners and managers of Northern finance capital. Third, however unpleasant it is to accept, the distinction between productive and unproductive capital inflows remains within the exploitative and competitive hierarchy of the international division of labor. Development through productive capital inflows remains highly exploitative. Successful development merely enables a given country to climb up this hierarchy at the expense of less-developed nations. For instance, Singapore, which was relatively unscathed by the financial crisis, was a beneficiary of the forced disposal of nonliquid businesses and their assets in other Southeast Asian countries at fire-sale prices.

My point here is that the drive and imperative for speculative profit making not only animates *foreign* currency speculators and portfolio investors but operates in the very heart of industrializing Asian economies. It is the very spirit of financial globalization, which will always favor capital flows that can be withdrawn instantaneously, because patience is not a virtue of hyperprofitability. Once this imperative has set in, private-sector interests in developing countries will desire the rapid development of capital markets as the fast and easy track to making large sums of money. Even if the developmental state tries to stem rapid capital outflow now and then, the state will not and cannot stop outflow in the long run, not only because the state's strength is based on market-opening progress but also because in the official drive toward national economic productivity, it has inculcated the imperative for hyperprofitability in the people through various technologies of biopower. Training into consumerism through rising standards of living, and the proliferation of new needs and desires through the global culture industry and media advertising, are other means for the inculcation of this imperative. In the final analysis, the distinction between productive and nonproductive forms of capital dogmatically assumes the

purity of the people and forecloses how the people were formed and constituted by technologies of biopower and cultural and ideological instruments
to actively want these capital inflows. Simply denouncing the political and
economic corruption of the indigenous elite as the internal neuralgic point
that makes the nation vulnerable to speculative and nonproductive forms of
foreign capital obscures the constitutive relation between state and people
in these regions. For instance, why do most of these corrupt regimes remain
in power even after the financial crash? Why does business largely continue
as usual after the crisis has waned? As important as it is to attribute responsibility to external forces such as currency speculators and the IMF's and
World Bank's neoliberal economic policies, finger-pointing and economic-
nationalist sentiment can also hinder the more difficult task of coming to
terms with how both statist and popular elements within the affected countries were also responsible for the conditions that generated the crisis.

Strictly speaking, such an accounting of responsibility for the crisis
wrought by financial globalization can no longer assume that it is a form of
trauma. Despite surface similarities to colonial trauma such as the crisis's
systemic or structural character and its origins in material political and economic conditions at the national and transnational level, the power and
politics of global money cannot be understood in terms of the breaching
of a protective barrier. In global financialization, money is not merely a
force of destruction (*Destructionkraft*), as Marx claimed (Marx and Engels
1932/1970, 59; 94). It is also clearly productive in ways that go beyond Marx's
understanding of production. There is no longer any barrier separating the
inside from the outside because from the start, national economies are actively opened up by their states to the outside. Transnational capital flows
fabricate the economic well-being of these collective subjects and their individual citizens from the start. It makes no sense to speak of trauma unless
trauma is no longer pathological and the result of an external imposition
but a normal state of existence, a power that is operative from the start, at
the origin.

Within this framework, we need to distinguish between the different modalities of constitutive exposure and their levels of operation: first, at the
macrological level of global political economy, states undertake aggressive
policy initiatives to open up their markets and attract foreign capital. As
Saskia Sassen has argued, the state's active internalization of the legal, eco-

nomic, and managerial rules, standards, and concepts required for cross-border business transactions and capital mobility within the framework of international finance and corporate services leads to its partial denational-ization, since it is effectively welcoming its own disciplining by transnational legal and corporate regimes (Sassen 1998, 200). Second, at the level of the biopolitical production of the individual and the population, techniques of discipline and government craft the bodies of individuals as bodies capable of work and create their needs and interests as members of a population. Third, at the level of social reproduction, global mass-consumer culture also leads to the proliferation of sophisticated consumer needs and desires. These processes prepare the ground in which the desire for hyperprofit and the speculative drive can take root in individuals. They constitute the conditions of possibility of the political and economic self-determination and sovereignty of collective subjects and the self-mastery and security of individual subjects. At the same time, this condition of possibility of strength and power also implies a radical vulnerability.

The physiology of power of financial globalization differs from the colonial model of power presupposed by postcolonial cultural critique in at least two ways. First, it does not work through external imposition or impingement on a preexisting subject. Second, it does not operate in the first instance at a mental, psychical, or ideational level, even though it prepares the ground for processes of ideological subject formation to take root. Marxist categories of analysis such as alienation, ideology, and reification still have an explanatory value provided that we understand the reification of consciousness (Lukács) as originary rather than something that befalls the subject under conditions of alienation, since the laboring subject of needs is itself a product-effect and not an original ground that subsequently becomes alienated. I would like to suggest that this physiology of power and its violent consequences should be understood not through the motif of trauma but in terms of what Jacques Derrida called in his final writings "auto-immunity." Autoimmunization is a perversion of the process of immunity. In immunization, a body protects itself by producing antibodies to combat foreign antigens. In autoimmunization, however, the organism protects "itself against its self-protection by destroying its own immune system" (Derrida 1998, 73n27). Autoimmunization is therefore a form of suicide where the organism immunizes itself against its own immunity.[20] The autoimmune or suicidal character of hyperdevelopment through globalization lies in the fact that the constitution of the self's very selfhood requires the exposure of the self to the alterity and heteronomy of capital flows. In defending itself against this other, the self is doing nothing other than compromising its own selfhood, since its selfhood comes from the other. In Derrida's words, "The autoimmune consists not only in harming or ruining oneself, indeed in destroying one's own protections, and in doing so oneself, committing suicide or threatening to do so. . . . It consists not only in compromising oneself [*s'auto-entamer*] but in compromising the self, the *autos*—and thus ipseity. It consists not only in committing suicide but in compromising *sui*- or *self-referentiality*, the *self* or *sui*- of suicide itself. Autoimmunity is more or less suicidal, but, more seriously still, it threatens always to rob suicide itself of its meaning and supposed integrity" (Derrida 2005b, 45).

I have written at length elsewhere on the autoimmune character of postcolonial national culture (*Bildung*) as the opening up of the body to the supplementation of an image (*Bild*) (Cheah 2003). I conclude here with a brief outline of the autoimmune character of development through foreign capital and the cultivation of human capital. Financial flows are autoimmune processes. On the one hand, inflows of money strengthen the well-being of the national economy and are therefore a source of power and security that can be drawn on in self-defense against any external threats. On the other hand, however, since this integrates the nation into a circuit of capital market processes where other actors who have even more money can attack and weaken the nation through currency speculation, what is medicine is also poison. Hence this constitutive alterity needs to be divided into two so that the self can provisionally act in defense of itself, to protect itself against this other that is also in fact itself. Hence, in the Malaysian case, capital controls were established and justified through Prime Minister Mahathir's pious distinction between immoral forms of capital flows that lead to abnormal economic activity such as currency trading, short selling, and trading with borrowed shares and other forms of speculation, which are "unnecessary, unproductive and immoral" because they do not finance any real trade, and moral and productive forms of financial flows that contribute to the real economy. Bad flows of money are manipulative. They lead to "no tangible benefit for the world. . . . No substantial jobs are created, not products or services enjoyed by average people. . . . Their profits come from impoverishing others. Southeast Asians have become the targets because we have the money but not enough to defend ourselves."[21] Mahathir superimposes this moralistic distinction onto a Euro-American imperialist conspiracy against developing Asia: "But now we know better. We know that economies of developing countries can be suddenly manipulated and forced to bow to the great fund managers who decide who should prosper and who should not" (quoted in Gill 1997, 124). But this obscures the point that any given state of global economic hegemony is sustained by the power of capital flows, and that all financial flows and profits, whether they come from production or speculation, involve exploitation.

But at the same time, and this is the real meaning of the crisis, there does not seem to be any way out of this circuit of exploitation. The long-term solution that is invariably suggested is sustainable development through the cultivation of human capital through state education policies. Here is the politically correct advice of the World Bank based on focus group results from Indonesia and the Philippines on schooling for the poor:

> Beyond the crisis, the education system will shape the region's future workforce and the competitiveness of its economies. Sustaining high quality and broad-based educational expansion is central to equipping workers with the skills for high productivity manufacturing and service industries and to train them over the course of a working life. . . . Institutional and policy reforms are required to foster the high quality schooling which includes the skills that will propel East Asian countries into the knowledge economy of the next century. (World Bank 1998b, 290)

Here we hit against the autoimmune character of governmentality. Governmental technologies build human capital to strengthen the national economy. But in so doing, education's primary function is also reduced to the government of human resources in the interests of creating a more efficient and intelligent pool of commodified labor for the global economy. Yet, as the example of the East Asian model of development illustrates, this is the only way to ascend the hierarchy of the international division of labor.

Unless we can somehow leap out of the networks and circuits of capitalist globalization, the inflow of foreign capital is something that no developing country in the postcolonial South cannot not want. Since we are all inextricably woven into and implicated within the web of the productive power and politics of money, postcolonial cultural critique should at least begin by questioning the continuing dominance of the colonial paradigm of power as an external imposition. This is not to say that this type of power no longer exists. It clearly does. But it is no longer the main modality and form of power in contemporary globalization. One fundamental task of post-colonial critique would be to interminably track the autoimmune processes of finance capital at every turn, looking at how and when the medicine can become poison in the interest of postponing or stalling these noxious effects and lengthening the respite of postcolonial nations outside the OECD so that, hopefully, they can become as powerful as possible within the rules of this new game of power. At the same time, the consequences and effects of any increase in power for a given postcolonial nation-state within the international division of labor also need to be interminably circumscribed, because the strengthening of a state necessarily leads to the further instru-mentalization and exploitation of its own citizens, especially marginalized minorities, and other peoples.

Notes

This chapter first appeared in *positions: East Asia Culture Critique* 16, no. 1 (spring 2008).

1 "In traumatic neuroses the operative cause of the illness is not the trifling corporeal injury but the affect of fright—the psychical trauma. In an analogous manner, our investigations reveal, for many, if not for most, hysterical symptoms, precipitating causes which can only be described as psychical traumas. Any experience [*Erleb-nis*] which calls up distressing affects—such as those of fright, anxiety, shame or physical pain—may operate as a trauma of this kind; and whether it in fact does so depends naturally enough on the susceptibility of the person affected. . . . In the case of common hysteria it not infrequently happens that, instead of a single, major trauma, we find a number of partial traumas forming a group of provoking causes. These have only been able to exercise a traumatic effect by summation and they be-long together in so far as they are in part components of a single story of suffering. There are other cases in which an apparently trivial circumstance combines with the truly operative event [*eigentlich wirksamen Ereignis*] or occurs at a time of peculiar susceptibility to stimulation and in this way attains the dignity of a trauma which it would not otherwise have possessed but which thenceforward persists." Breuer and Freud, "Vorläufige Mitteilung," 84–85; 6. I have modified the translation where ap-propriate. The text and its translation will hereafter be cited as "VM," with the page numbers of the translation following that of the German.

2 Freud, *Jenseits des Lustprinzips*, 31; 303. The text and its translation will hereafter be cited as *JL*, with the page numbers of the translation following that of the German.

3 For the distinction between fear (which is directed toward a known object), anxiety (anticipation of and preparation for danger, both known and unknown), and fright, see *JL*, 10; 281–82.

4 Freud also suggests that if a trauma causes a gross physical injury, then the chances of a neurosis developing diminish because any painful or feverish illness will lead to a distribution of libido to the injured organ and bind the excess of excitation.

5 The psychoanalytic concept of *Projektion* refers to the treatment of internal excitations that produce too much unpleasure "as though they were acting, not from the inside, but from the outside, so that it may be possible to bring the shield against stimuli into operation as a means of defense against them" (*JL*, 29; 300–301).

6 Fanon, *Black Skin, White Masks* (1967), 143–44. Hereafter cited as *BSWM*. Fanon quotes, but does not give a reference to, two passages from Freud's *Über Psychoanalyse: Fünf Vorlesungen* (8–9, and 25; 14 and 27). But see Macey 1999, 103–4, for the argument that Fanon has misread Freud because Freud is in fact distancing himself from Breuer and defines trauma in terms of fantasy instead of real experience.

7 I am using the phrase "structural trauma" in a way that is different from Dominick LaCapra's use of the term. For Fanon, the trauma of colonialism is historical, but it works through an imposed structure that can be abolished. LaCapra, however, uses "structural trauma" to refer to an ontological trauma that arises from "transhistorical absence (absence of/at the origin) and appears in different ways in all societies and all lives. . . . It may be evoked or addressed in various fashions—in terms of the separation from the (m)other, the passage from nature to culture, the eruption of the pre-oedipal or pre-symbolic in the symbolic, the entry into language, the encounter with the 'real'" (722). He distinguishes it from historical trauma, which is the trauma arising from specific historical events that affect specific subjects.

Although I appreciate the dangers of conflating historical trauma with structural trauma in LaCapra's sense, I cannot subscribe to his sharp distinction between the two forms of trauma, since I believe that historical examples can actively transform theory. To insist on a sharp opposition between the two is to subscribe to a Platonism where there is an a priori unchanging structure that can be figured in advance of concrete instantiations. I am grateful to Michael Rothberg for alerting me to this essay. In his perceptive response to an earlier version of this chapter, delivered at the University of Illinois Urbana-Champaign on February 8, 2007, Rothberg used LaCapra's distinction between historical and structural trauma to suggest that my characterization of global capitalism in terms of autoimmunity risked installing global capitalism as an eternal structure. But autoimmunity is precisely the constitutive undermining of every presence according to a law of radical contamination. As I suggest later, progressive movements are radically contaminated by the technologies that sustain global capitalism, just as global capitalism is also contaminated by progressive movements. Methodologically, the motif of autoimmunity would prevent any sharp distinction between structural and historical trauma, without thereby freezing a given historical example into a permanent structure.

8 "The collective unconscious is not dependent on cerebral heredity; it is the result of what I shall call the unreflected imposition of a culture. . . . The Antillean partakes of the same collective unconscious as the European. . . . Without thinking, the Negro selects himself as an object capable of carrying the burden of original sin. The white man chooses the black man for this function, and the black man who is white also chooses the black man. The black Antillean is the slave of this cultural imposition. After having been the slave of the white man, he enslaves himself. The Negro is in every sense of the word a victim of white civilization" (BSWM, 191–92).

9 "Since the racial drama is played out in the open, the black man has no time to 'make it unconscious.' . . . The Negro's inferiority or superiority complex or his feeling of equality is *conscious*. These feelings forever chill him. They make his drama. In him there is none of the affective amnesia characteristic of the typical neurotic" (BSWM, 150).

10 I am here setting aside the fact that in *Beyond the Pleasure Principle*, Freud's discussion of trauma led to the formulation of the death drive and not the preservation of life. Fanon does not take the death drive into account in his transposition of the concept of trauma.

11 "The book, it is hoped, will be a mirror with a progressive infrastructure, in which it will be possible to discern the Negro on the road to disalienation" (BSWM, 184).

12 The revised version of the essay in *A Critique of Postcolonial Reason* updates the list of proxies to include the national subject of the global South, the rural woman who is the consensual recipient of microcredit, woman as subject of development in UN Plans of Action, and, last but not least, "the postmodern postcolonialist" who engages in "hybridist postnational talk, celebrating globalization as Americanization" (Spivak 1999, 361). I have discussed Spivak's account of power and her critique of Foucault in greater detail in Cheah 2007.

13 See Mbembe 2001, especially chaps. 1 and 5; chap. 5 draws on Fanon.

14 See Amin 2003, 17–21, for a differential mapping of the former Third World into capitalist East and Southeast Asia, industrializing Latin America and India, and Africa and the Arab and Islamic world. Cf. Mbembe 2001, 52–53, on the nonfeasibility of the Southeast Asian route of rapid industrialization through the welcoming of global financial flows for African countries.

15 It is part of the hubris of critical theory influenced by psychoanalytic thought to assume that psychoanalytic concepts such as trauma or the death drive are immediately applicable to contemporary situations such as globalization and its politics. Such a gesture privileges psychoanalytic concepts as universally valid across all historical contexts and situations. Furthermore, the application of psychoanalytic thematics in the study of geopolitical events and political institutions is reductive. Since it dogmatically reduces everything to the psyche as the basic unit of analysis, psychoanalytic cultural theory does away with the need for different types and

levels of concrete analysis that are appropriate to the specificity of a given object of study. In short, such a use of psychoanalysis is against the spirit of the creolization of theory. My argument is that Fanon transformed the psychoanalytic concept of trauma by transposing it into the colonial situation and, more importantly, that postcolonial theory, which has been so influenced by Fanon's analysis of the psychical functioning of colonial power, needs to be rethought because in postcolonial financial globalization, the primary modality of power is not psychical. A more thorough and concretely grounded study of the relation of psychoanalysis to power relations would need to situate the institution of psychoanalysis and its concepts and practices within the rise of biopower in a way that Foucault suggested in the first volume of *The History of Sexuality*.

16 Jeffrey D. Sachs, *Asiaweek*, February 13, 1998, quoted in Gill 1998, 191–92.

17 On the buildup of mobile capital, see Wade 1998, 1538–39; and Chandrasekhar and Ghosh 1998, 68.

18 See Wade and Veneroso 1998a, 9. Cf. Jomo 1998, 6: "The problem was ultimately one of greed: the combination of much lower foreign interest rates and seemingly fixed exchange rates caused borrowers to gamble and not prudently pay the cost for some insurance by hedging."

19 See Wade and Veneroso (1998a, 16; 1998b, 31–33) for the argument that since East Asian societies have a high savings rate, foreign capital is not needed to finance development as long as there is government support for agreements between banks and firms about debt refinancing. Hence these countries can regulate the capital account to minimize the risk of short-term foreign capital flows and to reestablish stable growth.

20 Derrida 2003, 94. The *pharmakon* is an older name for autoimmunization (124).

21 Mahathir Mohamad, keynote address at IMF–World Bank meeting, Hong Kong, September 13, 1997, quoted in Gill 1997, 125.

☙

FOUR

MATERIAL HISTORIES OF TRANSCOLONIAL LOSS
Creolizing Psychoanalytic Theories of Melancholia?

Liz Constable

> The tension between historical facts, and psychoanalytic
> truth, between subject position and subjectivity, between the
> performative and the constative, is the dynamic operator that
> moves us beyond the melancholic choice between either dead
> historical facts or traumatic repetitions of violence.
>
> Kelly Oliver, *Witnessing: Beyond Recognition*

"He died of disgust" (Il est mort de dégoût). These plangent words are uttered by Papicha, a celebrated cabaret singer and dancer in contemporary Algiers, and one of three main female characters in Nadir Moknèche's second film, *Viva Laldjérie* (2004).[1] Moknèche's film offers an intensely powerful and intricate cinematographic weaving together of image and sound that narrates and imagines the sociopolitical and affective reverberations of Algeria's civil war violence of the 1990s in three women's lives in contemporary Algiers, 2003. Contemporary Algiers, the city's public and private spaces, becomes a central character in the film, a character whose open spaces (particularly the ocean and the skies) open up luminously synesthetic sound-scapes through the pianist-composer Pierre Bastaroli's soundtrack, which combines what he describes as an intentionally nonexoticizing, non-Orientalizing piano score inspired by Debussy and Saint-Saëns with Algerian song, or *raï*, sung by Cheba Djemet. Focusing on the social life of affect in a transcolonial, war-traumatized, contemporary Algiers, Moknèche's film raises essential questions about what vernacular cultural production in transcolonial contexts does *to*, or *with*, the knowledge provided by psychoanalytic perspectives on the social and psychic legacies of traumatizing loss. Moknèche himself invites such questions when he writes that he hopes the film will serve as a "collective therapy," but he does not further discuss the film's modes and means of reinterpreting psychoanalytic approaches to loss (Marsaud 2007). By addressing these theoretical questions through an analysis of the film's dislocating and reframing of psychoanalytic concepts, I hope to open up for discussion the potentials and pitfalls of rethinking and rewriting psychoanalytic theories from minor perspectives.

As Shu-mei Shih and Françoise Lionnet point out in their introduction, among the many critical vocabularies generated by Euro-American Theory, Freud's work on mourning and melancholia has generated a significant body of scholarship that theorizes melancholic formations not as a problematic "one size fits all," but instead that recognizes that "one form of melancholia is never the same as another, as each arises from distinct social, economic, political, and cultural situations" (see Brown 2002; Eng and Kazanjian 2002; Cheng 2001). To put it simply, the universalization of melancholia actually occludes the melancholia of racialized and sexualized subjects. Starting from this point of departure, my analysis turns to one historically specific alternative genealogy for understanding a situated sociopsychic response to loss. The genealogy I trace starts from the material histories of contemporary Algeria, as mediated by Moknèche's film of 2004 and as mediated by decolonization discourses on the social life of affect, in particular Frantz Fanon's and Kelly Oliver's writings. Moknèche, Fanon, and Oliver all engage productively with psychoanalytic accounts by drawing from subjects of history whose experiential realities of the asymmetrical impacts of colonization, and subsequently globalization and neocolonialism, offer the material grounds for a situated encounter with, and reconfiguring of, psychoanalytic accounts of loss: that is, a creolizing of psychoanalytic accounts. By designating this process a creolizing of psychoanalytic accounts, I understand the ways that Moknèche's, Fanon's, and Oliver's discourses of decolonization on affect challenge the epistemological, historical, and geopolitical inclusions and exclusions formative of "theory as such," and challenge the ways that psychoanalytic accounts *can* end up circulating as theory. The creolization of theory, as I use it here, designates, following Édouard Glissant, the dynamic processes of an ongoing differentiation of both identities and ideas through contact and diffraction; the self-alteration that opens spaces for theorizing, from minority perspectives, through and with the differences that result from the entanglements of identities and ideas in colonial and global histories of domination and dissymmetry. In what follows, first, I examine the problems emerging from psychoanalytic theory's belated work in theorizing the sociopolitical dimensions of psychic pain and in taking into account the social underpinnings of the psyche, before moving to a case study of Moknèche's mediation in *Viva Laldjérie* of the social life of affects of transcolonial loss.

When Papicha, played by the Algerian singer Biyouna, spits out this laconic, visceral explanation of her husband's death during the decade of civil war in Algeria, spectators see a melancholic, tearful, and enraged Papicha on-screen.[2] After a visit with her adult daughter, Goucem, to the cemetery to place dead flowers on the tomb where her husband is buried, she has sought out the familiar and reassuring space of a bar in Algiers, La Madrague, where she sits alone and retraces memories of her husband's death in 1995. In the film's diegesis, the melancholy, rage, and pain expressed in her words "He died of disgust" have been reactivated by a banal and yet intensely humiliating event for Papicha. A short taxi ride in Algiers has placed her in the unexpected company of fellow passengers whose conversation is sparked by a newspaper article announcing the reopening in Paris of a famous Algiers nightclub, Le Copacabana, where Papicha sang and danced before the years of civil war. Her fellow passengers' taunting incomprehension of the rationale for reopening the nightclub, as opposed to a mosque on the same site, matches in intensity Papicha's own disgust and indignation: disgust that she should find herself in the company of passengers who remind her of the all-too-palpable legacies of the Front Islamique du Salut (FIS), gender-based discrimination, violence, and terror, of the 1990s.[3] These legacies remain in vestigial yet violent form in the inhospitable sociopolitical and cultural climate for women in contemporary Algiers, and most poignantly for her, in the inhospitable environment for her life's work as a celebrated female artist and singer. Although the film does not provide precise information about the circumstances of her husband's death, the multiple references to Papicha's fear of being recognized by Islamists suggest that her husband died as a result of Islamist terrorist violence. As spectators, we sense this, as opposed to knowing it, because throughout the short trip outside of Algiers to the cemetery, in the streets, and then at the cemetery, the film shows Papicha needled by the fear that she is being recognized by Islamists.

The scene I have described foregrounds an affective response (disgust) that figures the "cause" of one person's death, while the tautly visceral affective resonances of disgust blister the surface of Papicha's own verbal outcry about that death: "He died of disgust." But whose disgust does this comment refer to? This is one of the important questions the film poses for a discussion of psychoanalysis reinscribed through, and re-embedded in, the material histories of minority cultural formations. Moknèche's film opens up for analysis spectators' and critics' assumptions about the links that connect affect to social context, and social context, in turn, to individual and collective subjects' responses to psychic pain. As soon as I articulate these initial questions, they fan out into multiple, related investigations about the film's representations of the relational power of the transmission of affect, investigations into the movements of affects across intersubjective and intrasubjective relations, and across intergenerational relations. Does the reference to disgust designate others' disgust directed against Papicha's husband, or the mortifying self-abjection that he, in turn, bears as a result of the disgust "dumped" in him? And as Papicha's disgust-puckered words remind us, the disgust also lives on in her, as a transgenerational legacy of affect. The legacy of years of gender-based discrimination and of fear and terror inhabits Papicha's movements through public space and shapes her reactions. Others' aggressive contempt lives on in her as fear. And where Papicha develops an intensely fearful, yet equally intensely contemptuous, response to those who seek to deny her the possibility of creating her own meaning, others' disgust has another counterpart in her own reactive contempt, fueled in turn by her husband's death.

I begin with the analysis of this sequence because Moknèche's film challenges so powerfully long-held assumptions about affectivity, and more specifically assumptions that affective responses reside in individuals, as opposed to being socially induced energies that cross over and function relationally to structure relationships between subjects and across generations. Equally important, Moknèche's cinematographic focus on the sociohistorical matrices for the affective reverberations of collective trauma and melancholy raises a closely related theoretical question about the encounter the film stages between psychoanalytic perspectives on affect, on the one hand,

and the capacity of vernacular cultural production to reinterpret, dislocate, reframe, and reshape psychoanalytic theories, on the other. The disgust, this sequence suggests, is not the possession of one subject, or of one generation, and cannot be defined in terms of psychological interiority. No, instead, the disgust is both the repugnance directed at her husband by Islamist fundamentalists who sought to censor his activities and his own revulsion at their objectives; it is also passed on, a transgenerational transmission of affect from Papicha's husband to Papicha herself, who spits out the words sodden and blistered with revulsion and scorn. Disgust functions dynamically and bears a crucial *relating* function in this sequence and throughout the film.[4]

Moknèche's film, through its focus on the social life of affect, prompts me, as I stated earlier, to ask what this film suggests that vernacular cultural production does *to*, or *with*, the knowledge provided by psychoanalytic accounts or theories. How does vernacular cultural production reframe and rewrite the foundational fictions and concepts of psychoanalytic theory? How does vernacular cultural production resituate or dislocate psychoanalytic theories in the process of bearing witness to affects resulting from transcolonialism? *Transcolonialism* is the term Lionnet and Shih use to designate the "shared, through differentiated, experience of colonialism and neocolonialism (by the same colonizer or by different colonizers), a site of trauma . . . the shadowy side of the transnational" (Lionnet and Shih 2005, 11). What is the potential, and what are the potential modes and media, of a psychoanalysis that bears witness to the psychic *and* the social dimensions of affective realities of transcolonial, transnational subjects? Would such a reframing of psychoanalytic theory through vernacular cultural production be usefully understood as a creolization of psychoanalysis? How, then, would we define the meaning of a creolized psychoanalysis? How does psychoanalysis, rewritten from the perspective of the minor, avoid reinscribing hegemonic theoretical narratives that appropriate or distort experiences of nonhegemonic subjects? In the case of *Viva Laldjérie*, how does psychoanalysis reinscribed from the minor bear witness to the affects that emerge at the interface of the psyche and the sociohistorical in transcolonial contexts where histories of domination, dispossession, loss, and terror remain unmourned?

When I draw attention to the distinction between historical accounts and affective realities of experiences of transcolonialism, I am referring to Kelly Oliver's work on fictional witnessing, quoted in the chapter's epigraph, and to her argument that the responsive, and responsible, witnessing of past painful loss requires a double approach, or what I am calling an elliptical approach (in this case, historical and psychoanalytic), to generate "the dynamic operator that moves us beyond the melancholic choice between either dead historical facts or traumatic repetitions of violence (Oliver 2001, 16).[5] Witnessing, as Oliver's work argues, starts from the more finite context of the historical and works with the subject positions, identities, and identifying concepts available in that historical moment.[6] And yet responsive witnessing, sensitive to the insights of psychoanalysis, recognizes that all these historically determined categories can be epistemological traps whose criteria for what is real also exclude and preclude unarticulated and unknown affect that nevertheless shapes psychic and social structures. For that reason, ethically responsible witnessing to past pain, she argues, needs also to function in the psychoanalytic sense of bearing witness to something that cannot necessarily be seen, and that is beyond recognition or knowability (another's pain, another's enslavement), and that engages the incommensurability between the sociohistorical and the psychic while also recognizing the fully social nature of the psyche. Here, those subjects who have undergone dehumanizing forms of oppression bear witness to a pathos beyond recognition and to something other than the horror of their objectification. Witnesses to social and psychic oppression do not demand simply to "be seen" or to "be recognized." Their demands go beyond the question of recognition and engage the infinite responsibility of witnessing "beyond recognition" (where entirely different epistemological criteria prevail for deciding what is real).

Kelly Oliver's work on witnessing beyond recognition suggests that cultural artifacts can be considered as modes of witnessing beyond recognition, and therefore also as epistemologically elliptical, or multipolar, modes of theorizing. As epistemologically elliptical modes of theorizing, cultural artifacts understood this way have the representational and affective capacity to make visible the simultaneous interactions and articulations of the social and the psychic. They have this capacity precisely because their nondocumentary modes of representation figure and gesture toward (if they do not represent) the tensions and contradictions generated in people's lives by traumatizing losses, which open onto the psychic, yet social, wounds of history.

In referring to affects, I adopt the distinction that Teresa Brennan (2004) makes between feelings as "sensations that have found their match in words" (19) and affects as socially induced emotions and energies that are "thoughtless" (116), a type of "intelligence of the flesh" (140) that interrupts thought and defies the concept of the emotionally self-contained subject. Affects, Brennan argues, have effects independently of the individual experiencing them, because affective energies cross over between subjects, and, to give the example I used from Moknèche's film, the aggression of one person can be the anxiety of another.[7] Moknèche's cinematographic witness to the workings of social affect, and to the social sources and paths of psychic suffering, takes us to another crucially important dimension of asking what we might discover when we examine vernacular cultural production as an elliptical or multipolar mode of theorizing, which rewrites psychoanalytic perspectives on loss. Brennan's work departs from a long-held consensus across various critical approaches that considers affect and affective energies as self-contained and located in the individual. Instead Brennan emphasizes the transmission of affect, the ways "the emotions or affects of one person, and the enhancing or depleting energies these affects can entail, can enter into another" (3). Whereas social theorists have accepted for a long time that the ideas or thoughts of a given subject are dependent on culture, time, and social power structures, Brennan suggests that contemporary theorists still resist the proposition that a subject's emotions are not its own or that a subject is not affectively self-contained.[8] Pointing out that in the approaches to affect in many non-Western cultures, movement of affect between subjects is a given, Brennan argues: "The fact is that the taken-for-grantedness of the emotionally self-contained subject is a residual bastion of Eurocentrism in critical thinking, the last outpost of the subject's belief in the superiority of its own worldview over that of others" (2). If, as Brennan's work on the social transmission of affect and energy suggests, the assumption of an emotionally self-contained subject is one of the lingering vestiges of Eurocentrism in critical thinking, her hypothesis provides us with further impetus for examining Moknèche's film—and other vernacular cultural production about the affective realities resulting from transcolonial experiences—as multipolar or elliptical fictional witnesses to social affect and as potential creolizations of psychoanalytic theories.

I have organized the analysis that follows into two sections. In the first, I discuss the potential incompatibilities between psychoanalytic theories and

matizing losses, on the one hand, and a responsive and responsible ac-
nt of losses resulting from gender-based discrimination, violence, and
crimes in Algerian women's lives, on the other. Her words take us di-
y to the role of psychoanalytic theories in bearing witness to the "site of
ma . . . the shadowy side of the transnational" (Lionnet and Shih 2005,
umbled, tangled, inextricable, unidentifiable bits of painful affect: the
, suffering, and losses described here, unlike straightforward experi-
s or memories, have left an impact on the psyche and the body that in
registers as emptiness, an affective void that impedes identification and
ng of feelings and blocks the narrating or telling of a story. Although
ll pain necessarily becomes traumatic, as pain becomes traumatizing, it
s itself and can result in a loss of meaning, an uncertainty about how to
d describe oneself. As a result, the affects emerging from pain that be-
s trauma mark the psyche while remaining incomprehensible to trau-
ed subjects themselves.[9]
d yet right away, the question implicitly posed by the absent English
for *koulchite* opens up the theoretical questions implicit in rethink-
sychoanalytic concepts from minoritized perspectives—a creolized
oanalysis—where, that is, minority perspectives provide the explana-
heoretical narratives, and not just the raw material for others' theo-
use the term *creolization* (of theory) first to identify the critical points
arture and objectives of research scholars whose minor and minori-
erspectives (their points of departure) prompt them to provide ex-
ory accounts of—or to theorize—the mediation of social phenomena
h local, vernacular viewpoints and vernacular modes of representa-
hich are in themselves the results of encounters. Therefore the points
rture of creolized theory are not static entities but instead *relational*.
t in creolized theory is the question that Françoise Lionnet and Shu-
ih articulate when they ask, "How do the two terms *minority* and
inflect each other, when theory as such is Eurocentric?" (Lionnet
h 2005, 12). Encounters and the resulting inflection and diffraction
ities creolize theory. As with postcolonial theory, creolized theory
ges the epistemological, historical, and geopolitical inclusions and
ns formative of "theory as such." And yet creolized theory no longer
s the vertical axis of colonizer-colonized power relationships within
-state and instead departs from the axis prevalent in postcolonial

responsive witnessing to the affective realities of
national trauma; in the second, I propose a case s
a cinematic creolization of psychoanalytic theori
a theorizing whose medium is vernacular cultura
ond section, I situate my case study within discuss
tions raised when cultural artifacts re-embed ps
unmourned loss in material history, and resituate
terial conditions of minoritized perspectives.

From *L'Interdite* (1993) to *Viva Lal*
Shifting Historical Contexts and S
of Psychoanalysis in a Min

In Malika Mokeddem's semiautobiographical n
den Woman) (1993), an Algerian physician, Sul
fective realities of Algerian women she encou
Aïn Nekhla, Algeria:

> In front of the doctor they're nothing more
> ing *koulchite*. I scrutinize *koulchites*. Jumble
> piled up in an inextricable tangle. I try to fi
> untangle, I sort. I get discouraged. My exas|
> pincers, and clumsiness lies in wait for me
> here in the South of Souths, the doctor is (
> drugs.
>   Loss of meaning is a *koulchite* in prepa
> each cell of the body of fate. (Mokeddem

She describes these affective realities starkly
also states, "I'm not a psychoanalyst, and h
doctor is deprived of even the most vital d
chite in preparation" (Mokeddem 1998/1993
description of the fictional rural setting in
could not be further removed from the r
and temporal transnational realities of tl
filmic representation of urban Algiers, M(
multiple potential incompatibilities betwe

tra
cou
wai
rec
trai
11).
pain
ence
turn
nam
not a
burie
see a
come
matiz
A
word
ing p
psych
tory t
ries. I
of dep
tized
planat
throug
tion, w
of dep
Implic
mei Sh
theory
and Sh
of iden
challen
exclusio
privileg
a natio

analyses. Creolized theoretical accounts work with the constitutive trans-national relationalities of cultural entities in contact zones, from the diverse modes of relationality (minor to minor, and relations emerging through vernacular responses to the colonizing impact of multinational capital and cultural globalization). Following Glissant's *Poétique de la relation* (1990), creolization's starting point lies in the initial encounters of *métissage*—the intermixing of groups, languages, and cultural forms produced through the social organization of colonialism and slavery. However, it is important to emphasize that creolization, as I am using the concept here, goes beyond métissage and designates instead the dynamic processes of an *ongoing* differentiation of identities emerging through contact, by diffraction, and the self-alteration implicit in *la relation*, an understanding of creolization that opens spaces for theorizing though, and with, the differences (translations and mediations, clashes and discords) resulting from encounters.[10]

With these basic markers in place for an understanding of creolizing of theory, Mokeddem's character, Sultana, points to the positive potential, as well as to a potential critical impasse, of a creolized psychoanalytic perspective that could take into account the interdependence of psychic and sociopolitical contexts in shaping the psychic, corporeal, and affective dimensions of women's potentially traumatizing losses in Algeria of the 1990s. What do I mean by the potential critical impasse? Mokeddem's female physician refers to the women's pain through the term *koulchite* (the term is left untranslated). The linguistic-cultural impasse points to a number of ways in which it would be legitimate to protest that psychoanalytic approaches to traumatizing losses are not necessarily equipped to provide a responsive and responsible account of losses resulting from systemic, ongoing trauma of gender-based discrimination, violence, and war crimes in these Algerian women's lives.

First of all, psychoanalytic theory developed through a primary matrix of the family drama or family romance, and its accounts presuppose an individual psyche fundamentally at odds with the social, and presuppose individual instincts in conflict with social interdictions. In psychoanalysis's founding narratives, the concept of a social psyche (a subjectivity whose psychic life cannot be explained apart from its social contexts) is missing, and this theorizing of psychoanalysis as social theory has only more recently been undertaken primarily from various different minor perspectives: feminist theory, queer theory, and anticolonial and postcolonial theory (Brennan 2004; Cvetkovich 2003; Fanon 1952/1967, 1963; Oliver 2002, 2004).[11] As a result, in the case of the wartime losses and gender discrimination that Mokeddem's novel and Moknèche's film recount, unless the foundational psychoanalytic concepts (such as affect, the unconscious, trauma, melancholia) undergo significant revision and rethinking—as has been undertaken by these critics—these concepts would seem, at first, less well equipped to account for loss that is systemic in nature, and less capable of bearing witness to the social sources of psychic suffering.[12]

Here the potential mismatch emerging from psychoanalytic theory's belated work in theorizing the sociopolitical dimensions of psychic pain and in taking into account the social underpinnings of the psyche is likely to be compounded by the cultural and historical embeddedness of its normative foundational fictions. Indeed, much of the important context-sensitive and imaginative rethinking of psychoanalysis that *has* addressed the collective dimensions of loss and collective trauma has been undertaken in post–World War II Europe, in Germany and France, as opposed to previously colonized nations.[13] And so even the psychoanalytic approaches that have addressed the sociopolitical contexts for psychic pain may well require a radical disembedding of core cultural assumptions to bear witness to the losses of subjects in a decolonized nation. However, just as a creolization of theory shifts emphasis away from postcolonial theory's primary focus on colonizer-colonized power structures, and instead toward the multiple ongoing construction of relational identifications at work in the *mise-en-relation* of what Édouard Glissant refers to as the *chaos-monde*, a similar shift has been undertaken by the psychoanalytically informed social theorists I mentioned earlier. Brennan, Oliver, and Cvetkovich, who have developed Fanon's analyses of affective imperialism, have foregrounded the relational movements of affect in their rethinking of psychoanalytic understandings of oppressive power structures.

Oliver, building on the writings of Fanon, argues persuasively that if the occupation of body, material world, and psychic space in oppressive sociopolitical structures (colonial and neocolonial) is *total* in a systemic way, it is because *affective* imperialism functions to secure and renew asymmetrical power relations. But what exactly does this mean? We might usefully return first to Fanon, to a passage where he contrasts the effects of foreign occupation on an occupied population in wartime (the German occupation of

France in World War II) and in a colonial war (Algeria): "Under the German occupation the French remained men; under the French occupation the Germans remain men. In Algeria there is not simply the domination but the decision to the letter not to occupy anything more than the sum total of the land" (Fanon 1961/1963, 204). Where Fanon underscores the occupation of the "sum total of the land," the extensiveness and far-reaching nature of the total and systemic colonial occupation he defines here is one that Oliver interprets through Fanon's interpretation of psychic life and social structures as interdependent, an understanding she elaborates subsequently through her concept of the colonization of psychic space, to which I will return. Oliver emphasizes Fanon's consistent linking of economic and psychological oppression and, critical to my analysis here, foregrounds, as other readers of Fanon have not done in such a sustained way, his attention to minds and bodies as *interrelationally constitutive* through the transmission of affect. In referring to Fanon's interrelational embodied subjects, Oliver gives a strong reading to Fanon's emphasis on the circulation or movement of affect between minds and bodies, the capacity of bodies to "dump" or "project" unwanted affect into other bodies. The implications of such an understanding of the transmission of affect (as social in origin, biological and neurological in impact) redefine affect away, as I noted earlier, from notions of interiority and toward a fully socialized concept of the projection and uptake of affect. In turn, this makes accessible for analysis the psychic and physical interactions between and among bodies in producing and maintaining oppressive structures of power. As Oliver and Brennan contend, in social contexts thick with negative affects (anxiety, fear, or grief, for example), thick with the affects that subjects seek to live *without*, the urge intensifies to maintain one's sense of self, and identity, through depositing disturbing affects in the other. Oliver concludes that Fanon's writings on the social psyche point us to the understanding that "the colonization of the body and of the material world is also always the colonization of psychic space" (Oliver 2004, 49). Her focus on exposing for analysis colonialism's "affective imperialism" becomes tremendously useful in envisioning the possibility of a creolizing of psychoanalytic theories of loss. First she does this by emphasizing a fully interrelational social psyche, and then by foregrounding the projective and introjective movements of affect between minds and bodies as constitutive of relational subjects in oppressive sociopolitical structures.

I frame the second part of my analysis by pairing two texts whose contexts of production open and close a decade of civil war in Algeria to advance a hypothesis about the shifts in context over that decade when it comes to encounters between psychoanalysis and vernacular cultural production. Mokeddem's *L'Interdite* (1993) is written from the middle of Algeria's years of civil war, and Nadir Moknèche's *Viva Laldjérie* (2004) appears a decade later. In terms of the sociopolitical and historical background, there are substantial commonalities: both works focus on the effects on women of the armed conflict between the Algerian government and the various Islamist rebel groups between 1991 and 2002. Both text and film address Algerian women's affective reactions and responses to Islamist fundamentalists' attempts to use violence and terror to pressure women into conforming with an extremely restricted and prescribed role within the fundamentalist framework. Although the fundamentalist movement in Algeria has been active from the 1970s onward, the 1980s and 1990s represent the periods of intensified fundamentalist pressure on women in Algeria. In 1984, after a significant political victory, the fundamentalists made the state enact an extremely regressive family code that granted women the status of minors.[14] When in 1989 the Algerian constitution was modified to allow the formation of political parties—a measure adopted in response to popular protest against the single-party military-backed government—the fundamentalists united under the Islamic Salvation Front (FIS), and its armed wing, the AIS. The formation of the FIS marks the beginning of an intensification of political violence against women, an escalation of gender-based discriminatory violence that only increased after 1991, when the government canceled the second round of national legislative elections and the state banned the FIS. In rebellious reaction, the fundamentalists formed themselves into several armed groups, such as the MIA (Islamic Armed Movement) in the mountains and the GIA (Armed Islamic Group) in urban areas. The targets of their violent attacks were members of civil society opposed to fundamentalist perspectives, foreigners, journalists, artists, intellectuals, female relatives of members of the security forces, police, and government, and all women who did not follow the fundamentalists' prescripts: working women (particularly women whose profession entails the beautification of women, such as hairdressers and seamstresses), unveiled women, and single women.

Where novel and film share a sociopolitical and historical background, however, the context of production has shifted in significant ways. The shifts are implicit in the differences between the two titles. Where *L'Interdite* foregrounds a dichotomizing framework of oppressor and oppressed—one that emerges also through Mokeddem's reference to rural Algeria as the "South of Souths"—*Viva Laldjérie*, in the vernacular mixture of Arabic and French specific to Algiers, borrows the words of a popular football slogan of "One, two, three, Viva Laldjérie," a composite name introduced into spoken Algerian by combining the French word *Algérie* and the Arabic word *El Djazair*. By giving this film a title drawn from the everyday, creative practices of vernacular speech that differentiate themselves from both Arabic and French—creolization as differential dynamic—Moknèche's film announces its representation of a society that over the last decades has become increasingly shaped by the electronic media's circulation of global cultures and ideas, and that embeds Algerians in a composite global geography, to which Moknèche's film constantly draws our attention. My reference to creolization as a differential dynamic should not be misunderstood to sidestep the geopolitical and economic inequalities that structure his fictional Algiers, and certainly Moknèche's Algiers is embedded in, and divided by, asymmetrical power structures, but the potential poles and points of identification and disidentification, and modes of inclusion and exclusion, are now multiple.

To point to two examples, in the sequences where Goucem (Lubna Azabal), Papicha's daughter, and Papicha watch satellite television together, Moknèche's film uses a strategy of elliptical juxtapositions on a geopolitical level and juxtaposes their daily experiences of fundamentalist discrimination against women in Algiers with their viewing of U.S. media reports about body image, weight loss, and cosmetic surgery. In another sequence, Papicha finds her roast chicken dinner wrapped in a newspaper article about the hunt for Osama bin Laden, and once again the film draws out an implicit comparison between two contexts that shape in quite different ways the experiences and implications of terrorism. In doing so, the film foregrounds the double and multiple frames of reference that the characters use to situate their interpretations and situate themselves. For women living in an increasingly composite Algeria, questions relating to self-image and self-description are intensely fraught, and the stakes of those identifications are complex. The self-altering national changes that have reconfigured nationalist-colonialist binaries and undone dichotomous identities within the nation have simultaneously been accompanied and countered by polarizing religious Islamist solidarities that triggered the civil war and gender-based violence of the 1990s. The mutually constitutive yet conflictual simultaneous developments—internal pluralizing and also internal polarization—emerge against the stark economic and labor realities of contemporary Algerian society that provides the context for Moknèche's film, where, despite oil revenues, a third of the population today faces unemployment and becomes part of the population of *hittites* (those who support the wall, from the Arab word *hit*).

As the Lebanese journalist Samir Kassir remarks, in today's Algeria and in contemporary Arab-Muslim societies, enveloping the gendered particularities of loss of meaning, he observes a "deep sense of powerlessness . . . fuelled by unassuaged grief for past splendour" (Kassir 2006/2004, 4). Kassir argues that such potentially intolerable frustration, which "manifests itself more in *perceptions* and *feelings* than in statistics" (1; italics mine), finds its source in the serial layers of domination reverberating through a contemporary Algeria, which is internally divided through colonial historical inclusions and exclusions and now minoritized in relation to global economic and geopolitical imbalances. Kassir's observations identify what I am calling, following Kelly Oliver's work on psychoanalysis as social theory, a historically grounded melancholic sociopsychic environment shaping the affective realities of contemporary Algerians (Oliver 2002, 2004). And yet, as is evident in Moknèche's title, *Viva Laldjérie*, although the film represents a melancholic sociopsychic environment of post–civil war losses, at the same time it is not a film whose primary affect is melancholy. I am not simply stating that the film deals with the trauma of the reverberations of the civil war violence without representing that violence directly, although this is indeed the case. Instead I am pointing to the ways in which an examination of its mode and means of treating traumatizing loss embodies a reinterpretation of psychoanalytic perspectives on loss. And here to return to Kassir's commentary is helpful.

On the one hand, Kassir interprets contemporary Algeria's globally minoritized condition as generative of a situation where Algerians cannot *not* measure, as he puts it, their own anxieties about their future identity against Western "certainties" (projections, assumptions, fears) about "the Arab world" (2). At the same time, Kassir argues that the potentially unbearable loss of meaning, and what I am calling a transcolonial social melancholy, that can result from such comparative self-assessment is accompanied by a vibrancy of visual, music, and video subcultures developing not only in Algeria but throughout Arab-Muslim cultures. The energetic, vernacular, new media culture emerges as one of the results of increasing integration of other visual, aural, and information cultures, and the incorporation of different new media cultures has gone hand in hand with the development of transformative vernacular cultural production in these areas. Kassir suggestively contends that "while the economic and political structures, blocked by internal and global balances of power, play a decisive role in perpetuating the deadlock," if one looks to what he calls "the culture of creation," loss of meaning, or transcolonial social melancholy, is far from an accurate or complete description of the affective realities that contemporary Algerians would recognize in themselves (91).

He goes one step further and suggests that the lack of interface between thriving vernacular cultures of creation, on the one hand, and a more stagnant social culture, on the other, indicates a missed opportunity: "Perhaps that is where we should seek solutions: in the galvanizing effect that new media can have on cultural development, and that culture can have on durable economic development" (91).

Kassir's hypothesis about the vernacular cultures of creation reinvigorating and responding to the debilitating effects of transcolonial social melancholy in Arab-Muslim societies takes me directly to the questions I want to address about the ways Moknèche's film engages with social melancholy and the resulting potential loss of meaning—with, that is, the affects marking what I am calling the historically grounded sociopsychic realities of a contemporary, culturally globalized, yet economically impoverished and traumatized Algeria post–civil war.

Creolizing Responses to Unmourned Loss:
The Colonization of Psychic Space and Traumatic Loss
in Nadir Moknèche's *Viva Laldjérie*

Viva Laldjérie is Moknèche's second film. His first film, *The Harem of Madame Osmane*, appeared in 2000, and he has recently directed a third film, *Délice Paloma* (2006). Born in 1965, Moknèche spent his childhood and adolescence in Algiers and then studied law in France. After a period of travel, from 1989 to 1993, he studied drama at the Chaillot National Theater and with Ariane Mnouchkine at the Théâtre du Soleil. During this period, he began making films, and between 1993 and 1995 he studied film at the New School for Social Research in New York, where two of his short productions won first prize at the university film festival.

Viva Laldjérie focuses on the lives of three women—mother and daughter, and neighbor friend—living as single women in a residential hotel, the pension Debussy, between rue Debussy and boulevard Saint-Saëns in Algiers after the civil war, a city still staggering from the collective trauma of violent terrorist activity and still subject to outbreaks of Islamist violence against those who resist the fundamentalist agenda. Each of these female characters, through the past or present occupation Moknèche has chosen for them, through their living situations as single women, and through their kinship relations, provides the filmmaker with the opportunity to pinpoint specific facets of Islamist gender prescriptions and the women's quotidian responses to them. Papicha, or Mme Sandjak, a former dancer and cabaret singer (played by the singer Biyouna), is widowed, having lost her husband in an Islamist attack. She lives in fear of further attacks but is reluctant to settle for the inactivity and the seclusion of the life she is obliged to lead in the absence of her professional outlets. She attempts to perform in the community again and to reopen Le Vieux Copacabana, the nightclub where she used to perform, galvanized into action by nostalgia when she learns that the club is being closed to make space for a mosque. Her daughter, Goucem (Lubna Azabal), lives with her mother, works in a photography store and studio, and is involved in a long-term affair with Annis Sassi, a married doctor, who has a gay son. Finally, Fifi (Nadia Kaci) lives next door to Papicha and Goucem and works as a prostitute from her hotel apartment, where her telephone answering machine message states provocatively for a social environment laced with social strictures, "With Fifi, nothing is taboo" (Avec Fifi, pas de tabous).

It would be difficult to imagine three female characters whose daily lives and work in Algiers represent more direct noncompliance with fundamentalist political agendas than Moknèche's three women. As such, each character embodies the tensions and contradictions of contemporary Algerian society. Exotic dancing, cabaret singing, work in a photography shop and studio, sex work: each of these women's working lives defies fundamentalist prescriptions first because they are *working* lives. But Moknèche goes one step further in creating female characters whose working lives bring them to focus on their appearance, on image, and on the pleasure-in-artifice they experience through shaping their self-representation. How they look, and how they can change their images, and the playfully shameless satisfaction in creating looks and images for themselves and others are central concerns for each of these women. In creating these characters, Moknèche has created three women whose everyday lives constitute quotidian acts of defiance toward fundamentalist prescriptions although that defiance certainly does not overcome the stigma of the related fundamentalist gender-discriminatory stereotypes against all women who beautify themselves or help others to do so (hairdressers, seamstresses, estheticians, photographers, and so on).

By locating his characters in Algiers after the civil war, Moknèche sharpens the film's focus on the cultural specificity of the role of images, and self-image, in contemporary Algerian women's lives, and does so by contextualizing the topic within the background of collective trauma. When I use the term *collective trauma* I refer to the ways that the manic defenses—derealization of pain, amnesia—adopted in the face of traumatizing loss, violence, and terror end up undermining the potential for networks of solidarity, collapse public space, and make the dialogue, reflection, and negotiation crucial to community virtually impossible. Collective trauma, in the context of Moknèche's Algiers, has not completely dissolved public space. And yet the threats of outbreaks of violence have the potential to result in the social dissolution of public space and to retraumatize and shrink the sociopsychic space through which individual losses are experienced. Here the social shapes the psychic, and the psychic experiences a second and secondary traumatic loss. Kai Erikson describes collective trauma as follows:

> By collective trauma . . . I mean a blow to the basic tissues of social life that damages the bonds attaching people together and impairs the prevailing sense of communality. The collective trauma works its way slowly and even insidiously into the awareness of those who suffer from it, so it does not have the quality of suddenness normally associated with trauma. But it is a form of shock all the same, a gradual realization that the community no longer exists as an affective support and that an important part of the self has disappeared. . . . I continue to exist, though

damaged and maybe even permanently changed. You continue to exist, though distant and hard to relate to. But we no longer exist as a connected pair or as linked cells to a larger communal body. (Erikson 1994, 11)

Moknèche's characters are rebuilding their lives and their kinship connections within just such a precarious public space, a reduced though not entirely dissolved public space. The sequences focusing on Papicha, stuck in her hotel apartment, isolated in private space, spectator rather than performer, yearning for the public community spaces of her former dancing career, convey that sociospatial isolation most powerfully. Constrained architectural space becomes a metaphor for the collapsing of the psychic space or the colonization of psychic space through gender-based constraints on the three women's ways of making meaning.

Then, as Moknèche comments in an interview with the historian Benjamin Stora, the collective trauma takes on a culturally specific dimension around self-representations and images for contemporary Algerians, a dimension inseparable from their history of colonization and decolonization: "Algerians have a tricky relationship with images, their images. They started by seeing themselves through the colonial eye, a mass of undifferentiated people, then when independence came, as social realist archetypes: the Combatant, the Farmer, the Worker. Never as individuals with their own personality."[15] Moknèche describes the reactions to his film crew in Algiers when they started filming in 2003, and he comments, "Their relationship with their image had changed. I get the feeling people are starting to love themselves, maybe accepting to look at themselves." He then switches to discuss images of the city itself: "Since its independence, Algiers has practically not been depicted, a city always lacking contemporary images of itself. The reference self-portrait remains colonial or folkloric."

For women living in contemporary Algiers, their relationship to images, and to self-images, is even trickier, and the loss of "affective support," as Erikson puts it, at the level of the social environment resulting from collective trauma is reinforced by the impact of gender-based discrimination that dissolves the social environment crucial for women to sustain the emergence of psychic self-representation and self-images. At this point, Kelly Oliver's rewriting of psychoanalytic theory as social theory becomes germane. Oliver argues that most of the cultural critics using psychoanalytic concepts of projection, abjection, and exclusion have used these concepts to diagnose and account for "the effects on, and motivations of, the colonizer or oppressor. Much attention has been paid to how marginalized people operate as the abjected other of/for dominant culture." She continues: "Less attention has been paid to the effects of colonization and oppression on the psychic dynamics of those othered or marginalized within dominant culture" (Edwin and Oliver 2002, Oliver 2002, 49). From this starting point, Oliver's two most recent books have proposed a psychoanalytic social theory that "starts from the position of those who have been abjected and excluded by the traditional Freudian model," "a psychoanalytic social theory that reformulates psychoanalytic concepts as social and considers how subjectivity is formed and deformed within particular social contexts" (Oliver 2004, xvi). As Oliver points out, cultural critics working with psychoanalytic concepts such as melancholia, abjection, and trauma frequently use them in what I will refer to as either a cling-wrap approach or a patchwork approach. Either critics stretch and expand psychoanalytic concepts initially developed with regard to the individual and apply them to address social phenomena, or they combine psychoanalytic concepts with social theory, usually Foucauldian approaches, but nevertheless leave the psychoanalytic concepts fundamentally unchanged.

Oliver rethinks psychoanalytic concepts in a substantively different way through expanding the social formation of the psyche beyond the understanding of the social prevalent in object-relations theorists (who define the social in terms of the primary caregiver) to include, instead, the larger sociohistorical context and political economy. As I mentioned earlier, Fanon's writings play a key role in Oliver's account of the economic, material, and bodily (affective) relations that link colonizer and colonized, subject and object. Through Oliver's use of Fanon's account of the sociopolitical etiology of the colonial "affective aberrations" that he argues are produced relationally or dynamically in colonial structures, she demonstrates persuasively how unwanted affects end up transferred onto, or injected into, another person, the recipient, whose own affects are changed as a result. For Fanon, the colonizer's phobia, when unchallenged by society, becomes a "common phobia," naturalized as a socially acceptable attitude that in turn generates and fuels the colonized's obsession (to be recognized and accepted by the very subjects who oppress them).[16] The point that Fanon's writings prompt Oliver to make is that oppressors occupy other bodies through their projections, and then, through repression, the oppressors "defend" themselves against aspects of themselves they don't want to acknowledge. Here Oliver's reading of Fanon makes compellingly clear Fanon's reasons, as well as her own, for insisting that social theories of oppression are incomplete without a psychoanalytic concept of unconscious desire. Minus a theory of the unconscious, minus a theory of the social transmission of affect, and minus a theory of sublimation as an alternative to repression, it is much more difficult to account for the ways that subjects act against their own self-interests or their own well-being. As Oliver explains:

> To understand the relationship between oppression and social context and affect, we need to postulate the existence of the unconscious. Without this postulation, we become complicit with those who would blame the victims, so to speak, for their own negative affects. Even if sociological or psychological studies demonstrate a higher incidence of depression, shame or anger in particular groups, this information cannot be interpreted outside a social context and without considering subject position and subject formation. . . . The psychoanalytic notion of the superego is useful in diagnosing how and why those othered internalize the very values that abject and oppress them. (Oliver 2004, xxii)

An analysis of a short dialogue from Moknèche's film will bring into focus the tricky relationship his female characters have with images in contemporary Algiers. Oliver's linking of oppression, social context, and affect speaks directly to this situation through her redefinition of sublimation and trauma. And, as my analysis will demonstrate, Moknèche's cinematic rendering of his characters' responses to unmourned losses embeds Oliver's argument, in turn, in the material histories of contemporary Algeria.

Walking through the cemetery to place flowers on her husband's grave, Papicha manifests constant anxiety about being recognized and followed. Catching sight of a man in the cemetery, she says anxiously to her daughter, "There's a man who's looking at me in a strange way. I think he has recognized me" (Il y a un homme qui me regarde de travers. Je crois qu'il m'a reconnue). Her daughter Goucem is impatient, as if she doesn't credit her mother's fears as legitimate or realistic, as if she is familiar with this anxiety, and as if this situation has played out one too many times. She walks over to the man and asks him, "Sir, do you recognize this woman?" (Monsieur, vous reconnaissez cette femme?), to which he responds in the negative. On hearing this, spectators understand better Goucem's impatience, because Papicha exclaims with hurt and indignation, "He didn't recognize *the* Papicha?" (Il n'a pas reconnu la Papicha?). The switch in Papicha's feelings from apprehension about being recognized to hurt and indignation that she hasn't been recognized as the formerly celebrated nightclub singer and dancer encapsulates the complexly contradictory relationship to image and self-representation that an oppressive sociopolitical environment has generated for this woman-artist. Moknèche's skill as a filmmaker lies in presenting an individual's living of social contradictions through a humorous mother-daughter dynamic. Recognition for her in this particular sociopolitical environment can mean indictment, endangerment to her life, and yet her own ways of making a meaningful life require that recognition; Papicha lives this social contradiction resulting from traumatizing loss as a personal dilemma. Oliver's work on social melancholy addresses the living of social contradictions as if they are individual dilemmas when she writes that "there is a complicated relationship between cultural values and our sense of ourselves as agents; this relationship goes beyond the internalization of abject images" (Oliver 2004, xxii).

To understand Oliver's explanation of the "complicated relationship" between cultural values, our sense of ourselves as agents, and the role of images entails analyzing what she means by "the colonization of psychic space" and how she redefines psychoanalytic perspectives on potentially traumatizing loss through a concept of social melancholy. As I indicated earlier, Oliver's rewriting of psychoanalysis as social theory draws substantially on Fanon's analysis of the movement of affect, not just from one idea to another, as Freud posits, but from one body to another: "the aggressiveness which has been deposited in his [the colonized subject's] bones" (Fanon 1961/1963, 42). When Oliver refers to psychic space, the psychic for her does not designate interiority, because Oliver argues that social support is inherent within psychic identity, an idea I will return to later. Oliver brings Fanon's map of the affective aberrations produced by colonial power dynamics together with Julia Kristeva's reading of social history as inextricable from psychoanalytic concepts to study the effects of an absence of social support on psychic space. From Fanon and Kristeva together, she suggests that oppression functions as "the colonization of psychic space that results from a lack of social support" (Oliver 2002, 49). But how shall we understand this?

For Oliver, relationality is primary and foundational to subjectivity, and this understanding determines her notion of psychic space. What Oliver designates by *relationality* is not intersubjectivity, since relationality precedes subject-object relations. For Oliver, taking the relationality of subjectivity to its limits means "going beyond intersubjectivity and admitting that there is no subject or individual to engage in a relationship with another subject—to engage in an intersubjective relationship—prior to relationality itself" (Oliver 2004, xviii–xix). From this point of departure, she sees the psyche, as do Kristeva and Fanon, as an "open system," where energies, materials, and information move between the system and its environment through permeable boundaries.[17] The openness of psychic space depends on the transformation of affects into language and representation. But—and this is crucial to Oliver's reinterpretation of Kristeva's psychic space—for that meaning-making series of negotiations, transferences, and translations to occur, and for subjects to make their own meaning, psychic identification with a supportive space *within the social* is crucial. Here Oliver reroutes Kristeva's more classically psychoanalytic account of female melancholic depression through a social theory account of female melancholic depression: social melancholy.

Where Kristeva argues that Western cultures' tendencies to abject maternity can entangle women's identificatory processes in that same abjection (installed within the psyche) and can undermine meaning-making processes, Oliver leverages Kristeva's theory away from its familial foundation and reads her *against* the familial grain. In Oliver's revision, if identification with supportive space within the social necessarily precedes the articulation and representation of affects in language, and if that social support underpins the meaning-making processes that allow subjects to make language their own, what happens in the absence of that support in the social? Absence of support, inattentive support, and indifference, as much as denial of support or violent repression in social space, can all collapse psychic space and produce what Oliver sees as a double alienation implicit in oppressive contexts that "results not just from finding yourself in a world of ready-made meanings but from finding yourself there as one who has been denied the possibility of meaning making or making meaning your own without at the same time denying your subjectivity" (Oliver 2002, 56).

From this observation, the link back to Papicha's paradoxical nonchoice of being recognized or not being recognized becomes clear. Either Papicha is recognized as a dancer-singer but then recognized as a potential target of gender-based violence to be eliminated, or she is not recognized as Papicha, and the meaning of her life as an artist is erased: both options entail erasure, self-erasure, and her situation exemplifies exactly the process of the colonization of psychic space that Oliver describes. Papicha is faced with a nonchoice: were she to choose to give up her life's work, her way of making meaning in the world, she would collapse her meaning into those imposed on her in the culture around her; and, of course, she would also throb with a debilitating isolation because she is not translating or making meaning within social space.

As a result—this next point is crucial—the paradoxical nonchoice that confronts her is what Kristeva and Oliver define as a trauma. Different to classical psychoanalytic definitions of trauma, trauma develops here when subjects experience "the inability to find the social space in which, or language with which, to express one's own body and meaning" (Oliver 2002, 57). In redefining trauma this way, Oliver also departs from the traditional psychoanalytic understanding of sublimation as the process by which an individual converts affects into words and meaning. As we have seen, for Oliver, that process of essential meaning making is necessarily more accurately understood as *social* sublimation because "the ability to sublimate has everything to do with social context, support and subject-position."

When we approach Moknèche's film with an understanding of social melancholy generated by the colonization of psychic space—a shrinking of psychic space that threatens to collapse the possibility of making meaning—this interpretation reroutes and thereby creolizes the psychoanalytic concept of melancholy because it accounts for, and bears witness to, the minoritized perspectives of women's affective lives in a decolonized contemporary Algeria reverberating with fundamentalist gender-based discrimination. Equally important, if the importance of *mourning* can be understood, from psychoanalytic perspectives, to reside in the disencumbering of the psyche from attachment to past loss to enable reengagement in external attachments—to enable being alive, as a subject, to the presentness of the present—Moknèche's soundtrack plays a vital role in marshaling music's ability, through rhythm and beat, to open up frozen or immobilized psychic formations. Papicha's own reclaiming of her voice figures within the film's diegesis the role of music in the film's soundtrack that reconnects the isolated psychic to the social in ways that reach toward the affective pain that lies beyond the parameters of social paradigms of recognition.

To consider *Viva Laldjérie* as a vernacular creolization and theorizing of psychoanalytic perspectives on unmourned transcolonial losses inserts Moknèche's filmmaking in a trajectory where Édouard Glissant's work imposes itself as a crucial theoretical voice whose writings have creolized psychoanalytic approaches to unmourned loss. Glissant points, as do many other scholars of the Caribbean, to the reliance of communities in the Caribbean (who have lived in the shadow of a past history of transplantation and repeated collective trauma without a shared public witness) on the psychic survival strategy of a passive amnesia, or a derealization, of their past (Glissant 1981/1989; Dash 1998; Suk 2001; Nesbitt 2003). When communities derealize the past to "go on," history remains nonhistory (Glissant 1981/1989; Dash 1998), and painful affect fills subjects with an unmourned symbolic loss, a loss of meaning, that carries the potential to retraumatize all over again and to be affectively transmitted transgenerationally. Children bear and take on the unresolved affective states of their parents' generation, and unmourned loss can reverberate as buried affect from generation to generation.

What is important to signal both in Moknèche's cinematic re-embedding of psychoanalytic perspectives on loss, and in Glissant's analogous work, is the effect of reinterpreting loss through material histories. As I mentioned earlier, collective derealization as a response to unmourned loss has been studied most fully in post–World War II Germany and France. It is undoubtedly the social psychological study of psychoanalysts Alexander and Margarete Mitscherlich, *The Inability to Mourn: Principles of Collective Behavior* (1967/1975), that lays the foundations for subsequent psychoanalytic understandings of the group psychological processes involved in what Melanie Klein called a "manic defense" of a lost ideal. As their study points out, the German people, faced with overwhelming causal triggers for a melancholic onset of self-recrimination and loss of self-esteem in the aftermath of World War II, does not, in fact, experience a collective self-impoverishment or self-devaluation. Nor does it go through a process of mourning for the victims whose death Hitler's aggression had caused. The Mitscherlichs hypothesize that the German people avoided the self-devaluation of pending melancholic guilt through "breaking all affective bridges to the immediate past" (26), through a massive and yet unconscious

self-protective psychic mechanism that derealized or denied affective identifications with everything that constituted the reality of the Third Reich. But,
as the Mitscherlichs show, the psychic mechanisms of derealization, while
extremely effective in warding off the onset of overwhelming melancholic
guilt and lacerating self-reproach, nevertheless result in a psychic immobi-
lization characterized by a pervasive sense of passivity.

Acknowledging the acuity of psychoanalytic theories, Glissant redirects
their analytic insights toward the experiences of the very subjects their traditional formulations exclude. He identifies processes of collective amnesia
and derealization analogous to those that the Mitscherlichs' work discovers
in post–World War II German subjects: affective traces that can barely be
identified or spoken about by Caribbean subjects, and have resulted in a
frozen mourning of collective trauma.[18] However, by embedding the modes
and media of this particular psychic loss in the material conditions of Caribbean cultures, this move leads Glissant away from temporality to a relational sense of space. The entire text of Le discours antillais argues that transplanted Caribbean subjects, whose melancholic impulse may be to try to
return to, or to restitute, the lost past, should resist the impulse to recover
unitary or single lost origins. Instead he posits the recognition of the impossibility of returning (to idealized lost origins) as essential to acceptance
and acknowledgment of the point of contact and mixture of different ances-
tries, languages, cultures — la Relation — as the locus of an originary métissage for Caribbean cultures. In positing the recognition of relationality as
origin, Glissant argues that a transversal epistemological point of departure
is more likely to lead them out of collective trauma than the (re)turn to the
past that functions through the vertical axis.

Moknèche, like Glissant, rereads psychoanalytic understandings of responses to potentially traumatizing loss from a minor perspective, and both
emphasize the simultaneous articulations of the social and the psychic in
rewriting psychoanalytic theories from the minor. Both refocus on articulating the synchronic together with the diachronic, and for both, the distinction between painful loss, on the one hand, and psychic pain that becomes
traumatizingly debilitating, on the other, is related to the absence or presence of an environment where empathetic witnessing of that painful loss
takes place through dialogue, through creativity, or through shared community rituals.[19]

What does our discussion of Moknèche's rereading of psychic life as inextricable from the social bring to an understanding of creolized psycho-analytic theory? One of the most basic ways of defining theory is that it provides ways of making visible and identifying the categories through which we apprehend reality; theories provide us with the conceptual building blocks for analyzing, organizing, and synthesizing the *interconnectedness* of social phenomena. An equally significant objective of all theories that seek social and political change (feminist, ethnic studies, postcolonial studies, queer studies, disability studies, creolized theory) is the reclamation of the power of naming and of language itself as the primary mediator to bring empirical phenomena into a sphere of legibility. So just as theory works to make visible modes of mediation and to identify the categories defining modalities of power, the political goals underlying theory from minor perspectives have the additional goal of identifying, making space for, and creating frameworks through which previously invisible, ignored, disdained, or misrecognized realities can be apprehended through language: the generation of new critical, creolized, literacies.

If there is a creolization that theory needs to undergo to become adequate to, and responsive to, the realities of our transnationalized present, it entails first an ongoing affirmation of relational work connecting fields of study (and their theories) far too often artificially separate by disciplinary, linguistic, or institutional boundaries. Anne Donadey's comparison of critical frameworks developed to address historiographic metafictions in African American studies, on the one hand, and Francophone postcolonial studies, on the other, communicates the importance for scholars of undertaking comparative connections defined as "minor to minor" *theoretical* relations (ethnic studies and Francophone postcolonial studies). In analogous ways, Moknèche's cinematic recounting of responses to unmourned losses through the material histories of his Algerian characters engages in a creolization of theory in one way I have not discussed directly although the epigraph gestures toward this. How? He gives form to the tensions between "historical facts and psychoanalytic truths," to borrow Oliver's words, or in my words, the tensions between the psychic and the social, that structure his characters' affective lives. And in doing so, his film brings out into the open the primary and constitutive relatedness of different theoretical perspectives, as opposed to one theoretical explanation remaining the ground from which another theory figures forth its "truths."

Notes

1 I thank Daphne Potts for her perceptive comments and analyses of Moknèche's film, and for our many inspiring conversations about film.

2 The Algerian singer and actress Biyouna appears in Nadir Moknèche's three films to date: *Le harem de Mme Ousmane* (2000), *Viva Laldjérie* (2004), and *Délice Paloma* (2006). Her roles in Moknèche's films have introduced her music to metropolitan French audiences, and in 2006 she released her second album, *Blonde dans la Casbah*, including songs in the vernacular of Algiers, a mixture of Arabic and French, and a musical blend of chaâbi (popular musical genre in Algiers), reggae, rock, and funk.

3 When the FIS won the first round of elections in 1991, the military intervened to stop the second round and banned political parties based on religion—interventions that triggered enormous unrest and that led Algeria into the years of civil war from 1992–2002.

4 See Hirschkind's (2006) epilogue for a useful discussion of the problems implicit in referring to an Islamist fundamentalist movement.

5 In using the concept of an elliptical or double-foci approach to the witnessing of past pain and loss, I am adapting David Damrosch's (1995) argument that the double foci of the geometrical form of the ellipse offer a useful methodological approach for comparatists to adopt in making sense of cultural and literary production in our contemporary world, where the paradigms of cultural unities, and the binaries of centers and margins, are no longer adequate to address the modes and means of dynamics underlying cultural production. Interlocking cultures and a multipolar world, he suggests, demand analytic approaches that are flexible enough to respond to cultural production that spans and emerges from various cultural foci.

6 Here I am drawing on Oliver's distinction between subjectivity and subject position: "Subject positions, although mobile, are constituted in our social interactions and our positions within our culture and context; history and circumstance govern them. Subject positions are our relations to the finite world of human history and relations—the realm of politics. Subjectivity, on the other hand, is experienced as the sense of agency and response-ability constituted in the infinite encounter with otherness—the realm of ethics. And although subjectivity is logically prior to any possible subject position, in our experience, the two are always interconnected. This is why our experience of our own subjectivity is the result of the productive tension between finite subject position and the infinite responsibility of the structure of subjectivity itself" (Oliver 2004, xiv–xv).

7 See Brennan 2004.

8 Among theorists who have gone against the concept of an energetically and emotionally self-contained subject and worked instead on the transmission of affect, see Jean Laplanche, Wilfred Bion, and Daniel Stern.

9 Freud defines what makes affect "traumatic"—as opposed to, for example, simply disorienting or frightening—in terms of excessive excitations that impinge on the psyche and remain lodged or encrypted as repressed foreign bodies, because the psyche does not manage to adequately discharge them (through representation, verbalization, or responsive action). See Breuer and Freud 1893. In my analysis, I am emphasizing the second part of Freud's description of what makes an affect traumatic: that is, I emphasize absence of response as the catalyst that converts painful affect into trauma, as opposed to the impingement of excessive excitation being necessarily "traumatic" in and of itself. In this understanding, painful affect can become traumatic and remain as buried affect, in the absence of adequate modes of response, which I will define as "witnessing." For a different interpretation of connections between theories of trauma and the creolization of theory, see Cheah, this volume.

10 See Prabhu and Quayson 2005 for a helpful analysis of the different uses of métissage, creolization, and hybridity in Glissant, Bhabha, Lionnet, and Vergès.

11 The work of three of these critics bears directly on Francophone colonial and postcolonial societies. From an anticolonial perspective, Frantz Fanon's work in the 1950s addressed the inextricable character of social structures and psychic life in French colonial societies. In the 1990s, the feminist philosophers and social theorists Teresa Brennan and Kelly Oliver take up this work.

12 When Fanon took up his post as psychiatrist *médecin-chef* at the Blida-Joinville hospital, Algeria, at the foot of the Blidean Atlas Mountains in 1953, he had a caseload of close to two hundred patients, 165 European women and 22 male Muslim patients. Here he tried psychoanalytic techniques with his patients but struggled: both the institutional context and his own inexperience thwarted the transferential dimension of psychoanalytic psychotherapy. In the same hospital, however, he developed modes of psychotherapy grounded in his growing understanding of the specifics of the cultural world—its modes of sociability and its belief systems—of his patients. See "In Algeria's Capital of Madness," chapter 6 in Macey 2002.

13 Mitscherlich and Mitscherlich 1967/1975.

14 To give some examples of the restrictions imposed in the Family Code of 1984: women lost the right to marry but had instead to be given in marriage by a Wali (a matrimonial tutor who could be a minor male relative); women lost the right to guardianship of their children; they also lost the right to divorce and had only an unequal share in inheritance. See *Shadow Report on Algeria* 2000.

15 The interview with Benjamin Stora is included in the production notes to Nadir Mocknèche's documentary, *Viva Laldjerie* (2004), from Film Movement (filmmovement.com).

16 See "Colonial Abjection and Transmission of Affect," chapter 3 in Oliver 2004, 47–59.

17 As Oliver (2002, 58) points out, Kristeva adopted the concept of open systems from the biologist Ludwig von Bertalanffy, who developed open systems theory in 1956.

18 See Glissant's first two sections in book 3 of *Le discours antillais*: "Inconscient, identité, méthodes," and "Langues, langue."

19 The psychoanalyst Peter Shabad writes that suffering turns into traumatizing pain when that suffering is unwitnessed or unacknowledged: "It suggests that being alone and not being able to convey one's experience immediately are intrinsic to the transformation of suffering into trauma" (see Homans 2000, 200).

FIVE

⚫

FROM MULTICULTURAL TO CREOLE SUBJECTS
David Henry Hwang's Collaborative Works
with Philip Glass

Ping-hui Liao

Diversity, which is neither chaos nor sterility, means the
human spirit's striving for a cross-cultural relationship, without
universalist transcendence.

Édouard Glissant, *Caribbean Discourse*

David Henry Hwang is certainly among the most innovative Chinese
American writers who have continued to explore the expressive, transformative potentials of mixed genres from diverse cultural traditions in por-
traying newcomers or diasporas as creoles and bricoleurs. His characters in
plays or musicals ranging from *FOB* to *Flower Drum Song* tend to construct
while at the same time deconstruct their identities in the process of creolization; they not only register but also appropriate the complex life situations
of entanglement with a world that is neither stable nor flat. According to
Hwang, "We are all visitors. We all travel. We all ask questions. We all hope
one day, looking into the eyes of another, to find part of an answer" (Hwang,
1000 Airplanes, in *FOB*, 294); in another interview, he indicates that "I do
feel that in terms of trying to create a model that is more representative of
what this country is becoming, both multicultural plays and multicultural
theaters are ultimately the wave of the future" (Hwang, "Evolving," 19). I propose to look at several of Hwang's collaborative works with the American
minimalist Philip Glass as nodal points of encounter between power and
its other to deepen thinking of the psychosocial structures of ethnic and
racial formation, to move beyond the boutique of multiculturalism, and to
be more receptive to images, ideas, and sounds from a plurality of orbits that
constitute new (albeit uneven) connectivities and meanings.

It is apparent that Hwang often appropriates multicultural theatrical motifs and advocates a politics of recognition along the lines of multiculturalism. However, the ways in which he considers the more dynamic process of becoming, of stepping out of one's ethnic realms to interact with
other worlds, suggest that he opts for a theory of creolization rather than
a multiculturalist minority discourse. Multiculturalism, in this regard, has
to do with combating mainstream culture, which seeks to assimilate or re-
press minorities. Creolization, on the other hand, involves a process of not
only rethinking colonial power relations but of entanglement and enrichment through discursive struggles to be other than and larger than oneself.
Hwang makes this point when he says that a theme he traces through all his
corpus is "fluidity of identity." "In a lot of my plays," he comments, "people
become other people." But he hastens to add that "it has a lot to do with the
nature vs. nurture question. To what degree do you have an inherited identity, and to what degree is your personality shaped by the influences and environment around you?" Evidently, his notion of becoming something other
than oneself, of creolization, is by no means naive, as it is upheld without
losing sight of material reality and power relations: "Would I be different if
I was born in China? Or if I had a different skin color in this country? I also
think it's interesting to explore racism and stereotyping between minority
groups in this culture, because that's really where the future lies" (Berson
1990, 94).

Over the years, the gap as manifested in Hwang's literary discourses between the nature and nurture positions, between fixed identity and transcultural hospitality, has operated in complex, if ambivalent, terms. On the one
hand, Hwang highlights the roles of racial heritage and the sense of cultural
belonging. On the other, he creates dramatic situations in which flexible
citizenships and race interchangeability become possible. A number of his
early works, *The Dance and the Railroad* (1981) and *Family Devotions* (1981),
for example, appear to construct characters and plots around the principle
of ethnic origin. Yet in the final analysis, they put into question such a conventional framework and suggest instead the idea of hybrid culture and of
identity as a contested category. Hwang's interests in collaboration with musicians and multimedia artists from other cultural traditions to transform
Chinese American narrative identities and to incorporate into his plays synthetic art forms such as the opera or musicals may have contributed to his
textual practice of creolization.

As made obvious by plays ranging from FOB (1979) to *M. Butterfly* (1986), Hwang was preoccupied with the reified subject positions or stereotypical images of the racial other. However, recently, as Hwang acknowledges in interviews or introductory remarks to his own plays, he has shifted attention to creole subjects in America. "Beyond *M. Butterfly* I find myself now trying to create a play that is more multicultural in the sense that now I'm trying to write about whites, Asians, and blacks," he writes ("Evolving," 18). He suggests in a different context that *The House of Sleeping Beauties* (1983) and *The Sound of a Voice* (1983) constitute his attempts to "explore different [Chinese American] areas, while remaining committed to working within the Asian community" (FOB, xii). *Rich Relations* (1986) is his first play "without characters specified as Asian" (FOB, xiii). But to map out Hwang's post–*M. Butterfly* trajectory, we will have to take a closer look at several of his collaborative works with Philip Glass regarding this sort of change. It is unfortunate that most readers are largely concerned with Hwang's masterpiece *M. Butterfly*, to the neglect of his later development (see, for example, Chang 1997; Eng 1994; Kehde 1994; Kerr 1991). To remedy the situation, I would like to examine the peculiar cultural politics of inclusion and creolization in works such as *1000 Airplanes on the Roof* (1988), *Voyage* (1992), and *Flower Drum Song* (2002, with Richard Rodgers and Oscar Hammerstein II). My concern is not simply with the nature and nurture problematic embedded in these plays but with the implications of Hwang's rhetorical turn from the phantasmatic to multicultural and creole subjects for ethnic studies.

In fact, such a tropical shift has already taken place in the prologue and coda of FOB. In the play, Dale (a second-generation American of Chinese descent) depicts the FOB (fresh off the boat) in disgusted terms. "What words can you think of that characterize the FOB? Clumsy, ugly, greasy FOB. Loud, stupid, four-eyed FOB. Big feet. Horny. . . . Someone you wouldn't want your sister to marry" (FOB, 6). The same words get repeated at the end of the play, but with a difference: against Dale's desire and indeed his acts of inhibiting, Steve the FOB has not only arrived but inhabited and "picked up English faster than anyone" to become a haunting albeit irritating presence (FOB, 49). At the core of Dale's derogatory description of the FOB lies a troubling sense of what the other is capable of doing invisibly behind our backs. The FOB or new immigrants step in to disrupt the political economy of the household, to upset the symbolic order, to the dismay of mainstream society. As Slavoj Žižek succinctly puts it, "What really bothers us about the 'other' is the peculiar way he organizes his enjoyment, precisely the surplus, the 'excess' that pertains to this way: the smell of 'their' food, 'their' noisy songs and dances, 'their' strange manners, 'their' attitude to work. . . . The basic paradox is that our Thing is conceived as something inaccessible to the other and at the same time threatened by him" (1993, 203). And as Frantz Fanon in *Black Skin, White Masks* and Dale in *FOB* know too well, "their" dangerous sexuality—hence "horny" in Dale's comments on the FOB. However, what actually disturbs our psychic balance, Žižek informs us by using several horrendous examples from the Bosnian war, is not something we can pinpoint to clearly defined observable property. It is the "I don't know what" in the other that irritates us, to such an extent that we are constantly fascinated and pissed off by the other as a phantasmatic object that eludes our gaze. To quote Žižek again: "Our relationship to this unfathomable traumatic element that 'bothers us' in the Other is structured in fantasies (about the Other's political and/or sexual omnipotence, about 'their' strange sexual practices, about their secret hypnotic powers, etc.)" (Žižek 1996, 105). *M. Butterfly* is best known for exposing these kinds of fantasies and traumas, as a number of critics have pointed out.

Hwang deliberately deploys spectacular sights and sounds in most of his early plays to engage the audience's fantasies, and he uses stereotypes or mythic figures such as Gwan Gung and Fa Mu Lan to consolidate as well as challenge those fantasies. Set against the strike of Chinese railway workers in 1867, the traditional Chinese opera steps Lone and Ma are practicing serve to displace the urgent matter at hand that frames *The Dance and the Railroad*. As Lone tells Ma, "We've already lost nine days of work. But we got eight hours" (FOB, 84). The workers are forced to compromise and to give in. The only protesting gesture they can assume is to stage "white devils" in their colonial drama and to trash them in acting: "I am a white devil! Listen to my stupid language: 'Wha che doo doo blah blah.' Look at my wide eyes—like I have drunk seventy-two pots of tea. Look at my funny hair—twisting, turning, like a snake telling lies" (81). Nevertheless the desire to be incorporated and naturalized is deeply embedded in the theatrical performances, which invariably stress cultural difference and nostalgia for Chinese grand tradition. As Robert puts it more blandly in *Family Devotions* (1981): "Look, Di-gou, people risk their lives to come to America. . . . Us

Chinese, we love to eat, right? Well, here in America, we can be pigs!" (*FOB*, 117). Or as Di-gou later dreams: "No one leaves America. And I desire only to drive an American car—very fast—down an American freeway" (*FOB*, 145). All these instants remind us of Jacques Lacan's observation of the Othering of the Other, of pulling the strings behind the scene (and screen) to run the show of stereotypical and phantasmatic images. Fantasy plays a vital role in the obscene, invisible structure of psychic power. Judith Butler's and Žižek's accounts of such an obscene power mechanism help explain the perverse power entanglements in which migrants are caught as creoles move to the metropole to be assimilated while differentiated, to desire membership but to be constantly reminded of the highly stratified and uneven structure of that symbolic ordering. Butler and Žižek move beyond Lacan and Foucault by highlighting the internal productive elements of fear, guilt, and anxiety that constitute the subjects in terms of primary vulnerability to forces outside and unknown—aliens, FOB, spectral apparitions, or sights and sounds from elsewhere. *M. Butterfly* powerfully stages the psychic life of power, of René Gallimard's subjection to his own fantasies, as it details the internalization process in which the former French diplomat recognizes himself as a Butterfly figure. He says: "I've played out the events of my life night after night, always searching for a new ending to my story, one where I leave this cell and return forever to my Butterfly's arms. Tonight I realize my search is over. That I've looked all along in the wrong place. And now, to you, I will prove that my love was not in vain—by returning to the world of fantasy where I first met her" (*M. Butterfly*, 91).

This constitutes a climactic scene in Hwang's writing regarding the phantasmatic subject, in which the figure of a psychic projection reconstitutes itself by feeding on its bad faith. Critics have used the scene to shed light on the fetishistic or fictional character of masculinity and sexuality (Kehde 1994) and to pinpoint unstable constructs such as homosexuality, cross-cultural dressing, and transvestism (Chang 1997; Eng 1994). However, in deconstructing the racial and sexual myths significantly related to a foreign body, the scene also renders the critique empty in spite of and against itself: Gallimard keeps returning to his world of fantasy. John J. Deeney has provided an illuminating, albeit misleading, account of Chinese readers' response to the play: "My experience in discussing Chinese-American writers among Chinese in Asia is that many of them react to these writers

[M. H. Kingston and D. H. Hwang] with indignation and even hostility"
(1993, 34). Reflecting on the other aspects of ethnicity and the aesthetics of
reception, Hwang thinks of the Asian American response as "more mixed
than it would be in the community at large" ("D. H. Hwang Worldnet," 5).
Among common audiences, especially those of Asian descent, there seems
to be a general consensus that Hwang has reinforced, instead of challenged,
dominant cultural misconceptions by characterizing "Oriental" males as
emasculated and manipulative. He is a bit concerned but not terribly both-
ered by that. He writes, "Any time you have a group that is not normally
portrayed with any regularity in the media in America . . . that group has
more of a vested interest in seeing that they are portrayed in a particular
way that might be acceptable to any particular Asian American looking at
that" ("D. H. Hwang Worldnet," 5). The issue at hand is delicate and controversial, and the writer certainly has his own relative autonomy in the principle of selection and significance. However, the perceived contestory nature
of racial and sexual politics may partly contribute to the shift of Hwang's
interests in multicultural subjects after 1988. In the remaining pages, I examine Hwang's collaborative works with Philip Glass as some of his gestures
toward mixed genres and new directions, with increasingly figures of cross-
cultural contact in the plays.

This is not to say that Hwang has not touched on the multicultural subjects in his earlier works. Maxine Hong Kingston tells us that "Hwang has
an ear for Chinatown English, the language of childhood and the subcon-
scious, the language of emotion, the language of home" (FOB, viii). "If no
playwrights like David Hwang came along," she continues, "a generation of
actors who speak our accents would be lost" (ix). In several places, Hwang
does talk about his ethnic background and even suggests that "at a certain
point I started to awaken to issues of color, in the late '70s when I was an
undergraduate in college" ("Evolving," 16). But he also states pointedly that
"I decided to write a play, Rich Relations, that didn't have any Asian in it"
(17). This is in part a response to the American minority cultures and their
problems: "I also wondered if a sort of literary segregation implied a cultural limitation." "It's interesting," he observes, "to watch the history of ideas
progress in the '50s, '60s, and '70s, and even today there's still a lot of vitality
to the idea that people of color, women, gays are determining our own literary destiny and not having it written for us." "On the other hand, I look at

Hollywood now, which has adopted this idea as a sort of segregation. That is, blacks should write about blacks and women should write kind of soft personal stories. And I wonder if it isn't also true that if we want to or if we choose to, we should be able to claim a full franchise as American writers the same as other American writers have and be able to address any subjects that we want" (17).

The title of his brief biographical account, "Evolving a Multicultural Tradition," is telling. The decision to write an "American" play without any Asian Americans in it is a major step in Hwang's literary, if not cultural, evolution. Here, as in other places, he oscillates between the nature and nurture positions, critical multiculturalism and liberal multiculturalism, or the politics of representation and the theory of creolization. On the one hand, he thinks that ethnic particularisms should be recognized and receive due attention. On the other hand, he advocates the notion of fluidity and multiplicity: to be "able to address any subjects that we want." Whether Hwang's version of multiculturalism is liberal, progressive, or even conservative is an open question. But, obviously, he has increasingly been motioning toward a politics of creolization or, in his words, "trying to create a play that is more multicultural in the sense that now I'm trying to write about whites, Asians, and blacks" (18). Here Hwang actually echoes Shih and Lionnet's observations in the introduction to this book on creolization as a "descriptive" as well as "speculative" concept that "emerges from the experiential" and "does justice to the lived realities of subaltern subjects, theorizing their experiences in terms of an epistemology that remains connected to those realities."

Together with Stuart Hall and Shih and Lionnet, Hwang reveals ways in which diaspora and creole subjects can be flexible while sustaining the test of material reality. To represent the creolized migrant subjects, Hwang works with musicians like Glass and Hammerstein II to transcend the racial divide and the notion of ethnic style as ideologically manufactured and dictated by the logic of the cultural market. To Hwang, the idea of Chinese American expression and its cultural politics of particularities proves to be self-depriving and misleading, too "empirical" and "systematic" to be productive. Music, as manifested by the collaborative operas and musicals, is a "distancing" mechanism and process that enables Hwang to move beyond a reductive vision and, in the words of a great composer of our time, Luciano Berio, "to enter into relation with the concrete, acoustical dimensions of its articulation: with the voices that sing it, and the instruments that play it" (Berio 2006, 22).

In light of the contingency of operatic works' indebtedness to live singing, playing, and staging, it is the performance that creates the discursive field in the only form of material being it can have (cf. Abbate 2001, ix). In other words, Hwang's use of mixed genres, of the synthetic operatic forms, suggests a point of departure in calling on the heterogeneous, the tonal, the experiential, and the polycentric, so that his works may touch audiences in more affective and immediate manners. That is a new politics of inclusion and subversion.

Let me briefly dwell on the issue of creolization and of inclusion before discussing Hwang's *1000 Airplanes on the Roof*. In response to the Francophone group-rights claim in Quebec, Charles Taylor proposes that in recognition of cultural differences and of the urgency to keep alive endangered cultural forms of life, certain privileges and immunities should be "revoked or restricted for reasons of public policy" (1994, 59). Criticizing Taylor for failing to understand that private and public autonomies are co-original, Jürgen Habermas has recently offered an alternative model: "The ethical integration of groups and subcultures with their own collective identities must be uncoupled from the abstract political integration that includes all citizens equally," for cultural and social differences must be interpreted "in increasingly context-sensitive ways if the system of rights is to be actualized democratically" (1998, 225, 210). Drawing on radical feminist debates, Habermas combines a concern with questions of normative justification with an empirical analysis of the social conditions necessary for the realization of democratic institutions. While finding his conception of rational reflection and ethical life too acultural, I do think that his distinction between private and public autonomy is helpful. "The individual rights that are supposed to guarantee women the autonomy to shape their private lives," Habermas argues, "cannot even be appropriately formulated unless those affected articulate and justify in public discussion what is relevant to equal or unequal treatment in typical cases" (210). "Safeguarding the private autonomy of citizens with equal rights must go hand in hand with activating their autonomy as citizens of the nation," he goes on to say.

This public autonomy includes discursive struggles for recognition in literary and political public spheres such as rearticulating black life history or reconsidering the racialization of immigrant acts (cf. Morrison 1989; Gates 1986; Lowe 1996). In such a way, Habermas adumbrates the equal rights to coexistence and the preservation of cultural forms of life. In addition to "rights to cultural membership," in Will Kymlicka's (1991) phrase, minority groups can "advance special moral reasons arising from the history of a country that has been appropriated by the majority culture" (Habermas 1998, 221). "Similar arguments in favor of 'reverse discrimination' can be advanced for the long-suppressed and disavowed cultures of former slaves" and, one should add, of peoples without histories. Habermas believes that only through sensitivity to diversity (difference exists as "facticity") and integrity (equal rights as "normality") can varying forms of life coexist in a multicultural society. It is crucial to maintain the distinction between the two levels of integration, for if they are collapsed into one level, "the majority culture will usurp state prerogatives at the expense of the equal rights of other cultural forms of life and violate their claim to mutual recognition" (225). "The neutrality of the law vis-à-vis internal ethical differentiation stems from the fact that in complex societies the citizenry as a whole can no longer be held together by a substantive consensus on values but only by a consensus on the procedures for the legitimate enactment of laws and the legitimate exercise of power" (225).

Jean-François Lyotard's notion of phrasing in relation to differential temporalities and communalities has jeopardized the Habermasian ideal of proceduralist consensus (see Lyotard and Thébaud's *Just Gaming* [1985], for example). However, it is important to remember that a politics of inclusion requires internal ethical differentiation and the desire to be liberated from injustice, on the one hand, and legal and political institutions that guarantee the coexistence as well as cultivation of cultural and religious identities. In brief, an internal relationship between liberalism and democracy, ethnicity (or ethicity) and publicity, should be asserted. If one is to do away with ethnic particularisms, the danger can be that one regards the problem of the Other solely from the perspective of the "inhabitants of affluent and peaceful societies" (Habermas 1998, 230), as in the case of Dale in relation to Steve in *FOB*.

Hwang's politics of creolization and inclusion is more complex; he makes the two levels of integration collide and implode. This is done in *1000 Airplanes on the Roof* through the figure of a person always on the run—having no identity, hence finding himself interchangeable with other things. And in *The Voyage* (which premiered on October 12, 1992, at the Metropolitan Opera House, New York), the subject of exploration is treated in a metaphorical way, to an extent that colonial histories are not taken seriously. In a kind of postcolonial retribution, the opera merges the past and future, the discoverer (Columbus or Commander) and the aborigine, but without really bringing both parties into contact with each other. *1000 Airplanes on the Roof* is a science-fiction music drama realized by Philip Glass, David Hwang, and Jerome Sirlin. The music was composed and directed by Glass, the script written by Hwang, with design and projections by Sirlin. The text marks Hwang's attempt to move beyond Chinese American subjects, as the protagonist (Mr. M.) can be anybody living in New York City. In fact, he reminds us of Kafka's K., E. B. White's speaker in "The Wall," Flaubert's Bouvard, T. S. Eliot's Prufrock, Beckett's Unnamable, and even Proust's Swann. Made up of fragmented interior monologues, the opera is about a man who is both a psychopath and a failure. "I've run everywhere to escape my memories," he says, "everywhere but into my mind itself" (*FOB*, 285). Everything turns out to be a lost object or merges with others and melts into air: "And time leaves me. I step temporarily outside its domain. The hands on the clock become fluid. Running off the face like water" (284). While the play contains specific references to New York—for example, "the gratings above the subway, in the nooks and crannies of the City" (282)—the rhapsodic motifs are largely about the frantic and conflictive tempos of modern urban life. Not only does the outside environment constantly change its shape on the speaker, but his relationship with his ex-girlfriend becomes something he can no longer comprehend. He sees and feels, but does not actually hear, a sound descending from somewhere ("from the hole where the sky had been"), a sound he fights to forget (283). He turns a deaf ear to what the other has said or will be saying: "Her mouth opened, lips began to form around words. I felt horror, terrible horror, at whatever was about to come from her mouth. Whatever had happened, couldn't be worse than what she was going to say about it" (282). "So at last, I attempted a sensible act. I ran" (282). He runs away and becomes things other than himself in music-image transfiguration. "For even as he gazes at the most ordinary of memories, he becomes aware of other images he is not supposed to see. In this way, the screens behind acquired a power greater than those in front.

The room is saturated with the presence of things hidden" (283); thus "he," the speaker, takes the shape of another person. The selfsame (or *idem*) identity collapses into multiple and always already slipping, as well as "trickling," subject positions or, in Paul Ricoeur's idiom, *ipse*-identities that constitute and reconstitute themselves in the narrative act.

Parts 3 and 4 of the music drama develop the theme of oneself as another, of seeing alternative selves in the mirror. "I travel past rows of faces, each varying slightly from my own. . . . I am following this line of faces, one transforming into another, until finally I am looking once again at him," the narrator says (293–94). "And I realize all this time, I have been looking into his face. Seeing in his eyes a mirror reflecting myself. And, all this time he has been looking into my eyes, and he, too, has seen himself" (294). This mutual gaze and its imaginary relationship constitute the narrator's peculiar cultural economy of movement—even though he finds himself caught up in the nonmovement as a clerk in the copy shop, "waking up again in a hospital bed, running" (288). The creole subject of running or travel reaches its climactic moment as the narrator imagines himself to be on a spaceship, making contact with extraterrestrial visitors. However, the fantasy of having been elsewhere, of having encountered a UFO, is shattered by a doctor in the hospital: "When I wake up, I'm in . . . a spaceship? What is this? Strapped to a table? No, wait. The smells are different. No rotten leaves. This time . . . I smell . . . Listerine. I'm on earth. In a hospital. The doctor looks down from above. In a voice far removed from my conscience he asks, 'Where have you been?'" (296). The narrator wakes to such a question and realizes, after all the phantasmatic scenes, his normality: "And I'm a normal man. A normal man, running" (302).

It may well seem a small step from the spaceship fantasy in *1000 Airplanes on the Roof* to the spectacular spaceship adventure in *The Voyage*. The three-act *Voyage* is an allegorical treatment of the multicultural subject of discovery and conquest. The opera was commissioned by the Metropolitan Opera House in commemoration of the five hundredth anniversary of Columbus's arrival in the New World. The amount of the commission ($325,000), we are told, probably stands as the largest ever awarded in the history of opera—one hundred thousand dollars more than Verdi's *Aida* in today's currency (Oestreich 1992, 22). The opera does not explicitly deal with Columbus as a problematic figure in postcolonial hindsight. As Oestreich succinctly points out, "In the poignant epilogue, Columbus's failings are acknowledged, in line with the current widespread devaluation of his achievements, but ultimately resolved in contemplation of the final seductive journey of death" (26). Regarding the script, Hwang says: "There's a lot about randomness and a sort of chaos, the degree to which the discoveries we make or the things we're able to achieve or the historical currents we get caught up with are not entirely of our own design, of our own will. We have this desire to reduce the amount of ignorance in the world, but we're traveling blind, and so many of the things we're trying to achieve have as much through chance as through anything else" (quoted in Oestreich 1992, 26).

As the curtain rises, we witness a wheelchair-bound scientist modeled on the theoretical physicist Stephen Hawking. The scientist sums up the argument of the opera: "The voyage lies where / The vision lies / There" (11). Offstage, the chorus sings the Music of the Spheres and then in varying and fragmented parts raises a series of questions in relation to black hole theory, singularity, finitude, and the disappearance of God. The first act is set during the end of the earth's Ice Age, with a spaceship hurtling out of control toward our own solar system. After the spaceship crashes (act 1, scene 1), the crew appears on the earth's surface, marveling at the "infant stages" of the planet. The commander asks the crew to forget their planet and to take the ship's directional crystals to explore the world in front of them. "If a day arrives when we may return / Any two brought together / Will point the way home," she advises them. Taking varying forms and jumping into different spaces and times, the crew members disappear and are transported to Europe, India, and Tibet. The commander lands in America, surrounded by a large group of natives, who view her as "a fantastic creature, barely humanoid, speaking gibberish" (18). As the commander is absorbed by the natives, performing the rites of spring, we hear the chorus of American cheering.

Columbus appears in the second act and in the epilogue, but his adventures are treated first in parallel to the travelers from another planet, with first mate, second mate, and Isabella reciting God's words, and then in relation to Isabella's multiple identities as the queen. In a concluding aria, Isabella dictates the meaning of voyaging: "I take many forms / I wear many faces / But all for the one righteous end / That the voyage you take / Is made in my name / And discoveries claimed for my honor / I am your Queen / I am your love / I am your one true God / Trust / Follow / Believe" (23–24).

Only in the epilogue does Columbus establish himself as an explorer, as the very personification of the metaphor of voyaging—physical and mental. Against Isabella's power over his body and her desire to claim him as a lover, Columbus declares that his journey is made in the name of science, not in honor of the queen. He remarks: "From the first amoeba / Who fought to break free of itself / To Ulysses, to Ibn Battuta, to Marco Polo / To Einstein, and beyond / All that we seek to know / Is to know ourselves / To reduce the darkness / By some small degree / To light a candle, jump a stream / That the sum of human ignorance / Might dwindle just a bit / And the deeds done in darkness / May wither one day perhaps even / Expire" (34). Rather than falling into the arms of Isabella, Columbus ultimately takes the journey of death: "But the journey that awaits / Is far more seductive than / All your last temptations / Finally / We take the voyage / When voyage / Takes us" (35).

The third act takes place in 2092. The idea of a black hole's pulsars is picked up again, and in a sort of repetition with a difference, two of the glowing crystals we saw in act 1 are being carried by a pair of archaeologists—twins, like the other set in the space station. While the space twins and earth twins are engaging in science topics, the commander's voice joins the inconclusive theoretical debates. Several years later, following the lead of the commander, space travelers bid farewell to this world and are ready to depart for a recently discovered planet, the source of life. As the commander suggests, the journey is never final: "Through the ages / All we have sought to know / What once had been believed unknowable / Continuing this tradition / We depart on our expedition / Which will not reach its end" (28).

If *1000 Airplanes on the Roof* and *The Voyage* can be used to illustrate Hwang's effort toward "evolving a multicultural tradition," we will have to consider the aporia of a cultural politics of creolization, that is, of the desire to be different while integrated. The narrator in *1000 Airplanes on the Roof* is fascinated with the notion of interchangeability, of running into and merging with the Other; however, to his dismay, his frenzied journey ends with the rediscovery of his normal everyday existence. In other words, he can imagine himself to be many things, but the doctor keeps holding him back by asking questions such as "Where have you been?" And *The Voyage* concludes with Columbus's contemplation of the meaning of scientific inquiry and the final journey of death. Perceived in such a light, these two works can be said to explore and to implode the gap between the notion of fluidity and the persistent reminder of ethnic identity, between the concept of exploration and the moral consequence of conquest. Ironically, Hwang is constantly remembered as the author of the award-winning *M. Butterfly*. His collaborative works with Glass are listed but not seriously treated except by Glass himself and a few music critics in *Writing on Glass* (Kostelanetz 1997, 262–63, 266–69, 271–73). Tapes or CDs of both operas have not to this day been released. Perhaps to better appreciate Hwang's works over the years, we should substitute the time frame of evolution with the idea of "in-betweenness" and creolization.

Hwang's recent and controversial rewrite of Rodgers and Hammerstein II's musical *Flower Drum Song* (1958), very much inspired by C. Y. Lee's life narrative under the same name (1961), is another instance of creolization in terms of appropriating Chinese and Western operatic traditions. In a story set in San Francisco's Chinatown during the 1950s, the second-generation Chinese American characters try to rework traditional lyrics and to transform them into American popular songs. Racial stereotypes are often turned inside out to produce comic and serious dramatic effects, laying bare the uneven race relations in the same vein. Newly revised flower drum songs suggest dynamic energies on the part of the Chinese diaspora to retell stories of discrimination and injustice while exposing the culture industry of exotic melodies as well as memories. There is no denying that Hwang's *Flower Drum Song* operates very much under the rubric of "global informational capital and social elites," as Timothy D. Taylor (2007) observes of the ways in which operas and transnational music have largely been produced and consumed; the musical nevertheless provides postcolonial (though not postimperial) cultural critique from within the entertainment industry. It readdresses racism, and rather than dwelling on America's internal colonialism and imperial past, it offers alternative stories about how Chinese immigrants have developed their art of survival and articulated a theory of creolization in bringing forth new tunes and accents. That may partly explain why the American white audience as well as the Chinese American population found the opera "offensive," though for differing reasons (see Lewis 2006). Though resisted and perceived to be a box office failure, the musical challenges us to rethink yet again whether we can allow for exchanges as change.

2

EPISTEMOLOGICAL LOCATIONS

SIX

☙

I AM WHERE I THINK
Remapping the Order of Knowing

Walter Mignolo

Colonialism is the very base and structure of the West Indian's
cultural awareness. . . . I am not so much interested in what the
West Indian writer has brought to the English language; for
English is no longer the exclusive language of the men who live
in England. That stopped a long time ago; and it is today, among
other things, a West Indian language. What the West Indians do
with it is their own business. . . . A more important consideration
is what the West Indian novelist has brought to the West Indies.
That is the real question; *and its answer can be the beginning of*
an attempt to grapple with that colonial structure of awareness
which has determined West Indian values.

George Lamming, "The Occasion for Speaking"
(italics mine)

Global Linear Thinking and Global Decolonial Thinking

An unintended consequence of global linear thinking was the coming into being of decolonial thinking. Global linear thinking describes, in Carl Schmitt's conceptualization, the history of the imperial partition of the world since the sixteenth century (Schmitt 2003). From the Treaty of Tordesilla, by which Pope Alexander VI created an imaginary line that divided the Atlantic from north to south and settled the dispute between Spain and Portugal for the possessions of the New World, up to the scramble for Africa among western European states that ended up in World War I, global linear thinking mapped not only the land and waters of the planet but also the minds.

Schmitt's history of global linear thinking has several important consequences for the imperial foundations of the modern-colonial world order
and the imperial foundation of knowledge. The act of the pope to divide the
planet and to offer it to Spanish and Portuguese monarchs was indeed one
of sovereign authority, not only political but epistemic. The act of tracing a
line dividing the Atlantic means that there is an epistemic sovereign: God
has the knowledge backing up the legality of the decision and He is also in
control of the rules and acts of knowing. Although by the mid-sixteenth
century the authority of the pope and the monarchs began to be disputed
by a group of legal-theologians in Salamanca, who called into question the
limits of divine and natural law (and of divine and natural knowing) in favor
of human law (which opened the doors to the secular move we encounter
in the eighteenth century), the fact remains that global linear thinking, as
Schmitt himself specifies in the subtitle of his book, goes hand in hand with
the origin of international law. I underline this point: the origin of international law in the constitution of the modern-colonial world.

The new *nomos* of the earth, in Schmitt's own formulation, was based
therefore in the papal partition of the earth as its historical foundation and
international law as the necessary consequence: who has the right indeed,
and what are those rights that Europeans may have over non-European
lands and people? A second consequence after the partition and the origin
of international law was the depiction of the planet on the world map, of
which Abraham Ortelius's *Orbis Terrarum* remains as the paradigmatic example. Never before Ortelius was the planet earth seen from "above," with
the sea and land masses discernible at a glance. But above all, the main issue
is not that the observer observes the planet from above but that the observer
is "above" the Atlantic, and the Atlantic becomes the natural center of the
world. The new nomos of the earth comes with a new observer and epistemic foundation. The Colombian philosopher Santiago Castro-Gómez described it as the hubris of the zero point. This second consequence sets the
stage for the imperial control and colonization of knowledge and of being:

> The co-existence of diverse ways of producing and transmitting knowl-
> edge is eliminated because now all forms of human knowledge are
> ordered on an epistemological scale from the traditional to the mod-
> ern, from barbarism to civilization, from the community to the indi-
> vidual, from the orient to occident. . . . By way of this strategy, scientific

thought positions itself as the only valid form of producing knowledge, and Europe acquires an epistemological hegemony over all the other cultures of the world. (Castro-Gómez 2007, 433)

Basically, zero point epistemology is the ultimate grounding of knowledge that, paradoxically, is grounded neither in geohistorical location nor in biographical configurations of bodies. The geopolitical and biographical politics of knowledge are hidden in the transparency and universality of the zero point. It is grounding without grounding, in the mind and not in the brain and in the heart. Every way of knowing and sensing (feeling) that does not conform to the epistemology and aesthesis of the zero point is cast behind in time and in the order of myth, legend, folklore, local knowledge, and the like. Since the zero point is always in the present of time and the center of space, it hides that it is local knowledge universally projected. Its imperiality consists precisely in hiding its locality, its geohistorical body location, thus pretending to be universal and therefore to the universality to which everyone has to submit.

The zero point serves as the measuring stick to creating the epistemic colonial difference and the epistemic imperial difference. Latin absorbed and recast knowledges that were either translated from Greek to Arabic or cast in the Arab-Islamic tradition. While Arabic remained crucial locally, it lost its global influence once the modern European languages derived from Greek and Latin became the languages of sustainable knowledge, disavowing the epistemic potential of non-European languages and knowledges. Being where one thinks then becomes a fundamental concern of those who have been relegated to a second or third place in the global epistemic order. "I am where I think" sets the stage for epistemic affirmations that have been disavowed. At the same time, it creates a shift in the geography of reasoning. For if the affirmation "I am where I think" is pronounced from the perspective of the epistemic disavowed, it implies "and you too," addressed to the epistemology of the zero point. In other words, "we are all where we think," but only the European system of knowledge was built on the belief that the basic premise is "I think, therefore I am," which was a translation into secular terms of the theological foundation of knowledge (in which we already encounter the privilege of the soul over the body).

"By way of this strategy," Castro-Gómez observes, "scientific thought positions itself as the only valid form of producing knowledge, and Europe acquires *an epistemological hegemony* over all the other cultures of the world" (2005, 43). From the fact that Western epistemology—that is, the episte-mology of the zero point—became hegemonic, it doesn't follow that who-ever was and is not thinking in those terms is not thinking. There is ample evidence to the contrary, evidence that is silenced both in the academic world and in mainstream media. The democratization of epistemology is under way (my argument intends to contribute to it), and *I am where I think* is one basic epistemic principle that legitimizes all ways of thinking and delegitimizes the pretense that a singular and particular epistemology, geo-historically and biographically located, is universal.

The Imperial Significance of Schmitt's Second Nomos

Schmitt's *The Nomos of the Earth* is more than a scholarly book concerned with the discipline of international law. On the contrary, it is through the history and the discipline of international law that Schmitt reflects on the present situation of Europe and forecasts the future. He was not a Nigerian looking at how international law and the nomos of the earth affected Africa or an Aymara in Bolivia reflecting on the origin of international law and the Spanish justification for appropriating his land. If we read Schmitt from the perspective of those who endured the consequences of the second nomos of the earth (spatializing the sites of knowledge) and we link those sites of knowledge (say the perspective from Nigeria or from the Bolivian Ayma-ras), we confront the question of the colonial epistemic difference that is absent in Schmitt's narrative and we enter the process of decolonizing that second nomos of the earth. We realize that Schmitt's narrative is half of the story—and a half of the story that silenced the other half. While zero point (i.e., imperial) epistemology is and shall be recognized in its splendors, it shall also be recognized in its miseries and arrogance. Decolonizing West-ern epistemology means stripping it of the pretense that it is the point of arrival and the guiding light of all kinds of knowledges. In other words, de-colonizing knowledge is not rejecting Western epistemic contributions to the world. On the contrary, this implies appropriating it because of its uni-versal value while at the same time rejecting the implied pretense that be-cause of its global contribution it will be *the* totalitarian universal system of knowledge, ruling out the possibility of pluriversal, dialogic, and epistemi-cally democratic ones.

In such a scenario, classical Greece loses its privileges as the origin of everything, and other starting points emerge. One that I am proposing here is the sixteenth century, when the population and system of knowledge in Anáhuac and Tawantinsuyu came into contact and conflict with African and European systems of knowledge, languages, and religions. The Atlantic in that regard, in the sixteenth century, marks a discontinuity with the classical tradition on which Western Europe built itself. If we accept that "we are where we think" and that the places we are follow from the place we occupy in the new nomos of the earth—that is, of the modern-colonial world—then several epistemic trajectories emerge and escape the control of global linear thinking.

Racial classification meant rational classification, and rational classifications derive not from natural reason but from human concepts of natural reason. But who establishes criteria of classification, and who classifies? Those who inhabited the epistemic zero point (*humanitas*)? And who are classified without participating in the classification? Those who are observed (*anthropos*). To manage, and to be in a position to do so, means to be in control of knowledge—to be in the zero point. That is precisely what global linear thinking is. Global linear thinking since the sixteenth century is imperial; it is imperial thinking that I have described elsewhere as the rhetoric of modernity and the logic of coloniality.

Three aspects in Schmitt's outline of imperial-colonial expansion concern my argument. While global linear thinking is imperial, the consequences of tracing lines to divide and control the world are not the same everywhere. I see at least three dimensions of global linear thinking.

First of all, nodes in global linear thinking have the particularity of breaking up linear time by dividing space by means of lines. Consequently, if we focus on historico-structural and heterogeneous nodes (that is, where global linear thinking creates frontiers and therefore conflicts), then the linear historical narratives lose their privileges. Linear time is no longer the only possibility for narrating the past, and the European perspective is no longer the only one that counts: there are people beyond the lines traced by European actors and the institutions that are enforced by their own international law. Nodes take us to see the past and the present as heterogeneous historico-structural configurations of imperial-colonial space. For example, the partition of India and the creation of the state of Israel took place in 1947 and 1948, respectively. How do you narrate, in a linear global chronology, these two simultaneous events—and by simultaneous I do not mean the same day, the same month, and the same hour? You cannot deny that these two events are strictly co-related in global linear thinking; linear not in a chronological sense but in the special sense of drawing lines and creating nodes.

Second, global linear thinking from its beginning in the late fifteenth century (*Tordesilla Treatise*) plays two simultaneous roles. On the one hand, the *raya* (line) divides the operational space forming imperial powers between Spain and Portugal in the sixteenth century; between Spain and France, England, and Holland in the seventeenth century; between England and the United States since the nineteenth century, when the idea of a Western Hemisphere affirmed the United States as an imperial contender (none of the South American and Caribbean countries have any say in the line that divides the Western Hemisphere from Europe). On the other hand, the raya divided imperial states (monarchic or secular nation-states) from their colonies. When colonies became independent states (in South America and the Caribbean in the nineteenth and twentieth centuries) or became overseas departments of France or *estado libre asociado* of the United States, like Puerto Rico, the raya was redrawn, allowing certain former colonies to cross the line and to get inside, reinforcing the fact that South America, although in the Western Hemisphere, is part of the so-called Third World. This is why today, for example, Samuel Huntington (1996) puts Australia and New Zealand in the First World and South America in the Third World.

Third, the geopolitical consequences of the line in the reconfiguration of the nomos of the earth went beyond geography proper. Space went hand in hand with people inhabiting it. Land, people, and being became packaged by imperial global linear thinking in what the Japanese scholar Nishitani Osamu theorized as two Western concepts of "Human Being": *humanitas* and *anthropos*. Anthropos does not refer literally to the native barbarians of the sixteenth century or the naked primitives of the eighteenth. It refers to every instance by which the actors and institutions, languages and categories of thought that control knowledge define humanitas and use the definition to describe the place they inhabit as the point of arrival in time and the center of space.[1] Since humanitas is defined through the epistemic privilege of hegemonic knowledge, anthropos represents difference, more specifically the epistemic colonial difference. Anthropos, then, is as much the barbarian or the primitive as the communist or the terrorist, and all those who can be placed in the axis of evil and who are friends of the devil. Illegal immigrants and homosexuals are today within the realm of the anthropos. The domain of humanitas is consubstantial with the control of global linear thinking: the lines have been traced from the perspective of humanitas, and it is in humanitas that the control of knowledge resides.

Epistemic and Ontological Colonial Differences

My goal here is not to redraw the map traced by Schmitt but to clarify two crucial functions of global linear thinking. The first was to establish the criteria for the making and remaking of imperial differences, the second for the making and remaking of colonial differences. They are both crucial to understanding the world order in the past five hundred years (1500–2000) and the radical transformations we (all us living) have been witnessing since 2000, of which 9/11, the collapse of Wall Street, and Israeli massacre in Gaza are telling signs (I return to these issues later).

We find both imperial and colonial differences in the canonical work of the legal theologian Francisco de Vitoria (ca. 1480–1546). Vitoria is without a doubt the founding reference for the creation of international law at the same time that he indirectly contributed to the historical foundation of modern racism. Vitoria has to solve two sides of the problem. On the one hand, he needed to debunk the sovereignty of the pope and the monarch to possess lands in the hands of non-Christians and to deal with the question of jurisdiction. To cut off the authority of the pope and the monarch, Vitoria stated that all nations on the planet (in this case, the Spanish nation and the Indian nations in the New World) were endowed with *ius gentium*, the rights of nations. Since Indians belong to the human community and were endowed with ius gentium, neither the pope nor the monarch could have *dominium* over them. Vitoria's second step was to deal with the Spaniards and the Indians, face to face in the New World. Since Spanish and Indians were equal on the principle of ius gentium, how could Spaniards justify their interventions in the Indians' life and habitat? After recognizing that Indians have the rights of nations, Vitoria demonstrates their deficiencies in rationality (although they have reason) and maturity (although they are human). Once Vitoria makes Indians somehow inferior (although human with rights), he installs a racial epistemic hierarchy, placing himself at the zero point of observation. That is the epistemic colonial difference.

Now what can the Indians do, since they have rights but are not quite apt to use reason rationally? Well, that was one side of the story. Vitoria and the Spaniards, and later France and Britain and the United States in the twentieth century, have the right to be where they think and to think that other people are uncivilized, underdeveloped, or that they are becoming, just emerging. However, from the sixteenth century to the twenty-first, many who were and are considered anthropos from the perspective of the humanitas (be it Vitoria and the church, the scientific disciplines, or the World Bank—that is, appropriating the language of the anthropos to remain themselves as savior and not to allow self-determination) are taking their epistemic destinies in their own hands: anthropos becomes humanitas not by conversion, civilization of developments by humanitas, but by assuming their humanity and being where they think.

A few decades after these debates in Spain, Quechua Guaman Poma de Ayala was living in Tawantinsuyu, which was being transformed into the Viceroyalty of Peru. He was where he was thinking, and what he was thinking responded to needs, desires, and visions grounded in the history of the Tawantinsuyu and not in the history of Western Christians, as was the case for Vitoria. While Vitoria participated in a discussion among Spaniards about the Indians, Guaman Poma de Ayala addressed Philip III from the perspective of Tawantinsuyu. He did not represent all the Indians, as Vitoria did not represent all the Spaniards. Undeniably, however, Vitoria was speaking in the middle of debates and issues affecting Spanish society and life. So was Guaman Poma. However, Vitoria has been recognized, praised, critiqued, and enthroned. Guaman Poma was ignored until recently and is still recognized only as a document, not as a political treatise at the same level as Vitoria's. That is the epistemic colonial difference supported by the ontological colonial difference: Indians do not think. That long history of racial epistemic prejudice is at work today in Bolivia, both nationally and internationally.[2]

That was yesterday, the late sixteenth century and the early seventeenth. Today decolonial thinking confronting global linear thinking is alive and well, although generally silenced or marginalized by the institutional control of knowledge that preserves and promotes global linear thinking. Take two examples. U. O. Umozurike, from the University of Nigeria, published a study titled *International Law and Colonialism in Africa* (1979), and the Guinean political theorist Siba N'Zatioula Grovogui followed up several years later with *Sovereigns, Quasi Sovereigns, and Africans* (1996).[3] In a way, they tell the story told by Schmitt. The difference is that while Schmitt identifies the main character of that story as global linear thinking, for Umozurike and Grovogui, the main character (although both authors focus on Africa) is global decolonial thinking. Now, *global* is appropriated and twisted here, for it is not used to defend a new imperial globalism but on the contrary to confront global modernity with global decolonialities. In spite of the differences we can trace in modernity both spatially and chronologically, from the sixteenth century to today, between the European Union and the United States, or between England and France, those differences are not of the same kind as the differences that modernity created by expanding into the non-European world. Because of the similarities in the internal differences of modernity, it was possible to maintain Western imperial dominance. But given the differences within the borders of Euro-American modernity and the fact that Euro-Americans enact coloniality outside of European imperial countries (Romania or Slovenia do not fit in this concept of Europe) and the United States, global decoloniality and global decolonial thinking did not posit itself as a new abstract universal. On the contrary, it defends the needed pluriversality of global futures. Pluriversal global futures are born from the common experience the non-Western world had with the expansion of the West. To be sure, there were local agents who facilitated the expansion, and that was part of the problem itself. Pluriversal global futures require epistemic democratization.

Now we have a system of sorts, an underlying structure that connects global linear thinking with cartography and the world map, the idea of the human and humanitas, and a zero point of observation (the invisible knower, God or the transcendental secular subject), that not only observes but also divides the land and organizes the known. Carl Schmitt's *The Nomos of the Earth* was written from that point of observation and with the concern of imperial countries, particularly after the humbling crisis of World War II and the Holocaust. The line of colonial differences traced the separation between humanitas and anthropos. The distinction was both epistemic and ontological, and they work and continue to work in tandem: because of the ontological status constructed by and from humanitas, the anthropos are both epistemically and ontologically disabled. As anthropos, they are not human enough, and therefore they are below the level of rational and sustainable thinking.

What does the anthropos do? He or she can submit, give in, and assume his or her inferior epistemic and ontological status vis-à-vis the model of humanitas. The anthropos can fight back and show that he or she is also human, claiming recognition. This is the path of assimilation, of being happy to be accepted in the palace of humanitas. By following this path, he or she admits defeat, represses what he or she was, and embraces something that he or she is by the fact of belonging by birth, education, language, and sensibility to the anthropos. The third possibility, and the most rewarding and hopeful, is for the anthropos to unveil the pretentious sense of superiority of those who inhabit the humanitas—not to claim recognition but to show how insane the inhabitants of the house of humanitas are, because they still believe that humanity is divided between humanitas and anthropos, and the authoritarian control of knowledge gives them the privilege of seeing themselves *as* humanitas and not as anthropos. In other words, the task of the anthropos is to claim epistemic rights, to engage in barbarian theorizing and knowledge construction, and to show that anthropos and humanitas are both parts of humanity. To do so is to engage in decolonial thinking, confronting the imperial privileges of imperial-global linear thinking. This is the beginning from which decolonial subjects engage in the process of decolonizing authority (e.g., the modern state, and the modern-colonial states in the anthropos side of the linear divide) and decolonizing economy. That is, imagining a future in which the complicities between the state, market, and epistemic imperial hubris (e.g., global linear thinking, hubris of the zero) will be accepted as one historical moment in the life of the planet and of the species, but a moment that is no longer sustainable.

The first step is to accept the interconnection between geopolitics and epistemology and between biography and epistemology. That is, the first step is to assume that *I am where I think* (which brings together geohistorical and corporal configurations on both sides of the dividing line between the diversity of humanitas and the diversity of anthropos). By placing geography and biography in the historical frame created by global linear thinking, decolonial thinking performs two operations. The first operation anchors new epistemic and ontological sites (the theories of the anthropos), and it unveils the geopolitical underpinning *of* humanitas's universal thinking. For instance, Descartes presented his philosophy, in the final analysis, in a way that contributed to an affirmation of a locus of enunciation in which the mind was detached from the body and from the geopolitical location of that body.

My purpose here is to articulate a discourse, the discourse of the anthropos in the process of appropriating humanitas. My goal is to show the illogical rationality and the hubris of the zero point that humanitas appropriates as it builds itself into the position of domination by means of its partitioning of the earth and its classification of peoples. And I take "I am where I think" as the basic proposition that can enable such reasoning both epistemically and politically.

Decolonizing Knowledge and Being: Thinking Decolonially During the Cold War and After (Bennabi, Kusch, Wynter)

In the first two sections, I mapped the imperial-colonial scenarios in which zero point epistemology emerged and was consolidated. *Imperial-colonial* does not refer only to conservative or right-wing ways of thinking. Let's take theology, for example, Christian theology. There is a history of theology obviously linked to imperial designs and interests. The papacy is an obvious example. On the other hand, we have theologies of liberation in South and North America, in Africa, and also a Jewish theology of liberation. My claim is that, as in the disputes between (neo)liberalism and (neo)Marxism, they are disputes within the same game, where the contenders defend different contents but do not question the rules of the game. In this section, I argue that shifting from *I think, therefore I am* to *I am where I think* is a shift in the geopolitics and body politics of knowledge that focuses on changing the rules of the game rather than its content. We can call it decolonizing epistemology or, if you wish, working toward epistemic democratization. Decolonizing is nothing more and nothing else than taking democracy seriously instead of using it to advance imperial designs or personal interests. We cannot leave the word *democracy* only in liberal and neoliberal hands. It belongs to all of us, and that is, precisely, what democracy shall mean. "We" (members of the political society, who are not in the sphere of the state or the corporations) are laying claim to democracy, and to decolonize knowledge and being is precisely to make a strong claim.

In what follows, I explore and explain what decolonizing knowledge and being may mean not in definitional terms (since once the definition is read, it is forgotten) but as the seed from which collective decolonial options grow, unfold, spread, and transform our thinking and doing with regard to global decolonial futures.

I will bring in an Algerian, an Argentine, and an Afro-Caribbean thinker to further explore both the interconnections between the geopolitics and body politics of knowledge and the way this exploration shifts the geography of reason: from being because we think (*cogito ergo sum*) to being *where* we think. "Being" here does not mean that I am now at my house in North Carolina or that you are in a cafe in Paris; it means where we are, each of us being located in the house of modernity-coloniality: to what region of the world and to what kind of people (classified from the perspective of the zero point) do we belong? Are we anthropos or humanitas, black or Indian, developed or underdeveloped, Jews or Muslims, Christians or Israelites? I am not saying either that there is a modern-colonial determinism. I am saying that it is our ethical responsibility to know and understand the house of modernity-coloniality we all inhabit. My task here is to help in cleaning up and restoring the house of knowledge that has been knocked down by the global storm blowing from the paradise of linear thinking.

What is the point of bringing Algerian (Malik Bennabi), Argentinean (Rodolfo Kusch), and Afro-Caribbean (Sylvia Wynter) thinkers into the conversation? Algeria, to make a long story short, was conquered and ruled by the Ottomans shortly after the completion of the Spanish Reconquista (in 1492) until approximately 1830, when it fell into French hands. That period ended with the decolonial liberation of Algeria in 1962. Quite simply, if your body came into this world before 1962 and lived in Algeria through the war of decolonization and during the Cold War, your feelings and your intellectual, ethical, and political concerns would have been very different from those of someone whose body came into this world at the beginning of the twentieth century in Germany, that is, in Europe, and went through both world wars and Hitler. Thus there is no reason to take for granted that thinking in the German language and dwelling in German history has epistemic privileges over someone thinking in the imperial-colonial language (French) rather than the native Arabic and dealing with issues of knowing, thinking, living, and history in the Third World, as Algeria was classified, from the perspective of First World zero point epistemology (which, of course, pretended not to be located and merely to reflect an objective state of things). Being where you think means, first and foremost, delinking yourself from the epistemic mirage that you can only be if you think *as someone else* who thinks precisely where he or she is, and who (implicitly or not) directs you to think and therefore to be not mere anthropos (i.e., deficient in your being), but to abandon that state of immaturity and to become like those who are already inhabiting the house of humanitas (a process Kant defined as *enlightenment*).

A similar argument can be made in the case of Rodolfo Kusch, an Argentine thinker of German descent. After independence from Spain (1810), and after being indirectly ruled by England (economy) and France (ideology), Argentina was controlled by the Creole elite of Spanish descent who implemented ideas and public policies that originated in England. Toward 1830, when Algeria was invaded and controlled by France, Argentina was at the inception of building a modern-colonial state. I say modern-colonial because independence from Spain meant the continuation of indirect imperial rule by England and France. From 1860 onward, Argentina's wealth increased due to its commerce with England. The building of railroads through the second half of the nineteenth century and the exportation of corned beef generated the golden years of Argentina's economy. The cycle of increasing wealth and prosperity lasted until 1930, when Argentina suffered the consequences of the stock market collapse. The crisis opened up the doors for a radical transformation that created the conditions for the advent of Juan Domingo Perón in 1945. Rodolfo Kusch's first book, *La seducción de la barbarie* (The Seduction of Barbarism), was published in 1953. The book's title is indicative of a shift that was taking place in the geography of reason: the imperial idea of civilization (humanitas) that was central to Argentine knowledge and being from 1860 to 1930 had collapsed. Perónism brought the masses (anthropos) into the picture, and Kusch picked up on that shift, on the potential of popular and indigenous thinking opposed to the privilege of civilized thinking (namely: progress, development).

Jamaica, Sylvia Wynter's dwelling place in the modern-colonial world, has been framed by the history of slavery in the Caribbean and by the confluence of racism and patriarchy. There is a pervasive concern among black Caribbean thinkers, from the Haitian Anténor Firmin to the Trinidadian C. L. R. James, and it is the question of humanity, of being human. That this concern is more central for Afro-Caribbeans than African (let alone European) intellectuals has its reason: if black Africans were cast by Christianity as descendants of Ham, after the sixteenth century they came to be equated with slavery. Slaves' lives became expendable, both as commodities and as a labor force that could be replaced by other enslaved Africans. Humanitas was the point of reference, and those who fell into the domain of anthropos paid the consequences. Sylvia Wynter confronts this issue through Frantz Fanon and by so doing appropriates the humanity of being, dwelling, and thinking in the location of the anthropos, unveiling in the process epistemic limitations of humanitas: while humanitas attributes to itself epistemic privileges, anthropos operates in the epistemic potential that comes from knowing both the reason of humanitas and the reason of those who in the eyes of humanitas are anthropos. Now, let me insist that anthropos is assumed as such, as an ontological category and as an epistemic one: know that from the perspective of the humanitas, *I am an anthropos*—which does not mean, of course, that I am. Being where one thinks implies first and foremost recognizing and confronting imperial categorizations of being and universal principles of knowing.

Malik Bennabi: Dead and Deadly Ideas and the Quest for Independent Thought

Living in Algeria and Argentina, respectively, Malik Bennabi (1905–73) and Rodolfo Kusch (1920–79) did not know each other, although they were both living, writing, and thinking during the trying years of the Cold War.[4] Their work gives us two monumental examples, similar and equivalent to Darwin and Freud, dealing with crucial issues in the colonial world, parallel to crucial issues in the imperial world to which Darwin and Freud devoted their lives and intellectual energy. Bennabi went through the trying years of Algerian decolonization (1954–62). Kusch went through the trying years of the rise and fall of Juan Domingo Perón (1946–55). They were one generation apart. As far apart geohistorically as they might seem, Bennabi and Kusch had a similar concern sprouting from their awareness of being where they were thinking, thrown as they were in the respective imperial-colonial histories of their countries (Algeria and Argentina) and their regions (Maghreb and the Middle Eastern Islamic world, South America or America, as Kusch preferred to say).

Both historical processes were points of no return, and in the societies affected by such turmoil, no one would remain the same. The memory of the community and the subjectivity of the generations born after the fact would be permanently affected, though differently so in different places. In the case of Algerian decolonization, and beyond the human tragedy, members of French civil society reacted in a variety of ways as James LeSueur has shown (2001). Given his location, Bennabi asked questions and developed arguments different from those of the French intellectuals: the meaning of the Algerian war, in France, was embedded in the history of France as a modern nation-state, Christian and capitalist, that had been competing with England for global control since the first half of the nineteenth century. In Algeria, by contrast, the meaning of the war was embedded in the region's enduring histories of colonialism.

Bennabi's questions deal with knowledge and subjectivity as these relate to the history of Algeria and North Africa and its dense layers, from Islamization before the Ottomans to the French displacement of the Ottomans. In that displacement, a radical change took place: Algeria entered, through French imperialism, the domain of Western capitalist imperialism. In other words, what happened in 1830 was not just a change of rulers; sultans were replaced by modern imperial states. Dwelling in that history, during the challenging years between the world wars in Europe and through the critical years of decolonization in Asia and Africa (between 1947 and 1971 approximately), Bennabi wrote two short and crucial essays: *The Question of Ideas in the Muslim World* (conceived in the 1950s, but finished and published a decade later), and *The Question of Culture* (1954). Both essays respond to a common concern among Third World intellectuals: gaining independence from a long history of coloniality of knowledge and of being. That is, decolonizing being and knowledge by being where one thinks. Consider this paragraph by Bennabi:

> Though it has emerged from the post-Almohad era since the last century, the Muslim World is still out of sorts. Like a rider who has lost control over the stirrup and failed to recapture it, it has been struggling to attain

its new equilibrium. Its secular decadence, condemning it to inertia, apathy, impotence and *colonizability*, has nonetheless preserved its traditional values in a more or less fossilized condition. It has emerged under such conditions at the time when the twentieth century reaches the peak of its material power but when all the moral forces have started disintegrating since the First World War. (Bennabi 2003b, 111)

I am where I think relocates thinking and knowledge to the intersection of the geopolitical and body-political imperial classification of places and racialization of people, languages, and ideas. It flatly rejects the assumptions that rational and universal truths are independent of whoever presents them, to whom, and why. It strongly contests the common knowledge and lazy intellectual response that what I just said is "Oh, yes, you are talking about situated knowledge." Certainly I am, but it is not the "universal situatedness"; rather, it is about the epistemic and ontological racism of imperial knowledge. To say that knowledge is situated in and of itself doesn't take us too far. It amounts to saying that "reality is constructed." Sure: but how is it constructed, by whom, why, what for, whose interest does it serve if we construct reality in one or another manner? And what are they thinking and saying to those who are affected by the construction of reality but not participating in such construction?

Thus, three hundred years after Descartes's death (in 1650, in Stockholm), someone like Malik Bennabi, in Algeria, had to deal with the consequences of Descartes's contribution to the foundation of modern philosophy and knowledge. Bennabi is now confronted with a problem similar to the one Descartes had, although of dissimilar configuration. In fact, while Descartes was dealing with a past controlled by theology and Renaissance humanism, both were within his own tradition. While Bennabi is confronted with a past grounded on Arabic language and Muslim philosophy (Al Gazhali, Ibn Sina, and Ibn Rushd), Descartes was confronted with a past of Latin and French: he wrote *Discourse on Method* in French and *Meditations on First Philosophy* in Latin. In both traditions, algebra and geometry were a common ground: both Muslim and Christian philosophers around 1200 were drinking from the same Greek fountains. Bennabi, like Descartes, is where he thinks; his being is formed in a double movement. Understanding, on the one hand, the local history of Algeria at the intersection of the Ottoman Sultanate and French empire—also at the intersection of the Arab and French languages, and at the intersection of Islam and Christianity—means being in a dense memory in which French indexes a marginal language, experience, and subjectivity. For Bennabi (and many thinkers, philosophers, and scientists around the world) the problem is how to disengage from the trap, or how to elide the entrapment of universalism. The problem is how to decolonize knowledge and being by affirming the geopolitical legitimacy of knowledge for the purposes of decolonization rather than knowledge for the sheer purpose of controlling the world by understanding its laws. Paradoxically, Descartes's brilliant move to depart from theology and humanism ended up trapping other knowledges and subjectivities alien to the personal and regional forces that motivated his relentless search for truth. The bottom line: there are different subjectivities, modes of being and of being in the world, inflected by the coloniality of knowledge and power. There is no reason, other than the coloniality of power, to think that Descartes's thoughts are more relevant to the well-being of humanity than Bennabi's. Since we are where we think, there is no reason (other than epistemic racism) to believe that—among all forms of creative thinking (not destructive thinking)—one mode of being where one thinks is better or preferable to the other. Transcendental truths (God, reason, rights, and knowledge) that are attainable and controlled by one ethno-class result in asserting one mode of being and one mode of thinking—that is, the imperial mode of being where one thinks.

Unlike Descartes, the problem to solve for Bennabi was not that of the overarching presence of theology and the soft arguments of tolerant humanists (in the middle of religious war and the assassination in 1610 of Henri of Navarre, founder of the College La Flèche, where Descartes studied) but that of the power of ideas in relation to bilingualism. Remember that one of Bennabi's concerns (and a concern of many Arabo-Islamic intellectuals) is why (as the Moroccan philosopher Mohammed Al-Jabri put it), Ibn Rushd (1126–90), sharing his time between Cordoba and Marrakech, reached a high level of rational thinking, only to have Arabo-Islamic philosophy "stop" there and reemerge five centuries later in France and Holland in the body of René Descartes at the time when Western Greco-Latin Christianity had already silenced Arabo-Islamic philosophy and sciences forever. That is the context in which Bennabi is concerned with the question of ideas in the Muslim world.

Bennabi's distinction between "dead ideas" and "deadly ideas" effectively illustrates the type of situation motivating the need to shift the geography of reason and to be where one thinks: "A dead idea is an idea whose origins have been betrayed, one that has deviated from its archetype and thus no longer has any roots in its original cultural plasma. In contrast, a deadly idea is an idea that has lost both its identity and cultural value after having been cut off its roots, which are left in their original cultural universe" (2003b, 105). Although Bennabi's approach encompasses a larger horizon of humanity and human history, the closer horizon generates his concern: to be a Muslim and at the same time a Third World intellectual means being in two subaltern positions in relation to imperial Christianity and Western secularism and in relation to the First World. What does someone dwelling in *exteriority* (dwelling in a subaltern place that has not been *created* either by Muslim or by Third World agencies) do? There are several possibilities. One could recognize that history is of the winners and accept and embrace First World, Western modernity, and secularism. Which, of course, is what ruling elites not only in Arabo-Islamic countries but also in South America and the Caribbean also did.

A parallel example comes from the Cold War era. It can give a better sense of the point I am making with Bennabi. We could ask: what does a Third World and black intellectual dwelling in exteriority do? And we can respond to the question by looking over the shoulders of Sir Lloyd Best (1934–2007). He starts one of his key essays, "Independence and Responsibility: Self Knowledge as an Imperative," by drawing *l'état de la question*:

> Since 1962, two visions of the future have been offered to Caribbean peoples. Both have been aborted. The first proved to be an illusion; the second turned into a nightmare. . . . They [the agents of the first vision] . . . urged us to produce what we consume and consume what we produce. This strategy involved a sharp increase in government ownership and operation of economic enterprise and hastened the emergence of the omni-competent state. . . .
>
> The second vision was that of the socialist state, with the means of production predominantly owned and controlled by a paramount Leninist party. (Best 1996, 3)

What I am driving at is that, beyond the significant differences between a Muslim in Algeria and a black in the Caribbean, they are both linked in the history of the modern-colonial world (since the expulsion of the Moors from Spain and the massive trade of enslaved Africans were two colonial sides of the same imperial beginning). In many and different local histories, Muslims and Africans were entangled with a variety of different Western European local histories (mainly those of the Atlantic countries from the Iberian Peninsula to England by way of France and Holland). Lloyd Best's major concern was "independent thought and Caribbean freedom," as he extensively argued in the eponymous essay. The first version of the essay was presented in 1966 at the Second Conference of West Indian Affairs, in Montreal. The scenario drawn by Best and the description of local elites in their dependency on Western education, technology, and science (which, if they are not necessarily deadly by nature, can become deadly, as with the idea of development) is similar to the one drawn by Bennabi. Where Bennabi saw dead ideas in the Muslim world, for Best the equivalent was not dead ideas of a historical civilization but disqualified ideas of black communities—no longer in Africa but in South America and the Caribbean: the communities and emerging civilization formed in the encounter among Africans from different kingdoms, languages, religions, and ways of life. It is that creolized crossroads that Best claims at the end of his essay:

> I have argued that we need independent thought. One of the most blatant manifestations of the colonial condition in the Caribbean—of the plantation mind—is the refuge which our intellectual classes take in a sterile scientism on the one hand, or in a cheap populism on the other. . . . One half of our intellectual classes is a-political. They are engrossed in technical exercises or they are busy dissipating their energies in administration and public relations—running the public service, running the Universities, running this, running that, running in effect, away from the issues.
>
> It is being proposed here, that being who we are, what we are and where, the kind of action to which we must be committed is determinate. . . . To acknowledge this is to set ourselves three tasks: The first is to fashion theory on which may be based the clear intellectual leadership for which the nation calls and which it has never had. The second is to conduct the inquiry on which theory can be soundly based. This is what may be called, in the jargon of my original trade, the creation of intellectual capital goods. Thirdly, we are to establish media by which these goods may be transmitted to the rest of us who are otherwise. . . . We may wish

to create a media of direct democratic expression suitable to the native Caribbean imagination. (1967, 29)

Where Best saw the failure and the nightmare of proposed solutions for the Caribbean by the national elite in complicity with external, imperial institutions and ideas (mostly Western liberalism and capitalism, rather than Western or Slavic Marxism or Chinese Maoism), Bennabi saw Muslim societies saturated by dead ideas that created the conditions for the advent of deadly Western ideas: "It is under such circumstances," Bennabi concludes,

> that the present Muslim society borrows modern and "progressive" ideas from Western civilization! This is a natural outcome of a process determined by the dialectic of things, human beings and ideas that has shaped Muslim history. Nevertheless what is unnatural is its inertia and apathy in this stage, as if it wished to stay there forever. Starting from the same point, other societies such as Japan and China have, on the contrary, succeeded to pull themselves out of their state of inertia by rigorously subjecting themselves to the conditions of new dynamics and new historical dialectics. (2003b, 45)

Here we have two Third World intellectuals, one a Muslim in North Africa, the other a black in the Caribbean, looking at the global conditions, being where they think, and dwelling in the *exteriorities* of the modern colonial world. We have here border thinking at its best and its consequence, *the creolization of theory*. These views have not been accounted for in the analysis of globalization and modernity. Certainly Anthony Giddens and Niall Ferguson are where they think: dwelling in the interiority of British and imperial European histories. Although they too are *where* they think, their thinking (propelled by the book market and the coloniality of knowledge) generates the effect that in reality they just think, *as if* they are nowhere in particular, as if instead of inhabiting the interiority of self-fashioned imperial histories they were standing at the top of the hill looking down and dominating the valley.

The dialectic between dead and deadly ideas tells the story of the imperial and colonial differences in the modern-colonial world, for the dialectic is operative not only in the sphere of the liberal state and capitalist economies looking for new surrogate states opening new markets, but also in their internal contestation: Marxism. Bennabi is clear in analyzing the consistency of Marx's analysis within his own cultural sphere to which industrial capitalism unfolded: "If Marx had analyzed such situations he would certainly have done so based on the logic of a dialectic whose constituent elements were all part and parcel of one and the same cultural universe that was his own universe" (2003b, 81). In contrast, Bennabi continues, "in the colonized and ex-colonized countries, such situations are the complex result of a dialectic obtaining in an original cultural universe as well as of the dialectical relationship between the latter and the alien cultural universe, that of colonialism" (80).

In my view, Bennabi's *The Question of Ideas in the Muslim World* is nothing less than an agonic quest for independent thought. The need and anxiety have not yet gone away, today, among Muslim intellectuals (as well as intellectuals of the former Third World around the globe). Listen to the Iranian intellectual Amr G. E. Sabet. In introducing his argument, Sabet makes clear that in the investigation he presents, he is not making any claim in favor of any "Islamization of knowledge," and neither for its secularization. His argument aims, he stresses, at the integration of knowledge, "whether secular or religious, through a measure of *intersubjectivity*" (2008, 4). Furthermore, and this is crucial for my argument, Sabet notes that beyond looking for an integration of Islamic thought and social theory,

> this study seeks to link the former (e.g., Islamic thought) with *decolonization* in order to underscore Islam's liberating commitment not only toward Muslims but toward humanity at large. The decolonization process that had taken place during the post–World War II era remains, unfortunately, an unfinished, and even a regressing, project. (4)

Decoloniality (to distinguish it from decolonization during the Cold War) refers to a set of projects that, based on identities, are open to humanity at large, in the same way that Christian theology and secular liberalism were, although they did not recognize themselves as mere "identity." They recognized themselves as universality. For that reason, Sabet stresses, "In addition to political, as well as economic, independence there is *the essential need for the independence of thought, of the mental, the psychological, and the spiritual*; for the exorcising of souls and liberating of minds" (5, emphasis added).

Shifting the geography and the biography of knowledge and of knowing breaks the hegemony of five hundred years of theo- and ego-politics of imperial knowledge. The latter disguised its own geographic and biographical interests and motivation. While Adam Smith, Immanuel Kant, and Karl Marx were where they thought, their thoughts acquired a universal profile, unrelated to geohistorical and biographical configurations. The geographic and biographical politics of knowledge are categories of decolonial thinking confronted with, undoing, and moving away from the imperial control of imperial political theology and its translation into secular egology.

Rodolfo Kusch: Epistemic Potential of Immigrant Consciousness

In Argentina, Gunter Rodolfo Kusch was born in 1922 and died in 1979. He was the only child of Ricardo Carlos Kusch and Elsa María Dorotea Tschunke de Kusch, a German couple who moved to Argentina from Germany shortly after World War I ended. He was four years old when his father passed away. At the end of his teen years, Kusch was living in the middle of an exciting time in Buenos Aires, the decades of the 1940s and 1950s, when he witnessed the end of World War II, the Juan Domingo Perón and Eva Perón decade, and an intense intellectual and cultural life. A "native" intelligentsia was taking over, a native intelligentsia of European descent (mainly from Spain, Italy, and Germany). The "mestizo consciousness" that Kusch explored in his first book (*La seducción de la barbarie*, 1953) was a reflection built on the experience of a community of displaced Europeans who coexisted with a dense presence of the indigenous population that Kusch experienced in the northwest of Argentina and in Bolivia. By the time of Kusch, the Afro-population had practically vanished from Argentina's imaginary, but Kusch was aware of its presence in America (the consistent name he used in all his writing; he rarely mentioned "Latin" America, a telling statement that is consistent with the philosophical explorations he conducted throughout his life).

A demographic and sociohistorical shift was taking place as the history of Argentina was moving out of the so-called *década infame* (1930–40), and also an intense intellectual life led by Silvina Ocampo and the journal *Sur*, which she founded in 1931. Ocampo remained director of the journal until 1971. The journal was born and continued its life in the cosmopolitan mode it started. Waldo Frank and José Ortega y Gasset were two of Ocampo's enthusiastic supporters, and Argentine writers such as Jorge Luis Borges and Adolfo Bioy Casares were among her close collaborators. When Kusch published *La seducción de la barbarie* in 1953, he was at the beginning of intellectual and political debates that had turned their back on the influences of *Sur*, debates that had emerged in the last years of Perón's presidency and immediately after his fall and moved from the enchantment of Europe to the interrogation of the troubled colonial and therefore racial histories in America. In *América profunda*, published in 1962, Kusch intensified his philosophical reflections anchored in "an-other history." He described that "other history" as being distinctive in its profile and coexisting with the European history in America with metaphors such as "seducción de la barbarie," "América profunda," "América vegetal," and many others. Crucial to the understanding of Kusch's sustained meditations from *La seducción de la barbarie* to *Geocultura del Hombre Americano* (1976) and *Esbozo de una antropología filosófica Americana* (1978) is the coexistence of a European history transplanted to the history of "América profunda." The historical foundation of America is indeed a triple history: the survival of indigenous population, the survival of Africans' forced migration and the domination by Europeans and their descendents. On the one hand, Indian memories throughout the Americas needed to be reinscribed in conflictual dialogue and tension with the existence of peoples of European descent and institutions (economy, politics, and family) modeled on European social organization. It could no longer be an internal transformation as was the case for the history of Europe. On the other hand, the reinscription that could not avoid European interference was and continues to be a reinscription that reproduces the difference. For the indigenous people who decided, throughout history, not to assimilate, it was of the essence not to maintain the fantasy of a bygone past but to maintain the reality in a present in which the reinscription of the difference was crucial for just living. One can understand that if for any European it would have been difficult to live in the skin of indigenous people, there is no reason to think that indigenous people would have been happy to live in the skin of European men and women. The awareness that the states in South America were colonial states (or, at their best, modern-colonial states), while those in France, England, and Germany were modern imperial states, was a starting point both for the emergence of the "nationalist Left" (cf. Juan José Hernández-Arregui) and for the decolonial option (cf. Rodolfo Kusch), both options grounded in the subjective and historical experience of Perónism.

I could not have made the foregoing statement without reading and re-reading the work of Rodolfo Kusch. Furthermore, it is in that statement that Kusch's idea of "mestizo consciousness" can be understood. For Kusch, "mestizo" does not have anything to do with biology, with mixed bloods, with the color of your skin or the form of your nose. Mestizo is for Kusch a matter of consciousness.

There is no question that mestizo consciousness is a conceptualization that emerges from a body that experiences *existentia Americana* (as we will see), similar to what the Jamaican philosopher Lewis Gordon (2000) has termed and explored as *existentia Africana*. About fifty years before Kusch's first book, a sociologist of African descent, in the United States, was sensing, as a black person and not as an immigrant of European descent, a discomfort coming from the experience of a history different from that of Kusch. W. E. B. Du Bois found in the concept of consciousness a tool for the articulation of his experience translated into a term familiar in the human and social sciences. But his consciousness, that is, the way he was experiencing consciousness, was different: a person of African descent, in the Americas, experiences life and his or her own existence differently from a person of European descent. Both, however, share a common experience, the experience of the displaced in relation to a dominant order of the world to which they do not belong. The consciousness of being-such and the awareness of not-being-such (in the case of Kusch neither European nor Indian), or sensing a tension between being such and such (like Du Bois, being black and American, when an American was assumed to be white), point toward the sphere of experience that Gloria Anzaldúa articulated as "the mestiza consciousness/la conciencia de la mestiza." It is worthwhile to underline the grammatical twist in Anzaldúa. She is talking not about "mestiza consciousness" but about "the consciousness of the mestiza," which is how I would translate the Spanish title she inscribed in the last chapter of her book: "La conciencia de la mestiza." We should remember at this point that the title of Rigoberta Menchú's narrative, in Spanish, is *Me llamo Rigoberta Menchú y así me nació la conciencia* (1982), badly translated into English as *I, Rigoberta Menchú, an Indian Woman from Guatemala*. That translation preferred exoticism to philosophical and political meaning, and the trumpeting of Benjamin Franklin's exultation of the first person, "I, Rigoberta Menchú . . ." Last but not least, the Afro-Colombian Zapata Olivella (self-identified as mulatto) conceived a "mestizo consciousness" (notice that *mestizo* acquires, as in Kusch, a meaning that goes beyond the biological, a child born of European and Indian) to capture the historical essence of the basic three types of languages, religions, cultures, ways of life, sensibilities, and subjectivities that transformed Anahuac, Abya Yala, and Tawantinsuyu into what Kusch calls "America."

In retrospect, and in the more recent spectrum in which consciousness has been articulated decolonially (Du Bois, Anzaldúa, Menchú), it would be more adequate to rename Kusch's mestizo consciousness as "immigrant consciousness," the consciousness of the immigrant of European descent who arrives in the Americas around the end of the nineteenth century or the beginning of the twentieth and, instead of assimilating, reacts critically to the displaced conditions of European immigrants in a country that, by that time, is already in the hands of Creoles of Spanish descent and Mestizos with mixed blood and a European soul and mentality.

Immigrant consciousness, in other words, is the assumed condition of existence, an existence out of place: for people of European descent, for being in a place whose history is not the history of their ancestors; indigenous or aboriginals, who built their history in the land they inhabited, found themselves out of place when their form of life and institutions, education, and economy were displaced, destroyed, and replaced with ways of life and institutions of migrants from European countries; Africans coming from several parts of Africa, with their own different languages and beliefs, forms of life, and institutions found themselves in a land whose histories did not belong to their ancestors and, in contrast to the Europeans, in a land whose social structures placed them at the bottom of the social scale. Immigrant consciousness (double consciousness; mestiza consciousness; mulatto consciousness; intercultural consciousness, as indigenous people in Ecuador maintain today; maroon consciousness, as it has been established among Afro-Andeans in Ecuador) consists in diverse expressions and experiences of the same condition of existence: awareness of the coloniality of being; of being out of place in the set of regulations (e.g., cosmology) of modernity. Briefly, of the colonial wound. It is interesting to note that critical intellectuals came up with ideas such as peripheral, alternative modernities: a complaisant position that pretends to be dissenting but ends up reproducing the standards with superficial variations. Immigrant consciousness—

double, mestiza, indigenous, maroon consciousness—represents different manifestations of another paradigm: the paradigm constituted by forms of decolonial consciousness whose horizon is a pluriversal horizon conceived as transmodernity (Dussel 2002).

Sylvia Wynter: What Does It Mean to Be Human?

Frantz Fanon made a passing observation in *Black Skin, White Masks* that became a fundamental proposition being unfolded in the sphere of Afro-Caribbean philosophy:

> Reacting against the constitutionalist tendency of the late nineteenth century, Freud insisted that the individual factor be taken into account through psychoanalysis. He substituted for a phylogenetic theory the ontogenetic perspective. It will be seen that the black man's alienation is not an individual question. Besides phylogeny and ontogeny stands sociogeny. (Fanon 1952/1967, 11)

Now, the sociogenic principle, which I explain hereafter, is one aspect of languaging and knowing. It is therefore traversed by the differential of power embedded in the ranking of languages in the modern-colonial world order:

> To speak means to be in a position to use a certain syntax, to grasp the morphology of this or that language, but it means above all to assume a culture, to support the weight of a civilization. . . .
>
> The problem that we confront in this chapter is this: The Negro of the Antilles will be proportionately whiter—that is, he will be closer to being a real human being—in direct ratio with his mastery of the French language. *I am not unaware that this is one of man's attitudes face to face with Being.* A man who has a language consequently possesses the world expressed and implied in that language. What we are getting at becomes plain: Mastery of language affords remarkable power. (17–18, emphasis added)

Sylvia Wynter took Fanon's sociogenic principle to the next step. What is the next step? It is clear after Fanon that we cannot expect Western sciences and political theory to solve the problems created by five centuries of insertion of Western designs into the world beyond imperial Europe, and into colonial Europe itself: Ireland and southern Italy, for example, as well as the Soviet republics (i.e., colonies) of Central Europe. Briefly, and once more, by imperial Europe and Eurocentrism I mean three things, spatially, chronologically, and subjectively framed.

Spatially *Europe* refers to the Atlantic imperial monarchies and then nation-states (Spain, Portugal, France, Holland, England), and to the supporting cast (Italy and Germany) whose imperial dominions were lesser than the former, although they were not out of the game. It has been pointed out, several times, that the interconnections between marginal-capitalist countries in relation to central-capitalist countries went through a dictatorial political period: Italy and Germany never enjoyed extensive imperial domination; Spain and Portugal did, but lost it by the nineteenth century, when France and England were in ascendance and helping Spanish and Portuguese colonies to gain their independence.

Chronologically, *Eurocentrism* refers to a potent matrix of categories that connect and unify all areas of knowledge (what today we describe as the natural sciences, the humanities, the social sciences, and the professional schools, i.e., medicine, law, engineering, business, computing). That matrix is legitimized by Greek and Latin categories of thought and their translation and unfolding in six modern European imperial languages: Italian, Spanish, Portuguese, French, German, and English. Cast, defended, and promoted in the rhetoric of modernity, progress, salvation, development, et cetera, that matrix generated the image of its own totality, which authorized its promoters and defenders to disregard, marginalize, ignore, deprecate, reprove, rebuke, and attack all knowledge that did not obey the rules and principles of the (post)modern matrix of knowledge. At that point, the modern matrix (Eurocentrism) became also colonial.

Subjectively, the modern-colonial matrix of knowledge (coloniality of knowledge) has been created, perfected, transformed, expanded, and exported-imported by a particular kind of social agent: in general (and we can go through the biography of the great thinkers and scientists in the Western canon), they were male, they were Christians, they were white, and they lived in western Christendom, which, after the sixteenth century, was translated into Europe. That is to say: the modern-colonial matrix of knowledge has been linked to a kind of subjectivity emerging from the lived experience of white and Christian males who lived and studied in the six countries and languages I have identified. In the case of Kepler, for example, who was born in Cracovia and started his studies at the University of Krakow, it was, however, his learning and lived experience at the University of Bologna that provided the institutional push to his personal genius and intellectual motivation.

These three parameters map the hubris of the zero point uncovered by the Colombian philosopher Santiago Castro-Gómez. The hubris of the zero point describes a conception of knowledge that divides the knowing subject and the known object and gives to the knowing subject a locus of privilege: it is an observer that observes without being observed. In Christian theology, that place was reserved for God. In secular science and philosophy, it was transferred to the transcendental subject.[5]

Wynter's next step is to envision a *scientia* (I write it in the Renaissance style to distinguish it from the concept of *science* that unfolded from Galileo to Newton, from Newton to Einstein, and from Buffon and Linnaeus to Darwin) that disobeys the hubris of the zero point. I see this move as a *decolonial scientia* based on Fanon's sociogenic principle. Fanon's hypothesis, Wynter argues, is first of all a hypothesis derived from his awareness of reporting in the third person his own experience in the first person ("Look Mom, a Negro"!). The experience, in other words, of being through the eyes of the imperial other; the experience of knowing that "I am being perceived, in the eyes of the imperial other, as not quite human." Thus the decolonial scientia is the scientia needed not for progress or development but for liberating the actual and future victims of knowledge for progress and development. It is not the case, most certainly, of studying the so-called Negro problem from the perspective of any of the established social sciences or humanities. If that were the case, sociogenesis would become an object of study rather than being the historical foundation and constitution of future and global loci of enunciation. This scientia, built on the sociogenic principle (in this case the lived experience of the black man, although this is not the only colonial experience — colonial wound — that would sustain the emerging scientia), makes clear from the start that the mind-body problem (or the soul-body, if we take a step back from secularism to Christian theology) makes sense only in the domain of ontogenesis; it is only there that the problem can exist, Wynter states (2001, 13). That the sociogenic principle is not an object of knowledge but rather a locus of enunciation, and the energy that links knowledge with decolonial subjective formations, is stated by Wynter as follows:

Unlike the "common reality" of a wave phenomenon, however, the socio-genic principle is not a natural scientific object of knowledge. In that if, in the case of humans, this transcultural constant is that of the sociogenic principle as culturally programmed rather than genetically articulated "sense of self," with the "property" of the mind or human consciousness being located only in the dynamic processes of symbiotic interactions between the opioid and punishment system of the brain and the culture-specific governing code or sociogenic principle . . . and thereby experiencing ourselves *as* human, then the identification of the hybrid property of consciousness, which such a principle makes possible, would call for another form of scientific knowledge beyond the limits of the natural sciences—including beyond neurobiology whose natural-scientific approach to the phenomenon of consciousness is paradoxically based on our present culture's purely bio-centric and adaptive conception of what it is to be human. (47)

Thus if modern-imperial epistemology (in its diversity, but always imperial diversity) was spatially, chronologically, and subjectively located, scientia starting from the sociogenic principle becomes the project of decolonial scientia setting up new places or nodes of space, time, and subjectivity. That is, while modern-colonial epistemology was based on theology and secular philosophy and the affirmation of humanitas in Descartes's "I think, therefore I am," the rejection of the anthropos and the appropriation of humanitas by those who have been considered anthropos are an affirmation of being where one thinks and engages in decolonializing Western epistemology.

Spatially, decolonial scientia is located at the borders (territorial as well as linguistic, subjective, epistemic, and ontological) created by the consolidation and expansion of the modern-colonial epistemic matrix described earlier. This matrix, which emerged in the sixteenth century, guided by theology, in the imperial-colonial connections between Atlantic Europe and the Americas, folded and unfolded in the hands of England and France and projected itself into Asia and Africa from the late seventeenth century to the mid-twentieth. The leadership was taken up by the United States, where the use of the English language and the meteoric enlargement of scientific knowledge and technology expanded the basic principles and structures of knowledge. Consequently decolonial scientia is all over the globe (in the same way that modern-imperial science is), and it moves constantly from the so-called Third World to the so-called First World, and from the latest Western imperial countries to the "emerging empires" (China, Russia, and perhaps, in the near future, India and the Islamic Middle East; further in the future, one can see that in the Andes, under the leadership of Bolivia, the model of Tawantinsuyu will interact with the model of the liberal-colonial state).

Chronologically, decolonial scientia regionalizes—on the one hand— the chronological line of the imperial matrix of knowledge: this will be the way in which Europeans themselves conceived, narrated, and practiced their own conception of knowledge. And it reorganizes—on the other hand—chronology into global space: while in imperial scientia connections through times, including epistemic breaks and paradigmatic changes, followed one another in time, decolonial scientia links emerging nodes in space, the space of colonial and decolonial struggles around the world, to which follows today the massive migrations of the "barbarians" to the "civilized regions." Double consciousness and mestiza consciousness (Du Bois and Anzaldúa) are two key concepts that give substance to the ontogenic principle and thus capture the fact that people who fall on the side of the racially inferior and sexually abnormal are seeing themselves through the imperial other, that is, the imperial-modern subject holding and controlling knowledge and, therefore, determining who is authorized to know and what knowledge is useful to have (and for whom).

Subjectively, decolonial scientia is embraced by people who either endure the consequences of the colonial wound (that is, the colonial subject) or by modern subjects that detach themselves from imperial knowledge and subjectivity and embrace decolonial scientia. Contrary to the male, Christian, and Eurocentric dominating subjects and subjectivities, the decolonial subject is at the border of both non-European languages, religions, epistemologies, and hegemonic knowledge. Decolonial subjects are those whose consciousness are divided between knowing how one is being perceived from the socially normative and the experience of one's exteriority (rather than abnormality or inferiority). The consciousness of being in exteriority transforms the colonized (who feels abnormal, inferior) into a decolonial subject (who *is* in exteriority). At that moment, decolonization becomes a project of epistemic disobedience, independent thoughts, and decolonial freedom.[6]

Decolonial scientia has, then, three types of tasks ahead. One is to show that the hubris of the zero point enacted a geopolitics and a body politics of knowledge that consisted in denying that geohistorical locations and racial-sexual body configurations were relevant to knowledge. The zero point denied, in other words, the links between geohistory and knowledge and between biography and knowledge. The second is to explore the consequences that Western expansion (today called globalization) had for the population and the environment (i.e., natural resources needed by the imperial economy) targeted for conversion to Christianity, for civilization, for development, and now for human rights and democracy. It is necessary to look at responses globally and through time and avoid the imperial trap that looks at *local responses* to *global designs*. The third is to generate knowledge to build communities in which life (in general) has priority over economic gain, growth, and development; in short, knowledge that will subject economic growth to human needs rather than submit human needs to economic growth and development.

Redrawing the House of Knowledge at the Intersection of Global Linear and Decolonial Thinking

In the twenty-first century, the legacies of Western imperial epistemology and its colonization of knowledge and of being are being appropriated and thwarted in two directions: de-Westernization and decoloniality. They have one element in common, although both projects move in quite different directions.

De-Westernization was a concept introduced by Samuel Huntington. He was aware that while Western ideals will be defended, a global move toward de-Westernization would sooner or later dissolve Western dominance and transform it into something else. Not that Western civilization will disappear but that Western civilization will no longer be the pinnacle and the point of arrival, the point of reference, the locus of the zero point of knowing, the leader and judge of the rest of the world. That idea was picked up and turned around by a strong line of argumentation, in East and Southeast Asia, claiming de-Westernization not as an imitation of the West but as a continuation in a different direction of what the West had started.[7]

I propose two directions to disengage from the rules of the game and the edifice of Western epistemology. Disengaging is not the same as ignoring. We cannot disengage from something that is in all of us, today, around the world. By *disengage* here I mean and understand a double movement. On the one hand, it means the unveiling of the local and regional foundations of a so-called universal claim to truth that includes both the categories of thought and the logic that sustain all branches of Western knowledge, from theology to philosophy, from psychology and psychoanalysis to natural science, from political theory to political economy. On the other hand, it means delinking ourselves from a system of knowledge and subject formation that celebrates happiness based on individual success, accumulation of wealth, and constant consumerism.

What is the place of decolonial thinking at the time when global linear thinking has been displaced by new forms of control of authority and economy that depend not on partitioning and dividing the land but on controlling natural resources, military bases, nuclear weapons, and a polycentric capitalist economy? The concentration of decision power in the sphere of authority and economy is more overwhelming today than twenty years ago because of the polycentricity of capital accumulation and the devastating consequence for the life of the planet when political and financial leaders and the media are in a blind and wild race toward death, motivated by the belief in economic growth, global control, and happiness.

The management of knowledge and subject formation is not operative only in the sphere of authority (political and military armed control) and in the economic domain; it is a pervasive idea of a civilization and a way of life that permeates all spaces of society, private and public. There are hundreds of cases and examples, every day. I offer just one, from the front page of the *New York Times*, "Gatsby's Green Light Beckons a New Set of Strivers," February 17, 2008. There are many ways of reading a piece of art or literature. This article on *The Great Gatsby* and a teacher's experience with the novel is about the identification of young students (in their late teens) with the American Dream and the "fantastic" life that Gatsby made for himself. Susan Moran, the director of the English program at Boston Latin (who has been teaching the novel for thirty-two years), observes that her students "all understand what it is to strive for something, . . . to want to be someone you're not, to want to achieve something that's just beyond reach, whether it's professional success or wealth or idealized love—or a 4.0 or admission to Harvard." But other possibilities, some of them hinted at by Fitzgerald himself, are the individual and social costs of Gatsby's achievements, costs of which Gatsby himself is well aware. In this regard, the novel is a liberal critique of liberal values and of the very idea that "being someone" is the optimal horizon of life. Still other readings might be more decolonial, helping students to understand what Gatsby means in America and in the world at the turn of the twentieth century; what America means today at the beginning of the twenty-first century, when the enormous costs of a lifestyle based on success have become more obvious: success in personal achievements and personal achievements related to the success of one country at the cost of many others. The young Chinese student featured in the article has as her goal to attend Harvard, earn a degree, and return to China to help the country to "have a faster development."

That, too, is being where one thinks. The "where" is not just a geographic location but the map of desires and aspirations of a civilization driven by economic and social success, paying enormous costs in wars, refugees, unemployment, and new forms of slavery, rather than a civilization driven by the collective desire for well-being and the celebration of life in general, and not just human life as a singular privilege. To celebrate only the living we call "humans" at the expense of other sectors of life is to be already embedded in the civilization of death, in which we are immersed today. If nothing else, decolonial thinking and the decolonial option can contribute, in the broad sphere of education, to the understanding of the logic of coloniality that drives all of us toward a collective death dressed up as the triumphal growth of global economy.

Notes

I continue here the reflections I started in *Local Histories/Global Designs* (2000) and continued through the publication of "Delinking: The Rhetoric of Modernity, the Logic of Coloniality, and the Grammar of Decoloniality" (2007).

1 I admire and respect Schmitt's straightforward honesty. There is no intention of hiding, disguising, or justifying that humanitas was a European invention to its own benefit. The concept of humanitas, which has a long history in Western thought, acquired its extreme form from, and was consistent with, the victory of a philosophy of absolute humanity: "Only when man appeared to be the embodiment of absolute humanity did the other side of this concept appear in the form of a new enemy: the

inhuman" (Schmitt 2003, 104). The inhuman is of course the anthropos from the perspective of those classified as *inhuman*. Schmitt recognized the totality from his own perspective, but there is no room left for the anthropos to unfold his or her own discourse. Now we are doing it, creolizing theory is a contribution to that shift in the geography of reasoning.

2 For the concept of epistemic colonial difference, see Mignolo 2000; for the onto-logical colonial difference in tandem with the epistemic one, see Maldonado-Torres 2007, 240–71.

3 When international law (or the European nomos of the earth) is looked at from the perspective of colonial countries (that is, from its consequences rather than from its intention) the silences of Schmitt's account become apparent. See, for in-stance, Umozurike 1979; Siba N'Zatioula Grovogui 1996. Of course, there are other perspectives, although from the sixteenth century on, it began to be articulated in relation to what Schmitt describes as the modern nomos of the earth. Islam and international law are other cases in point see Sheikh Wahbeh al-Suhili (2005).

4 For an updated summary of Bennabi's work, life, and influence, see Walsh 2007, and for an analysis of his theory of civilization, see Boussalah 2005 and Benlahcene 2004. I am thankful to Ebrahim Moosa for calling my attention to the work of this Algerian thinker. I am here using two books by Bennabi written in the late sixties: *The Question of Ideas in the Muslim World* and *The Question of Culture*. Robert Kusch's works, written between 1952 and 1978, were recently collected in three vol-umes (Kusch 2000). An English translation, by María Lugones, of one of Kusch's fundamental books, *Pensamiento indígena y pensamiento popular* (1971), was pub-lished by Duke University Press in 2010 with the title *Indigenous and Popular Think-ing in América*.

5 Castro-Gómez 2005. A condensed version of his thesis on the zero point appears in "The Missing Chapter of Empire: Postmodern Reorganization of Coloniality and Post-Fordist Capitalism" (Castro-Gómez 2007).

6 It is precisely at this juncture that decolonial thinking and the creolization of theory meet.

7 See Mahbubani 2008 for a strong argument with historical depth in shifting the geo-politics of capitalist reason. There is an intellectual genealogy of this line of thought with Zakaria (1994). Needless to say, Bennabi was intuiting the path unfolding in East Asia that he contrasted with Muslim societies. Certainly he was not aware of the future of Muslim Indonesia.

SEVEN

TAIWAN IN MODERNITY/COLONIALITY
Orphan of Asia and the Colonial Difference

Leo Ching

In a recent class discussion about the popularity of Japanese anime and Korean wave in East Asia and beyond, a student asked why Taiwan doesn't have a significant influence in the emerging regional and global cultural industry, a kind of "soft power" that we are witnessing with Japan and South Korea. While haphazardly spewing out the names of Kaneshiro Takeshi, Jay Chou, Ang Lee, and Ah Mei as evidence of Taiwan's importance in the international cultural arena (note the difference between individual artists from Taiwan and the aggregated trend and genre from Japan and South Korea), my answer seemed tenuous and belabored. The student left unconvinced. Whereas Japanese, and increasingly Korean, cultural products have gained regional recognition and global appeal, Taiwan-produced culture seems invariably local, and regional at best (with the exception of auteurs such as Hou Hsiao-hsien and Ang Lee). In academia, especially in North America, the study of Taiwan can often be seen as a professional liability, a mere distraction from the more important studies of China or Japan. During Taiwan's long association with anti-Communism in the Cold War era, scholars with radical and leftist inclinations in both the United States and Japan have shunned the study of Taiwan. What Shu-mei Shih has heuristically called the "(in)significance" of Taiwan in globality is indicative of the minoritarian status of Taiwan not only in geopolitical terms but also in cultural and intellectual productions (Shih 2003). The (in)significance of Taiwan is symptomatic of the historical and structural imperatives of the postwar and Cold War American hegemony over East Asia that was in part produced, sustained, and reproduced by the disciplinarity of area studies. Even in the so-called post-area-studies moment of colonial-postcolonial studies, Taiwan, with its multiple colonial modernities, is rarely mentioned and almost never discussed in depth or at length. The (in)significance and insularity of Taiwan cannot be rectified by simply overturning the hierarchy and asserting its importance and universality. Instead one can begin by attending to the specificity of Taiwan in the world and its relationality to multiple modes of power and knowledge production.

This chapter is a modest effort to locate Taiwan in the theorization of the modern-colonial world and a gesture toward a colonial sensibility that is situated at the interstices of modernity-coloniality. I will begin by recapping the concept of modernity-coloniality as theorized by Latin American scholars, especially in their critique of Eurocentrism. This is not simply an attempt to introduce theory from the South but to underscore the importance of the geopolitics of knowledge, the idea that the production of knowledge cannot be separated from the geohistory of its condition of possibility. A detour into the subaltern theorization of modernity-coloniality brings a sharper relief to the Japanization of Eurocentrism in its own colonial endeavor. I argue that in the context of East Asian modernity, the coloniality of power is constituted and complicated by not only Eurocentrism but also Japancentrism. I argue that one prominent strand of Eurocentrism and Japancentrism is the Hegelian historicism with a strong spatial dimension. Finally, I reread Wu Zhuoliu's *Orphan of Asia* and suggest that its spatial itinerary and sensibility of despair constitute a counternarrative to both Eurocentrism and Japancentrism. From the perspective of the colonized subject, a world history with its modern rationality and teleology couched in Hegelian dialectics is simply, borrowing from Michel-Rolph Trouillot (1997) in a reverse context, "unthinkable." The colonial difference evinced in Wu's novel testifies to the continuous significance and relevance of Taiwan in the study of modernity-coloniality.

Modernity-Coloniality

It is impossible today to speak of modernity as a thing in itself separated from the political, economic, and cultural processes that violently incorporated the world as a planetary phenomenon. It is equally indefensible to assume modernity as an exclusively and originally European experience that conferred itself with permanent superiority over all other communities throughout history. We must recognize two key points: first, the coercive nature of modernity through imperialism and colonialism associated with the development of capitalism, that is, the involuntary nature of modernity for the non-West (Takeuchi 2005); and second, the falsehood of Europe's distinctive and inherent advantage over others, that is, the myth of Eurocentrism (Blaut 1993). In short, coloniality and Eurocentrism are two sides of the same modernity coin. Coloniality is the underside of modernity and its condition of possibility. Eurocentrism is none other than the various attempts to consolidate the myth of modernity as a proprietary Western project. Coloniality and the critique of Eurocentrism reject the history of modernity as linear and predestined and open up to a multispatial and relational dimension of an uneven modern-colonial world. The differentiated and overlapping contours of coloniality at large require us to take stock of the specific geohistorical and cultural conditions of modernity and its others. The spatialization of modernity enables us to confront coloniality in its multiple and interconnected manifestations. East Asian modernity (and Taiwan's position within it) would have to confront both the imperialist presence of the West and the colonial empire of Japan, but in different scales and historical conditions. Put differently, Taiwan in modernity-coloniality must engage in the critique of both Eurocentrism and Japancentrism, or more precisely a Japanized Eurocentrism.

Walter Mignolo has argued that there are two macro-narratives about modernity as theorized broadly in the humanities and the social sciences: the discourse of Western civilization and the world system theory (Mignolo 2002). The discourse of Western civilization marks the beginning of modernity in the eighteenth century mainly through the philosophers of the British and English Enlightenment and the German romantics. They traced European modernity to the mythical Latin or Greek origin; they reinterpreted all of world history and projected Europe's splendor onto the past. This is what Hegel would call "the end and center of world history." The Peruvian sociologist Aníbal Quijano calls this "the first Eurocentrism" (2000, 2). In short, modernity maintained the imaginary of Western civilization as a pristine development from ancient Greece to eighteenth-century Europe. The Enlightenment thus propagated the myth of Europe while excluding and ignoring as nonexistent all cultures that preceded it.

This discourse of Western civilization was challenged by the emergence of the so-called world systems theory in the 1970s spearheaded by a group of sociologists, most notably Immanuel Wallerstein. To put it simply for the purpose of our discussion, world systems analysis argues that the modern capitalist world system only emerged in the sixteenth century. This historicization of capitalism (what Wallerstein calls Historical Capitalism) relativizes and spatializes European hegemony only to the last five hundred years. By delimiting Europe's centrality to the last five centuries, the world systems theory removed the continent's "aura" of being the eternal "center" of world history. This is why Quijano calls modernity "the management of the world system's 'centrality'" (2). Mignolo, however, has taken issue with world systems analysis and suggested that Wallerstein's Historical Capitalism remains a Eurocentric criticism of capitalism. Mignolo argues that Wallerstein's conceptions of linear time and newness of capitalism are themselves the two basic presuppositions of capitalist ideology and modernist epistemology. These presuppositions allow for a third characteristic of historical capitalism: the image of capitalism as a totality that erased all other existing economic alternatives from the face of the earth (Mignolo 2002, 75). We should remember that until the eighteenth century, European modernity was still peripheral to the Hindustani and Chinese worlds. World systems theory has made visible the spatiality of Western history in the past five hundred years; it made visible the spatial articulation of power not as one linear succession of events.

From the perspectives of the Latin American scholars, the invasion of the Americas is thus crucial in the European creation of the world system. This system emerged from within the process of globalization that started in 1492 and intensified toward the end of the twentieth century. The history of modernity itself therefore began with the violent encounter between Europe and the Americas at the end of the fifteenth century. The conquest of the Americas allowed Europe to procure precious silver (and later gold)—through the process of slavery and indentured labor—so that it could purchase commodities from China and Hindustan, which did not desire anything from Europe, and accelerate the development of capitalism in Europe. The growth of the Atlantic circuit in the sixteenth century was crucial for the future development of Europe. It is precisely in this relationship between the Americas and Europe that Quijano argues that coloniality is constitutive of modernity. The Argentine philosopher Enrique Dussel puts it this way: "Modernity was born when Europe was in a position to pose itself against an other, when, in other words, Europe could constitute itself as a unified ego exploring, conquering, colonizing an alterity that gave back its image of itself" (1993, 67). Dussel therefore periodizes modernity in two phases: the colonial process of early modernity (1492–1789) and, since the time of the Enlightenment, the industrial globalization of mature modernity (1789–1989). The distinction here is important because if we conceive of modernity as emerging only in conjunction with industrial capitalism in the eighteenth century, then colonialism becomes derivative but not constitutive of modernity: modernity came first, and colonialism came afterward. Instead Quijano argues that the emerging Atlantic circuit of the sixteenth century made coloniality *constitutive* of modernity. In the sixteenth century, the spatial articulation of the Atlantic commercial circuit produced what he calls the coloniality of power. Quijano identifies coloniality of power with capitalism and its consolidation in Europe from the fifteenth to the eighteenth centuries. Coloniality of power implies and constitutes itself through (1) the classification and reclassification of the planet's population (the concept of culture becomes crucial in this task of classifying and reclassifying); (2) an institutional structure that functions to articulate and manage such classifications (the state apparatus, universities, the church, etc.); (3) the definition of spaces appropriate to such goals; and (4) an epistemological perspective from which to articulate the meaning and profile of the new matrix of power and from which the new production of knowledge could be channeled (Mignolo 2000b, 17). Coloniality of power is a means by which the entire planet, including its continental division (Africa, America, Europe), becomes articulated in the production of knowledge and its classificatory apparatuses. Eurocentrism becomes, therefore, a metaphor to describe the coloniality of power from the perspective of subalternity. What is crucial for my purpose is the idea that coloniality is both the underside of modernity and its very condition of possibility. Coloniality is therefore constitutive of modernity, and Eurocentrism is the management of Europe's purported centrality.

By locating coloniality as constitutive of modernity, Latin American scholars such as Quijano and Dussel and Latin American studies scholars such as Mignolo offer another perspective on modernity from those we find in colonial and postcolonial studies who privilege the British and French and South Asian experiences. Instead of interpreting colonialism as derivative of modernity in the eighteenth and nineteenth centuries, these scholars point to the conquest of America as the "original sin" of modernity and argue that coloniality is the very condition of modernity. I want to suggest that their insights are not accidental but integral to the production of what Mignolo has termed "the geopolitics of knowledge." The different history of colonialism and decolonization of Latin America and its spatial articulation with Europe compelled a different "thought" from European thinking: the creolization of theory. The geopolitics of knowledge is about both local histories and subaltern knowledges.

From the geopolitics of Taiwan and East Asia, how do we conceive the questions of modernity and coloniality? How does Taiwan's particular geohistorical-cultural position allow us to understand the interstices of modernity and coloniality? I suggest we begin by pluralizing the coloniality of power as theorized by Quijano not only in terms of Eurocentrism but also in terms of Japancentrism. (One can also add Sinocentrism to the colonial matrix, but for the purpose of this chapter, I will focus only on Eurocentrism and Japancentrism.) What I would like to argue is that Eurocentrism and Japancentrism are different, but complementary and complicit in their respective productions of the coloniality of power. If Eurocentrism constitutes a putative universalism, then Japancentrism represents a particularism that is, in the last instance, in collusion with a disguised universalism. Their difference, to borrow Walter Mignolo's term, is that of an "imperial difference"—a differentiation *within* the coloniality of power.

Imperial Difference: Eurocentrism and Japancentrism

As mentioned earlier, the eighteenth and nineteenth centuries saw the emergence of a Western civilization discourse that culminated in the first Eurocentrism. The development of the social sciences along with the natural sciences created a new global design. Ideas of Europe and its others were integrated into the concept of world history. Charles de Montesquieu, Adam Smith, Hegel, and Marx, among others, constructed the idea of Asia and African in contrast with Europe and incorporated Asia and Africa in a teleological vision of history. It is well known that Hegel showed how

world history is the self-realization of God (a theodicy), reason, and freedom. It is the process toward enlightenment: "Universal History represents
... the *development* of the consciousness that the Spirit has of its freedom
and also the evolution of the understanding that the Spirit obtains through
such consciousness. This *development* implies a *series of stages*, a series of
determinations of freedom, which are born from its self-concept, that is,
from the nature of freedom to become conscious of itself. . . . This necessity and the necessary series of the pure abstract determinations of the concept are the province of Logic."[1] In Hegelian ontology, development is what
determines the very movement of the concept until its culmination in the
idea. Development for Hegel is dialectically linear: it is a primordially ontological category, particularly in the case of world history. It has, moreover,
a direction in space: "World History travels from east to west; for Europe is
the absolute end of history, just as Asia is the beginning" (Hegel 1975, 97).
The distortion of history begins with the Encyclopedists (Montesquieu's *The
Spirit of Laws* is a good example) but continues with the English Enlightenment thinkers, Kant in Germany, and finally Hegel, for whom the Orient
was humanity's "infancy" (*Kindheit*), the place of despotism and unfreedom
from which the Spirit (*Volksgeist*) would later soar toward the West, as if on
a path toward the full realization of liberty and civilization. Since the beginning, Europe had been chosen by destiny as the final meaning of universal
history (Dussel 2002, 222).

If Eurocentrism constituted itself in the eighteenth century, Japancentrism emerged in the late nineteenth century and the early twentieth as
a non-European response to Eurocentrism. Japan's so-called revolt against
the West, with its variegated complexity and inherent contradictions, nonetheless has certain generalities. First, it constituted itself as a critique of
the West and its Eurocentrism. Second, it linked the revolution of Japan
with the revival of Asia (Najita and Harootunian 1998, 210). Fukuzawa Yukichi's "On Leaving Asia" (1885) and Okakura Kakuzo's *The Ideal of the East*
(1903) can be seen as the prototype of Japancentrism and its contradictions.
Whereas Fukuzawa sees the modern civilization and old conventions of
Asia as mutually exclusive, Okakura advocates the superiority of Asia's spiri-
tuality over the scientific progress of the West. Whereas Fukuzawa sees the
futility of resisting against the West and urges Japan to delink from China
and Korea, Okakura envisions the past as a way to create new paths for

the future and believes that Asia, not the West, should be the agent of historical change. Although Okakura's Asianism and Fukuzawa's de-Asianism appear to be articulating two opposing positionalities of Japan in relation to its Asian neighbors, it would be wrong to view them as incommensurable and irreconcilable. The two approaches converge on a Japancentrism that, regardless of their respective symbolizations of Asia, bestows on Japan a privileged position within the region in the emerging modern-colonial world system. First and foremost, the opposition between Fukuzawa and Okakura derived from the same sense of crisis: the confronting of Western civilization. It was this imminent threat that necessitated the rearticulation of the relationship between Japan and Asia as a modern problematic that constituted a rupture from the China-centered worldview. Fukuzawa sees Western civilization as a kind of epidemic, though it has greater benefits than measles. Okakura sees the West as inferior, as totally absorbed in the consideration of means rather than ends. Both were confronted with the opposing relation of East and West, and an existing Asia. More importantly, they also subjected Asia to symbolization away from geographic or environmental determinism (Sun 2000).

In these tumultuous times, Fukuzawa and Okakura render Japan in a unique role between East and West that ultimately constructs a hierarchical relation of nations that affords Japan a special status within Asia but does not fundamentally challenge the Eurocentric mapping of the world's peoples in terms of race and development. The archipelago therefore becomes an apt metaphor for both Fukuzawa and Okakura to imagine Japan's new role in the sea of empire. For Fukuzawa, "Japan is located in the eastern extremities of Asia, but the spirit of her people has already moved away from the old conventions of Asia to the Western civilization." This location and disposition will allow Japan to float in the "same ocean of civilization, sail the same waves, and enjoy the fruits and endeavors of civilization."[2] The eastern extremities of Japan's location also, in Okakura's view, bestowed Japan with "the unique blessing of unbroken sovereignty, the proud ancestral ideas and instincts [that] made Japan the real repository of the trust of Asiatic thought and culture." Japan is therefore the living museum of Asiatic civilization, where the historic wealth of Asiatic culture can be consecutively studied through its treasured specimens. However, Japan is more than a museum, "because the singular genius of the race leads it to dwell on all phases of the ideals of the past, in that spirit of living Advaitism which welcomes the new without losing the old." The history of Japanese art therefore becomes the history of Asiatic ideals, "the beach where each successive wave of Eastern thought has left its sand-ripple as it beat against the national consciousness" (Okakura 1903).

Okakura and Fukuzawa, despite their seemingly opposing stances, remain trapped in the East-West binary, where Japan emerges as the only civilized and privileged nation in Asia. Kōyama Iwao and Kōsaka Masaaki of the Kyoto school in the 1930s and 1940s formulated a more direct critique of Eurocentrism, especially its historicism. Here Naoki Sakai's critique of the complicity between the putative claims of universalism and particularism is useful in understanding the "imperial difference" between Eurocentrism and Japancentrism. According to Sakai, Kōyama and Kōsaka argue that a fundamental shift has taken place in the world since the late nineteenth century and the early twentieth. Until the late nineteenth century, history seemed to have moved linearly toward the further unification of the world that would allow for only one center. History was conceived as the process of Westernization (Europeanization). As Hegel's historicism puts it: "The history of the world was European history." Toward the late nineteenth century, Kōyama claims, the non-Western world began to move toward its independence and to form a world of its own, which included the recognition that "history was not only temporal or chronological but also spatial and relational" (Sakai 1998). The difference was between that of a monistic history (一元的歷史), which did not know its implicit reliance on other histories and thought itself autonomous and total, and world history, which conceived itself as the spatial relations of history. Kōyama also includes Japanese national history in the list of monistic history. Kōyama insists that another history, world history, which recognizes other histories, is about to emerge. This emergence should mark a fundamental change in relationship between the subject of history and its others; it should indicate that the monistic history in which others were refused their own recognition is no longer possible.

For Kōyama and Kōsaka, the unity of the subject of history, of pluralistic history, is unequivocally equated with that of the nation-state. The natural community (nation) must be represented by the state: only through the state is the natural community identified as the *nation for itself*. And only through this representation of itself does the nation become historical and generate its own culture, a historical world of its own. At this stage, a nation forms a history or historical world of its own with the state as its subject. While rejecting Hegelian philosophy as an extension of monistic history, Kōyama rigorously follows Hegelian construction (Sakai 1998, 491). The modern nation must be an embodiment of the will (自己限定性). The subject of the nation is, at the same time, self-determination (the determination of the self as such) and the determining self (the self that determines itself). The modern nation must externalize itself to be aware of itself and to realize its will. Hence it is, without exception, a nation representing itself in the state; it is the synthesis of a folk (irrational) and the state (rational). The nation is the reason concretized in an individuality (個別性, folk), so that the nation cannot coincide with the folk immediately. For the folk to transform itself into the nation, the folk must be negatively mediated by other folks. That is, the stronger folk must conquer and subjugate other weaker folks in order to form the nation (492).

The self-awareness of the state, as Kōsaka understands it, would be sustained by war. War is the test that validates or invalidates the state's moral status. It is through war alone that the world's historical meaning is made manifest (Najita and Harootunian 1998, 239). Kōsaka sees the Sino-Japanese War as a war of morality (Japanese morality over Chinese morality and the war between the Oriental morality and the Occidental morality) and as determining the world history of the future. To imagine the relationship between China and Japan in terms of the war of Chinese and Japanese moralities is to posit a dialectical relationship between the two. This means that, in the optimistic imagination, Japanese morality will eventually prove its universality as well as the particularity of Chinese morality. This would necessarily be a process in which particularities would be subjugated to the domination of a universality (Sakai 1998, 494). In the end, pluralistic world history proves itself to be another version of monistic history, especially when the subjects of world history are equated to nations. What annoyed Kōyama and Kōsaka in monistic history is not the fact that many were suppressed and deprived of the sense of self-respect in the world because of its Eurocentric arrangement. What they were opposed to was that, in that Eurocentric arrangement of the world, the *putative* unity of the Japanese happened to be excluded from the center. And what they wished to realize was to change the world so that the Japanese would occupy the position of the center and of the subject that determines other particularities in its own universal terms (495). Consequently, Kōyama and Kōsaka's theory reveals a thinly disguised justification, written in the language of Hegelian metaphysics, for Japan's aggression and continuing imperialism. It is this assertion of differentiation within the coloniality of power that I have referred to as Japancentrism's "imperial difference" from Eurocentrism. What is important to note is that Japan did not stand outside the West. Even in its particularism, Japan was already implicated in the ubiquitous West, so that neither historically nor geopolitically could Japan be seen as the outside of the West. This means that to criticize the West in relation to Japan, one has necessarily to begin with a critique of Japan. Likewise, the critique of Japan necessarily entails the radical critique of the West.

Orphan of Asia: Despair and the Colonial Difference

If Eurocentrism and Japancentrism are defined by the proprietary vision of modernity embedded in the nation-state and the appropriating and transforming of Hegelian dialectic historicism, Wu Zhuo-liu's *Orphan of Asia* can be read as decidedly countering Eurocentrism and Japancentrism. I have argued elsewhere that the spatial articulation of *Orphan of Asia* is critical in understanding the triangulation of China, Taiwan, and Japan in late colonialism. I have also suggested that the despair registered in the novel occurs precisely at the moment where radical changes (anti-Japanese colonialism or Chinese nationalism) are no longer imagined as viable options of resistance (Ching 2001). After reviewing the geopolitics of knowledge related to the understanding of modernity-coloniality and the articulation of the coloniality of power in Eurocentrism and Japancentrism, I want to suggest that a rereading of *Orphan of Asia* in its spatial movements and despair offers a counternarrative postulated by Western imperialism and Japanese colonialism from the perspective of colonial Taiwan.

I am not suggesting here that Wu Zhuo-liu was consciously or intentionally trying to counter the arguments of Western and Japanese philosophers through a nonproprietary and nondialectic narrative. Rather, if we juxtapose Wu's writing with that of Eurocentric and Japancentric thinking, an unexpected cleavage emerges. It is in this unintended and undeniable difference from the perspective and positionality of the colonized that the "colonial difference," as opposed to the "imperial difference," can emerge. According to Mignolo, "The colonial difference is the space where coloniality of power is enacted. It is also the space where the restitution of subaltern knowledge is taking place and where border thinking is emerging. The colonial difference is the space where *local* histories inventing and implementing global designs meet *local* histories, the space in which global designs have to be adapted, adopted, rejected, integrated, or ignored" (Mignolo 2000b, xiii). In other words, *Orphan of Asia* is symptomatic of the asymmetrical power relations in modernity-coloniality, and precisely because of its historical (im)possibility, it cannot imagine the worlds of Eurocentrism and Japancentrism. It is this (im)possibility and sensibility that alert us to the colonial difference.

Orphan of Asia chronicles the life of its main protagonist, Hu Taiming, in his quest for certainty in thought and in life. Spanning almost the entire fifty years of Japanese rule, the novel depicts Taiming as being swept and beaten by the currents of Japanese colonialism, Chinese nationalism, and localism, unable to find secure mooring. Instead of the vision of a world history or the insertion of Japan in that history, the spatial movement in *Orphan of Asia* is inescapably local, regional, and colonial. Unlike the spirit or the nation-state, the orphan's itinerary is neither teleological nor triumphant. Wu's protagonist shifts geographically in the triangulation of Taiwan, Japan, and China, not as a predetermined traversing of history but as compelled by the injustice and oppressiveness of the colonial condition. The triangulation is, after all, delimited and enclosed. The notion of the orphan is precisely the impossibility of belonging to the "family of nations" that undergirds the modern-colonial world system. It is also a colonial allegory: the coming into being of a consciousness of one's place (or lack thereof) in the differential structure of oppression: Japanese colonialism and Chinese nationalism. This is not the triumphant realization of the Hegelian Spirit in a teleological unfolding of history or a disguised relativization of Japan's position vis-à-vis the West. Rather, it is a psycho-traumatic realization of the impossibility of salvation within the colonial system. Whereas the Hegelian Spirit travels from the colonies (Asia and Africa) to the metropolis (Europe) in a process of self-realization, Wu Zhuoliu's orphan arguably moves in the opposite direction (from Taiwan to Japan, China, and back to

Taiwan), in an enclosed circularity of self-doubt. One narrates a linear un-folding of history, and the other one a circuitous return of subalternity. If the Hegelian Spirit represents the dialectic actualization of modernity, Wu Zhuoliu's orphan points to the nondialectic stasis of coloniality. Whereas the Spirit can view the world from above (the perspective of the colonizer), the orphan can only wander within the bounded spaces of the empire (the condition of the colonized). This is the colonial difference. The sensibility of the colonial difference is obviously a historical one: the mounting oppres-sion in the late-colonial period of mobilization and the disillusionment with Chinese nationalism as an anticolonial praxis. The orphan, Taiwan, is to play the role of self-consciousness that had failed in the continual dialectical re-affirmation: the Japanese-Taiwanese and Chinese-Taiwanese oppositions, despite the promises of colonialism and nationalism, do not transcend and transform into a higher being. The orphan remains deferred, detested and disempowered. For the orphan, modernity-coloniality means, above all, the state of being deprived of its subjectivity.

The nondialectic and nonaffirmation do not liberate the orphan; they do not lead to emancipation. However, they do point to what Takeuchi Yoshimi sees as "resistance" in Lu Xun's work.[3] Takeuchi sees resistance in Lu Xun's parable not as a modernist liberation but as a kind of stasis of inescapability. He writes of Lu Xun's slave:

> Salvation for the slave consists precisely in nonsalvation, in dreaming without awakening. From the slave's standpoint, the pursuit of salvation itself is what makes him a slave. If therefore he were to be awakened, he would have to experience the "most painful thing in life," the fact that there is "no path to follow" — the self-awareness that he is a slave. And he would have to endure this fear, for he would lose that self-awareness were he to give up and seek salvation instead. . . . The "most painful thing in life," awakening from a dream, occurs when the slave rejects his status as slave while at the same time rejecting the fantasy of liberation, so that he becomes a slave who realizes that he is a slave. This is the state in which one must follow a path even though there is no path to follow; or rather, one must follow a path *precisely because* there is no path to follow. Such a slave rejects being himself at the same time that he rejects being anything else. This is the meaning of despair found in Lu Xun; it is what makes Lu Xun possible" (Takeuchi 2005, 71).

It is useful to explore the correlation between Lu Xun's slave and Wu Zhuoliu's orphan. Similar to the slave and unthinkable as the Hegelian Spirit or the Japanese ethno-nation, the orphan suffers from (and therefore resists) the nondialectic and the nonsublation. As suggested earlier, the movement for Hu Taiming, the main character in the novel, is neither teleological nor dialectical. In this regard, Hu Taiming's despair, arising from his abandonment and nonattainment, points to a despair that "emerges in the resistance of following a path when there is no path, while resistance emerges as the activation of despair. As a state this can be seen as despair, whereas as a movement, it is resistance" (Takeuchi 2005, 72).

In "Can the Subaltern Speak?" Gayatri Spivak argues that the subaltern cannot speak, not because she has no voice but because the colonial apparatus has translated and appropriated subaltern speeches into its own discourse. Put differently, the subaltern cannot speak because there are no available macro-narratives available for the oppressed to speak from. The (in)significance of Taiwan cannot be remedied by overturning the slave-master or orphan-parent hierarchy. Instead, a proper grasping of Taiwan in coloniality-modernity demands a kind of horizontal thinking in global coloniality that rejects the authoritative verticalism of Eurocentric and Japancentric thinking. A critical comparative approach with other colonized spaces and histories in exploring the methodologies of the oppressed or the creolization of theory might be a good place to begin.

Notes

1 Quoted in Dussel 1993, 68.
2 Fukuzawa 1997, 351.
3 I am aware that this is a particular and highly selective reading of Lu Xun by Takeuchi, whose critique of Japanese modernity invariably romanticizes Chinese modernity and Lu Xun. I am interested, however, in the possible reading of Lu Xun's slave and Wu Zhuo-liu's orphan as articulating a different sensibility of a subaltern existence and possibility in the abyss of political impossibility.

EIGHT

TOWARD A DIASPORIC CITIZEN?
From Internationalism to Cosmopolitics

Étienne Balibar

To reflect adequately on transnational citizenship becomes increasingly difficult as global transformations progress, and as the political and ideological positions concerning these transformations set up a dense network of discourses and differences. It is now much harder to propose "conclusions" or "solutions" to ongoing debates that nonetheless help to clarify the choices faced by mobile citizens and the scholars who theorize their conditions. In this chapter, I want to begin by reacting to the motto of the "nomadic citizen" that has been pushed forward as a political-theoretical response by Alessandro Mezzadra from the University of Bologna, with whom I have started a personal conversation over the last few years. Mezzadra uses the term in a series of remarkable essays published in Italian, English, and French in response to the effects of transnational migrations on the equilibrium of political systems and the definition of their constituency.[1] To ask whether a nomadic citizenship, being at the same time a mobile or traveling citizenship and a citizenship for the travelers, is thinkable—a provocative formulation that, as you will see, I try in the end to qualify and displace—means to ask how the age-old figure of the citizen could be reconfigured in the age of global migrations, and if it proves inevitable, how it could also become an institutional reality.

Clearly the conditions for such an institution are multiple and unlikely to be matched simultaneously. They belong to the realms of law, politics, economy, culture, and also philosophy because the citizen is a "philosophical character," even in the technical sense of the term. Right from the beginning, the philosopher and its rival character, the Sophist, defined themselves in a relationship of intellectual proximity and critical tension with respect to the city or the polity, both deriving their function from the institution of the citizen and aiming at his formation. If these conditions were matched simultaneously, they would amount to a genuine revolution in the history of the political, or better said they would subvert the principle of the political institution, the *politeia* or the polity. It would not be the first such revolution, since the polity has already traversed several moments of collapsing and revival and has been marked by breaks as well as continuities. Some of the conditions that come to mind seem to correspond to the transformations and requirements of the global world in which we now live, but others are clearly running against some of its most entrenched structures—which, however, cannot be considered in each case simple structures of domination or oppression or cannot be reduced to this negative aspect. They combine possibility and impossibility in a confused historical pattern.

I want to partially discuss these conditions in four successive moments. First, I will return to the official definition of the "right of circulation" as a fundamental right of persons in contemporary legal and moral discourse. Second, I want to indicate what I will call, in a somewhat pretentious terminology, the ontological paradoxes and the anthropological effects of globalization that affect the constitution of the citizen. Third, having in mind the question asked by Deleuze and others, "Which is the people to come?" I want to elaborate on the antagonistic movements of territorialization and deterritorialization that produce contradictory effects on the idea of the "sovereignty of the people," therefore the basic institutions of democracy. Finally, I want to indicate some perspectives and instruments for the enlargement of the right of circulation and its political recognition, which point in the direction of a *civitas vaga*, or a citizenship of the roads and the changing places.

Freedom of Circulation as a Fundamental Right

Freedom of circulation (with its correlative, freedom of residence) was progressively recognized as a fundamental right, not without difficulties and in fact tragedies, and not without limitations, in the middle of the past century. It found an official formulation in the Universal Declaration of Human Rights of 1948 and the contemporaneous documents accompanying the

Proclamation of the Charter of the United Nations.[2] The official recognition of the freedom of circulation poses several problems.

First, there is a problem about its enforcing, and therefore also the obstacles standing before its enforcing. Some of these obstacles relate to the facts, or the realities, that make it difficult or unpractical to entirely liberate the circulation of persons. Legal theorists, who are often (albeit not always) also formalistic, tend to view these obstacles as contingent, external, while realistic politicians tend to view them as historical necessities, which locate circulation within the broader context of state formation, relations of power, and the control of populations and their movements. Other obstacles relate more profoundly to the internal tensions, perhaps the contradictions that affect the very idea of an absolute freedom of circulation: their status has to be compared with similar problems concerning, for instance, the freedom of expression or freedom of communication. Although there are considerable differences between states (including democratic states themselves; think of Europe and the United States) concerning the extent to which freedom of opinion and speech ought to be considered a constitutional principle, no one who is not an anarchist considers that *anything* could be expressed by *anybody* before *any* audience (including insults, provocations, threats, etc.) without regulation. At a certain point any freedom destroys itself.

Second, there is a problem about the status of the right of circulation as a principle or a fundamental right (which could also become a constitutional right, where fundamental rights become constitutionalized).[3] In the end, we will have to face the question whether, in a concrete situation, the more or less inevitable restrictions affecting a principle when it becomes a historical institution do not in fact empty it of its meaning or amount to its suppression. No doubt, similar questions could be raised concerning other fundamental principles. This is true in particular for the democratic principle itself, or the sovereignty of the people, when it becomes incarnated in parliamentary and executive representations. This is why a radical critique (Marxist or other) of democracy has a point, and a strong one: if the restrictions and regulations involved in the institutional realization of a juridical principle practically mean that it is reduced to nothing, the political or even juridical value of the declaration of this right as fundamental will become zero.

These problems are not independent from one another, as we understand immediately when we look at the performative statements in the Universal Declaration of Human Rights concerning the universality of the freedom of circulation. To begin with, article 13: "(1) Everyone has the right to freedom of movement and residence within the borders of each state. (2) Everyone has the right to leave any country, including his own, and to return to his country." When we compare this statement with others that are similar or emerge later, we find some remarkable characteristics.

Typically, the freedom of circulation is declared within a structure that could be called *antithetical or antagonistic*, where opposite freedoms are considered correlative, to produce a hypothetical unity or balance (in this case, to have the right to leave one's country or to return to it). Compare article 15 on nationality: "(1) Everyone has the right to a nationality. (2) No one shall be arbitrarily deprived of his nationality nor denied the right to change his nationality."

The freedom of circulation of persons forms an application of the right to personhood as it is proclaimed by article 6: "Everyone has the right to recognition everywhere as a person before the law." In Hannah Arendt's terms, this means that the right of circulation can be associated with a *right to have rights*, which I interpret as a basic injunction to allow access to the polity in a given state or community. Obviously, it is important to recall that these texts, both the Universal Declaration and the book in which Arendt famously coined the expression "a right to have rights" (part 2 of *The Origins of Totalitarianism*, 1951), belong to the same immediate aftermath of World War II, where international institutions and public intellectuals collaborated in an attempt at proscribing the politics of deportation and denationalization of whole populations, ending sometimes in extermination processes that, as Arendt was particularly clear in explaining, imply that individuals belonging to groups to be eliminated, declared "superfluous," be previously deprived of their juridical status as citizens and persons. But *determinatio negatio est*: as soon as the right to have rights must receive a practical application, it becomes qualified. This is where the question of the inversion of the statement of right emerges.

This qualification is entirely organized around the pivotal function played by the reference to the idea of *country*: a country, one's country. Each individual is supposed to have his or her own country, which refers to *membership* as well as *belonging*. I belong to the country whose membership I share with others, this is *my country* as well as *other people's country*, our shared membership makes us part of it as it also makes us its co-owners, as it were. That each of us is said to be able to change place, change nationality, change membership and belonging, "pass" from one country to another following certain procedures, does not alter this structure of belonging; on the contrary, it highlights that it is considered as the rule or the norm. Therefore the correlative, antagonistic, freedoms that have been elevated to the level of principles represent in fact a way to articulate the two sides of the border, the interior and the exterior of the country, the national and international status of the individual person. Not only is the border as an institution not abolished, but it is reinforced, or it receives a new democratic and liberal legitimacy, which policies of coerced denationalization and exclusion ("ethnic cleansing" *ante litteram*) had threatened.

In this sense, the right of circulation forms a counterpart for a certain "territorial" institution of the sovereignty of the people, as it is formulated in article 21: "(1) Everyone has the right to take part in the government of his country, directly or through freely chosen representatives. (2) Everyone has the right of equal access to public service in his country. (3) The will of the people shall be the basis of the authority of government; this will shall be expressed in periodic and genuine elections which shall be by universal and equal suffrage and shall be held by secret vote or by equivalent free voting procedures." This statement acquired its full meaning in the struggle against totalitarian regimes, the first steps of decolonization, and popular struggles against institutional segregation in countries such as the United States and South Africa.

Looking at the letter of these statements, we can also anticipate difficulties or latent tensions, which since then have become only too obvious. Let me indicate four of them:

First, some difficulties will emerge when borderlines become relativized and blurred, that is, when the difference between being here or there, from this place or that place, becomes more obscure or even meaningless, when populations emerge (or become more visible), which can be called nomadic in a new historical sense, or ubiquitous, if you prefer, since they quite normally share their time, or their *lives*, between different places and territories (something territorial states and their administrations hate and deny as much as they can).

Second, some difficulties are the consequence of a degeneracy of "popular sovereignty" as an effective constitutional principle, when the oligarchic and technocratic dimensions of democracies themselves are increased, or they delegate their power to national and transnational administrations that are not really subject to popular control.

Third, some difficulties—to which I want particularly to draw our attention—will derive from the fact that after the dramatic processes of the redrawing of borders in the twentieth century (which involved displacing huge populations, cutting and partitioning vast territories, changing the name and status of whole nations everywhere in the world), the borderlines and the very institution of the border received a new democratic and liberal legitimacy, and this process of relegitimization was based on a primacy of the individual, a sort of "international individualism." In the actual relationship between individuals and collectives, groups or communities, which forms the historical agent of the politics of human rights, that is, the complex process in which liberties are vindicated, basic rights are conquered, or, in the words of Claude Lefort, become "invented," it was the individual pole that was identified as the bearer of rights, whereas the collectives on which the recognition of these rights depends were exclusively identified with the (nation)-state. Basically, all the official definitions explain that it is the individual who circulates (travels or moves), and they identify a collective membership with a certain immobility or permanent residency. But already the concrete reality of the situation of refugees and displacements of populations that Arendt was reflecting on in "The Crisis of the Nation-State" would contradict this presentation. And this has become increasingly the case: neither subjectively nor objectively are mass migrations purely individual movements (even if it is always an individual who takes the risk of crossing the border, succeeds, or dies), but they are collective movements required and supported by groups, group identities, and institutions. Comparing both, we understand that one of the objectives of the Universal Declaration is to locate collective or mass movements— which are not reducible in practice to the aggregate of many individual travels—in the category of exceptional or catastrophic phenomena. This is also indeed coherent with the liberal understanding of labor migrations, however massive, regular, and organized they can be in fact, as a pure statistical phenomenon, where many individuals happen to move simultaneously along the same routes.

Fourth, some difficulties are already contained in the fact that, generally speaking, the Universal Declaration does not limit itself to a purely *formal* notion of right but also refers to the effectivity or materiality of legal principles, repeatedly explaining that a basic right does not in fact exist as such if the means to realize it are not given: this is the case when it comes to defining the right of property, freedom of expression, right to family life and protection of religious convictions, even the right to work (in article 23). But what is striking here is that the two complementary sides, or conditions, for the effective realization of the juridical norm, as it were, become located on each side of the border, in two different spaces. Article 19 (which could be generalized to several other cases of basic freedoms) says that the *formal*, *universal* character of the principle holds "regardless of frontiers" ("Everyone has the right to freedom of opinion and expression; this right includes freedom to hold opinions without interference and to seek, receive and impart information and ideas through any media and regardless of frontiers"), whereas article 28, which defines a certain legal and political order, clearly shows that it is the state, in practice the *nation-state*, that is the legal subject of social and international obligations and therefore implements the law or grants validity and reality to the universal principles ("Everyone is entitled to a social and international order in which the rights and freedoms set forth in this Declaration can be fully realized").

Ontological Paradoxes and Anthropological Consequences of Globalization

These big philosophical words should not frighten you. Here is what I mean by them. The phrase *ontological paradoxes* refers to the fact that the classical opposition between persons and things (or subjects and objects) on which our juridical discourse is based becomes now challenged, so that an exclusive disjunction of everything that exists, which should be either person or thing, but not both or something else, in the end produces social paralysis. The social practices that it wants to formalize are in practice less and less reducible to this dichotomy. The phrase *anthropological effects* refers to the fact that the differential treatment of individuals and groups or communities with respect to movement or circulation not only becomes a social problem, and therefore also a political problem, but at a deeper level questions the way in which the quality of being human as such is instituted in a globalized society that is both national and international. I mean: the human quality at the level of humankind (which is what the global space claims to be, and practically represents) becomes once again categorized and hierarchized so that its selective "reproduction" can be controlled. Certain forms of social intercourse are possible; others are impossible or very difficult, that is, they are associated with the necessity of taking enormous risks—which is particularly the case of traveling, not because or not mainly because of international terrorism or banditry, but because certain travelers are hunted by the police of certain states. This is an aspect of the risk society, to borrow Ulrich Beck's famous formula, that is only too often neglected, once again because what is supposed to be normal is residency, not nomadism.

The reason why I raise the discussion to the level of these ontological and anthropological considerations is the following: if we start with the idea that basic or fundamental rights such as the freedom of expression, freedom of association, or freedom of circulation cannot become institutionally implemented without some sort of regulation, we must also face the dilemma created by the transformations of the contemporary world. If the effect of globalization has been to progressively strip the right of circulation that had been universally proclaimed of its content, was it because it was inconsistent as a *universal* right? Or was it because the conditions have not been created that would allow a universal principle to remain valid when, paradoxically, it would concern in practice a greater amount of humans, a "multitude," if you like? Indeed, we should also ask whether this is absolutely new: which reality did the right of circulation, or the freedom to move, have in other epochs, in various parts of the world, and for various social categories? This makes a comparative study of the quantities, qualities, and modalities of circulation all the more necessary, to decide if the current transformations are completely unprecedented and unexpected. But we cannot avoid suspecting that the formulas in the Universal Declaration, already at the time, were a fiction, to which very different realities corresponded in practice: forms of massive control and restrictions of the freedom of circulation, particularly whenever it became a *collective* movement, in the case of labor migrations, or exchanges of populations and displacements following the end of colonial rule (think of the partition of India, primarily, and many other examples). This indicates that metajuridical statements concerning fundamental rights have a performative function that is in fact political, and whose political effects depend on deeper structures. These are the structures that I call ontological and anthropological.

Let me recall very briefly two kinds of phenomena that we all know characterize contemporary capitalist globalization. One: the liberal principle of *laisser faire et laisser passer* (free manufacturing and free trade) relates to objects and subjects with considerable disparities. Two: it is fraught with enormous inequalities and therefore associated with huge discriminations among persons with different social status. From this point of view, national membership, the belonging to nations and nationalities with unequal standing and unequal recognition at the global scale, is itself a social inequality of persons. I propose these axioms at a very general level, being aware that they would require a refined epistemological discussion: legal theorists, geographers, and urban planners are permanently busy with elaborating the categories for this fine discussion of differences, which I am afraid only too often escapes sociologists, political scientists, and philosophers. What we need is a topology of the different regions in the world, which is no longer reducible to dichotomies such as center and periphery, North and South, et cetera. Above all we need a topology of routes and borders to concretely articulate what we call circulation and communication, migration and travel, mobility and residency, displacement and settlement. Every discussion concerning freedom of circulation must also be a discussion on the changing configuration of the material global space. In his excellent essay, inspired in part by the Schmittian concept of the nomos of the earth, Carlo Galli (2001) has shown that there are *politics of the space* that produce *political spaces*. But it is equally true that there are politics of circulation that produce political regimes of circulation: their history is no less decisive for any social ontology and general anthropology of the present world, and in fact they cannot be separated. Geographers and sociologists like Nigel Thrift, Saskia Sassen, and Manuel Castells are working exactly on this subject.

It is here that we must always again start with a critique of the axioms of pure liberalism, which is also a way of acknowledging their ideological power. If we imagine that the global space of circulation is governed by the principle of laisser faire et laisser passer, we can no longer understand why there is such a disparity between different kinds of circulations, since "the dominant view among both classical and neo-classical economists is that both the free mobility of capital and labor is essential to the maximization of overall economic gains" (Carens 1987). On the contrary, we must adopt the point of view of a capitalist world system (I borrow the category from

Immanuel Wallerstein and his school) where social inequalities among regions and social categories are essential for the production of profits, especially surplus profits, which are the driving force of capitalism, and where political structures control the mobility and distribution of the labor force. Matters become difficult, but also more interesting, of course, when the economic and political imperatives that are supposed to converge at the global level and in the long run are in fact locally conflicting in the present—a present that, contrary to the ideal picture of the global market, might last indefinitely. This is very much the case with the displacement of persons and border regions of the world economy where global inequalities are concentrated. These "semi-peripheries," according to Wallerstein, are a privileged place to observe these political and anthropological consequences. Just think of the U.S.-Mexican border.

It seems, however, that today the typical disparity within laisser passer that limits or regulates the right of circulation is no longer reducible to an opposition between persons and things, subjects and objects, where things would circulate and persons would remain blocked, because the importance of "intermediary," transindividual beings that are neither persons nor things or partake of both categories has been enormously inflated. These intermediary beings, which we could call also *spectral beings* à la Derrida, in a sense reactivate what the ancient Roman law and philosophy called *actions*, distinguishing them from persons and things. But, quite different from the ancient category, most of these actions are practically actions without an agent, or without a single individual agent, who could be considered an exclusive owner with a liability concerning their consequences; they are impersonal actions of circulation and communication. What becomes intensified is not only the circulation of commodities, capital, and money but above all the circulation of *information* (which tends to dominate the circulation of commodities and capitals). On the other side, what becomes increasingly controlled, differentiated, and, for some categories, restricted, is the circulation of *persons*. The disparity is explained by reasons of economic efficiency or protection of national identities (even in republics with a "universalistic" ideology like France or the United States). This is a double crisis: an anthropological crisis of the category of person as a universal category, and an ontological crisis of the dichotomy of persons and things. How are they related?

Information, as we know, is neither person nor thing, but it can command or distribute both things and persons. Its communication is not so much a circulation as a hypercirculation: on one side, it replaces the circulation of persons, or it compensates for their immobility by making their work ubiquitous (so computer maintenance is displaced from Europe and America to India or Taiwan, etc.); on the other side, it reinforces the restrictions to the mobility of persons. For anyone who can be reached by Internet, there is no need to look for a job abroad, but for anyone who cannot use a computer there is not even a possibility of finding a job at home, as illustrated by many deindustrialized regions of Europe and probably also America.

Which brings in the other side: a gigantic inequality with regard to the right of circulation and the mobility of persons. What we need is a complete description of this inequality as a transnational social relationship. Its phenomenology includes *dissymmetries* (think of the access to passports and visas, the fact that certain strategic borderlines can easily be crossed one way, but not the other way) and includes differential *repression* (from this point of view, the so-called undocumented migrant emerges as an economic institution of globalization in its own right, an essential element of global employment and wage labor). Finally, this global inequality combines two antagonistic forms of coercion: coerced mobility, involving the risk of life and death at some borderlines or on some terrestrial and oceanic routes (think of the Canary Islands for the West African boat people), but also coerced immobility for categories such as unemployed youngsters of the deindustrialized suburban areas. This inequality should be compared with others, which affect the right to work, the right to a personal home and family life, et cetera. Its increasing consequences not only are socially and humanly destructive but create problems of insecurity, social conflicts, and ethnic hatreds.

I would like to insist on the cosmopolitical consequences of these social transformations. A first one is a decomposition of the category of commerce, which, in its classical meaning—common to Montesquieu, Adam Smith, Kant, and Marx—founded the cosmopolitan utopia: the idea that increasing interaction or intercourse among the human species would bring about a progressive cultural, intellectual, and political unity of mankind. A second one is the emergence of a new cultural economy of races, with, in particular, an opposition of nomadic and sedentary races (or quasi races), which the use of the name *migrant* as a racial category in many European countries would particularly illustrate. A third one, especially significant from the point of view of political anthropology, is the increasing reduction of the category of the stranger, or the "unwanted stranger," to the figure of the *enemy*, a social, cultural, religious, and in the end internal political enemy who calls for a politics of national, social, and cultural security. A new brand of *défense sociale* in the French conservative tradition has become officialized. This is more than a simple radicalization of the classical Hobbesian perspective from which nations, or "civil societies," relate to each other as individuals in a state of nature. It is rather a *reversal* of its political function: the foreigner whose figure becomes that of an essential stranger, whose difference becomes intensified, is no longer one with whom—according to circumstances—you can either wage war or make peace; he is one with whom peace as such is impossible, who will remain a threat to be permanently monitored. A permanent dialectic of difference, otherness, and recognition was involved in the classical idea of nationality, inherent in its definition of citizenship and state membership, which becomes now negated and transcended in a phantasmatic manner, although perhaps—as Arendt would suggest—the possibility of this negation was already present in nationalism. It would seem that in the globalized world where migrations have become both massive and permanent, no more room exists for the normal figure of the stranger as simple foreigner, distinguished from a commodity and an enemy. Hence the massive production of what the Algerian philosopher Sidi Mohammed Barkat (2005) calls the "body of exception." But this has spectacular consequences on the constitution of the legal order of nation-states: a relationship to strangers as such is necessary for their legitimacy (for this reason as well, civic actions that tend to prevent states from reducing strangers to the status of commodities or the condition of essential enemy are actions that *preserve* the legitimacy of the state).

The Citizen Territorialized and Deterritorialized

Basic dilemmas of citizenship, what I would call in Greek *politeia* or in French *droit de cité*, are opened again by the collapsing of the category of the stranger with the category of the enemy that goes along with restrictions of the right of circulation of persons, or some selected persons, while the circulation of things, especially the circulation of information, "actions of communication," intensifies. Such dilemmas force us to think anew about the origins, the functions and limits, and also the exceptions that affect the fundamental association between state, nation, sovereignty, territory, population. What is reconsidered is a whole concept of civilization, because it is the idea of a line of progress, which was supposed to lead from nomadism to sedentarism, or toward the subjection of nomads by sedentaries in history. This is one reason, among others, why the work of Deleuze and Guattari in *A Thousand Plateaus* has acquired such meaning and relevance today, even if they sometimes take the categories of the nomad and the sedentary in a metaphorical sense: this philosophical work indicates that the complexity of the relationship between nomadism and sedentarity has been retrieved and renewed and is located again in the core of the anthropological reflection on the unity of the human species.

Great theorists of sovereignty from Bodin to Schmitt, but also classical legal theorists in the nineteenth and twentieth centuries (Jellinek, Donati, Kelsen) who theorized on the *Rechtstaat* or *état de droit*, the constitutional state with its monopoly of legitimate violence in the hands of the public power, have shown that a triangular structure of interdependence exists between sovereignty, population, and territory. More precisely, a national sovereignty is associated with a population or a multitude that, already before the idea of the sovereignty of the people had been proclaimed by bourgeois revolutions, was conceived as a community of citizens, with an exclusive relationship between the individuals, their community, and their territory: this is the fiction of a mutual belonging to which I was referring a moment ago. The crucial instrument for the representation and the establishment of this triangular relation is the institution of the border. No doubt there can be considerable variations from the point of view of the individual rights of persons between ethnic states, where the territory is declared the exclusive property of a certain racial or ethnic-religious group, where the political notion of territory and the private notion of the property of land become identified, which may involve a distinction of different unequal classes of citizens with respect to their property rights and their right of settlement, and liberal states, where the private property of land is free, incomes can be settled and resettled, albeit with considerable social and economic disparities, et cetera. But the triangular structure encompasses all these variations. In this sense, all modern nation-states are also territorial states, and they are defined or conceive of themselves as communities of sedentary citizens, who are rooted in the territory.

This structural relationship shows that the relationship of individuals toward borders, using and crossing borders in their concrete lives, is an essential component of citizenship.[4] What therefore proves essential to the continuation of the nation-state is that it opens the right of circulation for some and closes it for others in a sovereign way. This can be done also indirectly, in a seeming limitation of the sovereign power, or a transfer of this power at a superior level, but without substantial change in its definition, as shown by the institution of common rules and a common police of the borders in the European Union. This means that the citizen is defined not only by the possession of rights such as habeas corpus and the electoral franchise, or duties such as taxes and military service, but also crucially as the bearer of a certain right of circulation inside and across the border. But we observe that a radical distinction between interiority and exteriority, spaces of liberty and spaces of coercion, although it is necessary for the very definition of the nation, becomes more and more artificial and is enforced with increasing difficulties. The European construction on this point is a good example: paradoxically, it leads to the increasing necessity of a police corps for the control of foreigners, because the creation of a wider space of free circulation has automatically created a growing population of illegal European noncitizens, a large number of which, everybody knows, are bound sooner or later to become European quasi citizens or full citizens (or parents of full citizens).

This situation calls for a renewed political anthropology of the droit de cité. Its first question should be: is citizenship originally a territorialized notion? Its next question would be: if the removal, displacement, relativization, and differentiation of borders, the change of their economic and cultural functions, produces trouble in the territorial association of state and community, where does this trouble lead? To which new figure, or probably, before that, to which new conflicts? History (but perhaps also the classical myths of Greek democracy) taught us that the origin of the polity or droit de cité lies in a territorial redefinition of belonging that limited, at least symbolically, the powers of *genealogies*, or transgenerational links conserved across migrations and diasporas, together with the name and the kinship relations. In the current crisis of the politeia, a new conflict of principles seems to be looming between the territorial definition of political member- ship and participation and a liberation from territory that should perhaps be described as a reterritorialization in a virtual space, the space of individuals who remain related to one another through common interests, private or public, in spite of their continuous travels and ubiquity; what we could call the *civis vagus*, the citizen of the roads.

But many problems are associated with such a representation. One of them concerns individual rights, especially fundamental rights. Historians of personal or subjective rights and the constitutionalization of rights have shown that there is a correlation between the territorial monopoly of the state and the effective granting of such rights or liberties. It was the state— admittedly, not without the revolution, more generally not without the re- sistance, the insurrectional exigencies of the citizens themselves—that rela- tivized or even eliminated the function of communities and membership in so-called natural communities, meaning communities of kin, religion, profession, language, culture, and so on, with their intrinsic hierarchies, and invented the idea of the personal or subjective rights of the individual. Paradoxically, or perhaps dialectically, the state created an institution of individual freedom that could become a condition for resistance to state power or the arbitrariness of the state. Such an institution was possible only because sovereignty and territory went together: the "myth of the state" in all its ambivalence also includes the idea that peoples as genealogical entities are nomadic, but individuals become territorialized. Or better still, the state produces a virtual decomposition of a preexisting people, a nomadic com- munity, and a virtual recomposition of the *ethnos* as *demos*, a community of citizens which is its "own" community. It is in this narrative that the great myth of barbarian migrations preceding the state and terminated by the state would take place. And it is this myth that becomes reactivated today in a threatening manner with the images of masses of migrants besieging the old nations. But it remains that we must face the difficulty of construct- ing an alternative narrative, perhaps an alternative myth, hopefully one that keeps or reformulates the relationship between individual rights and col- lective power.

When the relationship between nomads and sedentaries is torn apart by the changing regime of communications and migrations, the sovereignty of the people seems to become an impossible notion. At least it becomes contradictory with its classical definitions. This is, no doubt, the strong element in communitarian or republican discourses, which insist on the reciprocal relationship between a closure of the national territory—or perhaps supranational, as in the case of Europe—and the existence of a public sphere that is universalistic, open to each and every citizen. But this discourse is strong only if we suppose that the democratic powers and agency of the individual citizen today, within such limits, still exist in a more than spectral manner. It becomes dubious if the popular sovereignty, already delegated and expropriated in a number of ways, has become more and more a fiction, through the transformation of modern bourgeois nations into democratic oligarchies, and if these oligarchies are threatened themselves by problems of governance of a new type: namely, how to govern heterogeneous populations of nationals and nonnationals, or permanent and temporary residents with unequal rights, that is, by suppressing right away the possibility of equal treatment, thus reinforcing their belonging to antagonistic classes.

From an Enlarged Right of Circulation to a Diasporic Citizenship?

Every freedom—we can agree on this—involves regulations. It has to be limited, both not to harm its own beneficiaries and to avoid unbearable contradictions with other rights. But the condition is also that the restrictions do not amount to a negation, particularly for specific categories of persons, when these rights are presented as universal freedoms. If the principle of territoriality that accompanies the institution of national state sovereignty produces in the end a genuine exclusion from circulation for some individuals and groups, this will internally destroy the democratic idea of universal representation and the sovereignty of the people. It is this idea that supports the ideal of nomadic sovereignty in a global space, at least as a regulative principle, the overcoming of the repressive aspects of the territorial state. A citizenship at least partially independent from territory, which would still incorporate a complete system of subjective and objective rights, such as a right of circulation and a complementary right of settlement under reasonable conditions that make it feasible or manageable—such a citizenship would inaugurate a new historical moment in the progress of the idea of the citizen. It would raise the progress of the citizen to the cosmopolitical level by granting a more concrete character to the Kantian idea of hospitality while avoiding the shortcomings of the idea of a world federation, or a *Weltinnenpolitik* that still affects the "postnational constellation" in the Habermasian sense, where the distinction between internal and external space is not really politically mediated but progressively neutralized and suppressed.

Such cosmopolitical perspectives can become compatible even with a republican or neorepublican perspective that is part of the civic culture of progressive movements in today's democratic oligarchies. I suggested that there are already elements of internal decomposition in the community of citizens that forms the ideal people of modern nation-states. But they are not independent from globalization. In a manner that strangely recalls some considerations of Hegel in his *Philosophy of Right* (1820) about the "extreme" classes that escape the possibilities of integration of the modern state,[5] we can observe that developed capitalist states today also include extreme groups that tendentiously escape civic conversation and representation, albeit in a completely different manner: on the one side, we have a new class of transnational owners and executives who tend to escape the space of civic representation and conflict (but carefully preserve their influence on the administration) because they no longer have an interest in sharing with other citizens the concrete practices of urbanity, schooling, healthcare, and participation; on the other side we have an underclass of the precarious workforce, much of which is alien or maintained in an alien status and therefore excluded from full participation and especially from political rights. They are left outside political representation to avoid their claims of rights, rooted in their conditions of existence and their productive function, becoming formulated and voiced in the public sphere, producing an increase of social conflictuality that would also re-create a political agency. What makes this permanent exclusion possible is that social conflict now appears unbearable for many official citizens, particularly among the poor, who have become convinced that the political competition is a zero-sum game, in which rights can be granted to some only if they are withdrawn from others—or that their own identity would be in peril if other identities were recognized as legitimate components of the community of citizens.

Perspectives of the opening of citizens' rights to migrants, associated with a full recognition of the right of circulation and a measured institution of the right of settlement, no doubt face powerful objections. Some are practical; others are purely ideological. It is a crucial task of political philosophy today to disentangle these different aspects on the basis of a renewed reflection on the anthropological and ontological foundations of the notion of individual participation in the polity. I agree that a complete suppression of borders, or state control on borders, far from producing a higher degree of freedom, would lead to what Deleuze called a "controlling society," whose practical form could be a global system of survey of individual movements and lives. If there is no border, individuals may have to carry electronic bracelets, and their single moves will become permanently monitored. A broadened notion of citizenship includes not only what Mezzadra (2001/2004) rightly calls a "right to escape" but also a right to anonymity, or to *incognito* and multiple personality. On the other hand, if we accept Arendt's idea that the political community lacks preestablished ontological or naturalistic bases but is grounded only on the reciprocity of rights and duties among the participants, this is possibly where a new development of citizenship has to be elaborated: in the form of a reciprocity of rights and duties among sedentaries and migrants or nomads. Implied here is that the people cannot be taken as an already established notion but consist of an act of permanent creation and re-creation. Part of this re-creation consists of specific claims of rights, particularly concerning the democratic control of the use of borders, involving states on a multilateral basis, but also associations of citizens and migrants and international agencies of human rights.

This would explain, I hope, why, in the end, I prefer the expression *diasporic citizenship* or *ubiquitous citizenship* to the more fashionable *nomadic citizenship*. In part, this is a conventional choice. What I have in mind is not a global citizenship or citizenship of the world, as if it could be considered a single constituency, but rather a citizenship in the world, or an increasing amount of civic rights and practices, *in the world* as it is, the complex system of spaces and movements that form the reality of what we call "the world," for which we are trying to invent a civilization.

Notes

1 A dialogue that we had a year ago was transcribed under the strange title "Of Discos and Borders" (see Bojadzije and Saint-Saëns 2006).
2 This process, further refined but also transformed by international conventions

concerning refugees, is well presented in many recent books, among which see Benhabib 2004, from which I draw part of my inspiration.

3 See the classical history of the constitutionalization of rights in Stourzh 1989.

4 As convincingly argued by Enrica Rigo (2007) in the case of Europe.

5 This was written before the emergence of welfare states that to some extent resolved the contradiction within their own borders or projected it to the outside.

"THE FORCES OF CREOLIZATION"
Colorblindness and Visible Minorities in the New Europe

Fatima El-Tayeb

Disappearing Acts: Race and Europe

In her deliberations on the visual and the nation, Ming-Bao Yue recalls a typical incident in the life of a European of color:[1]

I was born and raised in Germany, speak the language natively, and am German by nationality. This reality has always been hard for the Germans to accept and growing up "Chinese" in Hamburg offered my own version of the "not-German-looking" episode. The incident happened in the 1970s when my brother and I took the subway home one day. We were chatting away in German and hardly noticed an older German male, sitting in a row behind us. He had obviously been eavesdropping for a while when he suddenly got up from his seat, walked over and interrupted our lively, if self-absorbed conversation. "Excuse me," he asked, and his tone revealed a mix of curiosity and annoyance, "how do you speak German so fluently?" I was totally unprepared for this interruption, but while I was still thinking of an appropriate reply, I heard my brother saying: "Well, that's because we've learned it." To which the man responded in a more hostile tone: "But how long have you been living here?" Before I could think of a reply, I heard my brother saying with a smile: "Oh, we've only been here about a year. You know, German is such an easy language!" Of all possible responses, this was certainly the last the man had expected, especially as Germans believe their language to be particularly difficult. The man's face paled instantly and, without so much as another word, he turned around and retreated to the other end of the subway car. (Yue 2000, 175)

The above scene likely needs no further explanation for either the European or the American reader. What prompted this interrogation of two German children by a German adult seems quite obvious: it was the children's "wrong" looks, their racial designation as nonwhite, which to the white German passenger on a Hamburg subway train necessarily translated into their being non-German. There appeared to be, in other words, an inconsistency if not an invincible contradiction between an aural truth, the sound of native German, and a visual truth, the sight of "Chinese." While the case seems clear, it might still warrant further inquiry: Why was the perfect German of the children not enough to make them readable as (minoritarian) Germans? Why did their answer, which seemingly confirmed the man's assumption (that they could not be German) anger him? Why did the supposed visual reality take precedence over the aural one? And why did the children assume that simply affirming their Germanness would not satisfy the man's curiosity and end the conversation? This chapter aims at answering these questions by putting them in the larger context of what I consider to be a particular European form of invisible racialization. By this I mean the peculiar coexistence of a regime of continent-wide, recognized visual markers that construct nonwhiteness as non-Europeanness with a discourse of color-blindness that claims not to see racialized difference.[2]

This chapter thus addresses issues of race and Europe, or rather race *in* Europe, two concepts rarely mentioned together, especially in reference to contemporary configurations. Considering the geographic origin of the very concept of race and the explicitly race-based policies characterizing both Nazi Germany and Europe's colonial empire, it could seem paradoxical that continental Europe is usually marginal at best in discourses on race or racism. But the narrative of Europe as a colorblind continent, largely untouched by the devastating ideology it exported all over the world, can be considered one of the most successful image campaigns in modern history: race seems to exist anywhere but in Europe.[3] Nevertheless, as I am far from the first to suggest, something is fundamentally wrong with this story. If anything, race seems more present in Europe than elsewhere, exactly because its post–World War II impact has been silent or, more accurately, silenced.

Encounters with the repressed presence of nonwhite Europeans—be it through a chance meeting on the subway or TV images of burning cars in neighborhoods that the average European has never visited—are not necessarily forgotten but rather decontextualized, denied any relevance for, and interaction with, others by being defined as strictly singular: everything always happens for the first time, giving each incident a spectacular character, signifying a threatening state of exception, but at the same time voiding it of any lasting consequences—uprisings in the French *banlieus* ignite debates on the end of Europe but no policy changes (instead the next incident is again met with utter incomprehension); a nonwhite person speaking native German, Polish, or Italian again and again appears as a curious contradiction, never quite becoming unspectacular and commonplace. Europeans possessing the (visual) markers of otherness thus seem forever suspended in time, forever "just arriving," defined by a static foreignness overriding both individual experience and historical facts.[4]

The continued inability or rather unwillingness to confront, let alone overcome, the glaring whiteness underlying Europe's self-image has rather drastic consequences for migrants and minority communities who are routinely ignored, marginalized, and defined as a threat to the very Europe they are part of, their presence usually only acknowledged as a sign of crisis and forgotten again in the ongoing construction of a new European identity. This dialectic of memory and amnesia, in the shape of an easily activated archive of racial images whose presence is steadfastly denied, is fundamentally European, I argue, in part constituting dominant notions of what *Europe* means: though rarely mentioned, race is present whenever Europe is thought, a dynamic that recalls a point Susan Suleiman made about the continent's historical (non)memory of the Holocaust:

> To forget is human, but amnesia is an illness—or worse still, an alibi. The question can then be formulated as follows: If forgetting is salutary as well as inevitable, both individually and collectively, under what conditions does it become a reprehensible amnesia? (Suleiman 2006, 217)[5]

One could add a set of more specific questions: if this amnesia is an active rather than passive process, how is it implemented, what purpose does it serve, and what are the intended and unintended implications for present-day Europe?

Not all these questions can be addressed exhaustively here, but it seems clear that contrary to common European wisdom, the repression of race

"Creating Security," Swiss People's Party, 2007.

discourse does not prevent it from being mobilized in various contexts, in unspectacular everyday interactions like the one introducing this chapter, in the Dutch umbrella term "black school" for struggling educational institutions with a high number of migrant and minority students, in the normalization of evocative terms such as "honor killings," or in the immediate readability of a Swiss People's Party (SVP) poster successfully used during the 2007 Swiss elections (the poster showed a group of white sheep kicking a black sheep off a Swiss flag; the caption read: "Creating Security").[6]

In each case, race is not mentioned but is referenced explicitly as a marker of not belonging, a strategy that relies on a shared iconography that remains unspoken. The resulting silence, however, is far from reflecting the implied indifference of Europeans to racialized difference but instead references and reinforces a common visual archive while simultaneously rendering inexpressible its workings:

Europe begins to exemplify what happens when no category is available to name a set of experiences that are linked in their production or at least inflection, historically and symbolically, experientially and politically, to racial arrangements and engagements. The European experience is a case study in the frustrations, delimitations and injustices of political race-lessness. (Goldberg 2006, 335)

Europe's dogma of racelessness relates directly to the various forms of creolization this book is concerned with, on the level of theory as well as activism. The growing presence of minority populations challenges the European narrative of purity, which in turn is deeply dependent on a type of theory that denies the experiential reality of racist exclusions within the borders of the new Europe, ensuring its own continued dominance by defending the continent's putative identity against groups who *are* European but are perpetually assigned the position of other, kept outside the borders of Europe, if not literally then culturally and socially. Racelessness can be read as a counterstrategy to the creolizing taking place in contemporary Europe, creolizing not (only) in the sense of a mixture of cultures and groups but as an active reworking of essentializing ethnic ascriptions. It is a strategy, furthermore, that in its negation of in-between spaces and identities draws heavily on dominant theories from poststructuralism to postcolonial thought.

I follow Stuart Hall, David Theo Goldberg, and others in arguing that paradigmatic models of racialization, aimed at establishing a set of criteria allowing us to unambiguously identify racist discourse, are inadequate in addressing and analyzing the European case. On the contrary, such models help to support Europe's colorblind status by showing how the continent is different from normative racialized nations such as the United States, while leaving unexplored the specific mobilizations of race in European processes of exclusion and hierarchization (Hall 1991; Essed 1991; Goldberg 2006).[7] The European case represents a form of racialization that receives relatively little academic attention both because it diverges from dominant models and because its strategy of denial is particularly hard to challenge: rather than explicit mechanisms by which race is implemented or referenced in political, social, and economic interactions within and between communities, the ideology of racelessness is the process by which racial thinking and its effects are made invisible. Europe can thus be placed in the larger context of ideologies of colorblindness that prohibit discourses around racialized oppression.[8]

In its European variant, colorblindness goes along with the convergence of race and religion as well as the externalization of racialized populations. Its success thus depends heavily on the investment of continental European theory in what Stuart Hall calls the "internalist" narrative of Europe, in which racialized others appear to have contributed nothing to a Europe that always remains both pure and self-contained (Hall 1991). The continued scarcity of minority voices in European debates, progressive and mainstream, and the almost complete absence of visible minorities from continental European institutions, academic, economic, or political, is a direct result of their being reproduced as outsiders without a legitimate stake in matters European. Intellectual discourse is as important in achieving this as are immigration and citizenship laws; both combine in a dominant narrative that creates a version of reality in which Europeans and migrants are clearly separable.

But while this narrative is still powerful, it will not be not tenable for much longer. Creolization takes place, and it does so in a process that not only involves majority and minority but fosters interactions between marginalized communities, Muslims, Roma, Afro-Europeans, in ways that also challenge diasporic notions of purity, moving from ethnic identification toward what Édouard Glissant calls "situational communities" (Glissant 1989, 142). The strategies used in this postethnic activism eclectically mix influences, countering the link of purity, authenticity, and legitimacy dominating European discourses of belonging by embracing the impure, inauthentic, illegitimate position assigned to them and making it the source of a new discourse rather than attempting to enter the existing one as legitimate subjects. This creolized movement of queering ethnicity is no "postmodern zapping between identities" (as one of the groups representing this new type of activism, the German Kanak Attak, states in its founding manifesto),[9] but is built around an acute awareness of the power disparities structuring Europe's racial landscape.

To deconstruct the entanglement of European intellectual thought and political racelessness, we must analyze its effects on those Europeans like Yue and her brother who represent the unrepresentable in this model. To address counterstrategies created by those who are erased from Europe's self-image, a fusionist approach is required. This is what I try to do briefly in this essay: I first look more closely at how European racelessness works and how it, rather than fading, managed the transition into a postnational Europe that is more than ever characterized by the diversity of inhabitants.[10] I then show how an analysis of these complicated interactions offers a chance to creolize theory, to rethink disciplinary and other boundaries. I suggest that elements of queer theory, diaspora studies, and queer-of-color critique might all offer insights both into a colorblindness that claims not to see race but actually allows Europeans not to see the racialized oppression they produce and into its effect on those populations whose presence is erased. The final section is devoted to these "invisible" minority communities and to the postethnic minoritarian activism originating among them, exemplified by a public art project that, taking advantage of racelessness' heavy reliance on nonverbal, visual tactics, pollutes public spaces by inserting an illegitimate minority presence.

Postnational Europe and Political Racelessness

In his response to Robert Kagan's theses on the decline of Europe and rise of the United States (Kagan 2002), Jürgen Habermas reframes this shift as a source of Europe's (moral) superiority over the new world power, in the process reducing the continent's colonial history to a successfully mastered learning experience:

> With the growing distance from imperial power and colonial history, the European nations received the chance of critically reflecting on themselves. Thus they could learn, from the perspective of the defeated, to see themselves in the dubious position of winners who are held responsible for the violence of an enforced and rootless modernity. This might have advanced the rejection of Eurocentrism and fed the Kantian hope for a *Weltinnenpolitik*. (Habermas and Derrida 2003, 3)

"Political racelessness" does not equal experiential or social racelessness, that is, the absence of racial thinking. Rather, it creates a form of racialization that can be defined as specifically European both in its enforced silence and in its attempt to externalize race by explicitly categorizing as not European all those who violate Europe's implicit but normative whiteness, thus allowing dominant society to forever consider the "race question" as externally (and by implication temporarily) imposed from the outside. The result is an image of Europe as self-contained and homogeneous in which racialized minorities permanently remain outsiders.[11] Within the circular logic of race as inherently un-European, it can be considered something that is not present unless brought in by non-Europeans, whose presence in turn always seems both sudden and marginal to the continent's core, even if it goes back hundreds of years. This logic has a number of rather obvious weaknesses. It denies the historical presence of populations of color (as well as the fact that their importance to the national imaginary is not necessarily proportional to their numbers), it ignores the genocidal policies that created a relatively homogeneous postwar Europe in the first place,[12] and maybe most importantly, it assumes that race is somehow connected to the presence of people defined as nonwhite (when on the contrary one could argue that race is present wherever people perceive themselves as "white").

As a result of this externalization of racialized populations, both public and policy debates lack a concept of minority identity and by implication of European racial diversity, preventing a comprehensive analysis of processes of exclusion based on similar modes of racialization. Accordingly, Europe's long-standing internal diversity is absent from most historical accounts, and terms like *migration, integration, culture,* and *xenophobia* replace the vocabulary and conceptual framework needed to adequately analyze processes of racialization within Europe (and the ways in which this racialization is an integral part of global economic policies inseparable from the after-effects of European colonialism).

A post–World War II discourse of colorblind universalism, rather than addressing this problematic tradition, further externalized issues of race from Europe's past and present by minimizing the importance of colonialism for intracontinental developments and by separating the Holocaust from the larger context of Western scientific racism (Hall 1991; Balibar 2004; Goldberg 2006), equating the ensuing silence around this history with the disappearance of its roots. As a result, a growing native population of non-European descent seems completely detached from developments preceding its arrival and thus from any legitimate claim of belonging to the national or continental community; its uselessness for a postindustrial economy increasingly outsourcing the cheap labor that brought the first generation of postwar migrants to the continent mirrored its invisibility in official narrations of a Europe that appears culturally diverse but racially homogeneous, fundamentally shaping the world but largely untouched by it.

If the discursive homogenization of modern Europe has been managed primarily in terms of the nation-state, however—that is, if racial minorities were framed as non- rather than second class-citizens—then chances for a more inclusive approach could seem better now than ever. The unifying Europe is widely perceived as leading the way toward a postnational type of society, and the shift from a national to a European polity and identity potentially offers a unique opportunity to reconsider not only migrant and minority populations' position in the emerging continent-wide community but also their contributions to the national histories that the European narrative is meant to both incorporate and transcend. A look at the continent's postnational turn from a minoritarian perspective warrants a pessimistic interpretation, however. So far it seems that instead of reconceptualizing Europe to include them, the unification process creates a narrative that not only continues to exclude racialized minorities but defines them as the very essence of non-Europeanness.

I would argue that this happens not despite but because of the rise in native migrant populations: the unification process coincides with an unprecedented and increasingly visible presence of Europeans of color, a product of growing labor and postcolonial migration since the 1950s.[13] In this context, the postnational appears as a way to circumvent the consequences of the increasingly native national presence of Europeans of color. That they were born in their countries of residence, their experiences if not passports defining them as European, makes their persistent categorization as migrants increasingly difficult. The current focus on a common continental identity instead emphasizes a cultural difference of marginalized communities that appears as both threatening to European identity and inherent to these communities across generations—a difference, in other words, that is racialized in the most unambiguous terms while never quite being defined as such. Key to the ability to define minority populations as nonmembers of the nation is the racialized European understanding of the concept of migrant, which (contrary to the use of the term in the United States) implies a strictly temporary presence, expressed most clearly in the concept of "guest worker," but at the same time indicating a permanent state.

That is, whoever is identified as a racial or religious other is necessarily conceptualized as a migrant, thus as originating outside of Europe, even if this origin is two, three, or more generations removed. It seems important to emphasize that this is a concept that indeed does not become unusable after a certain number of generations has passed or citizenship is acquired, but in effect has two separate meanings, which are, however, never explicitly differentiated: the term *migrant* in continental Europe means (1) a person who has migrated from one nation (usually outside western Europe) to another (within Europe), and (2) a European of color. Assimilation of the second and succeeding generations into the nation still largely depends on the ability to "pass for" a member of the national majority (notwithstanding that this ideal member of the national community against which assimilation is measured is himself or herself an artificial construct, based on the national imaginary rather than its reality). The Dutch Moroccan blogger Feiza Ahmed summarizes the conflict faced by nonwhite Europeans:

> I am asked frequently: "Where do you come from?" If I answer "The Netherlands" the follow-up question is almost mandatory: "No, no, where do you *really* come from?" Of course, this question is not asked if the person asking cannot see me. After all, my behavior or accent do not indicate that I am "foreign."[14]

Ahmed continues, pointing to the seemingly inescapable impact of visual markers:

> Say that I have children with a native white Dutch man with blond hair and blue eyes. The child will probably be a magnificent mixture, but one with dark skin. According to the official definition, my child will be a native citizen (*autochton*), since both his or her parents were born in the Netherlands. But despite an authentic Amsterdam accent and his or her autochthonous value system, people will keep on asking:
> "Where do you come from? The Netherlands? No, no, where do you *really* come from?" Through how many generations will this question persist? Unless the laws of genetics are turned upside down, my grandchildren and great-grandchildren won't have lily-white skin either.

"White" Christian migrants to the European Union from eastern Europe are also frequently racialized as not properly European. Nonetheless their situation is significantly different in that they are able to visually pass, though they are forced to remain silent in order not to betray their otherness; and, just as importantly, this otherness usually fades within a generation, and their children, white native speakers, are recognized as European.[15] The equation of native speakers with insiders, however, does not include those who do not pass the visual test of Europeanness. As the foregoing extracts as well as the subway episode cited earlier show, if the assumption of a necessary congruence between visual (or biological) and aural (or cultural) signs of belonging is violated, the visual tends to win out. Apart from the obvious racialization at play here, the European migrant construct, frequently reflected in continental migration studies, neglects the significant differences between a first generation that physically migrates and its descendants, who are in effect minority citizens but in continental Europe remain defined through the paradigm of migration: only temporarily present in their home countries, without access to the privileges that come with confirmed membership in the community of Europeans.[16]

Despite its primarily economic effects, the discourse justifying racialized inequality is strictly cultural. Since 9/11, clash-of-civilization scenarios have formed the dominant framework for debates on migration increasingly identified with the presence of Muslim communities across Europe, which in turn seem collectively represented by (and responsible for) the London bombings, the Danish cartoon controversy, or the assassination of the Dutch filmmaker Theo van Gogh. This attitude is not limited to populist discourse either; public intellectuals such as Hans Magnus Enzensberger, Martin Amis, and Pascal Bruckner strike a similar vein:

> One tends to forget the outright despotism of minorities who are resistant to assimilation if it isn't accompanied by a status of extraterritoriality and special dispensations. The result is that nations are created within nations, which, for example, feel Muslim before they feel English, Canadian or Dutch. . . . Thus they are refused what has always been our privilege: passing from one world to another, from tradition to modernity, from blind obedience to rational decision making. (Bruckner 2007)

Reactions like these contribute to the state of exception surrounding the European minority presence, professing a tense coexistence of incompatible cultures, each little incident potentially tipping over the delicate balance, Europe's destruction by the barbarians always imminent. With the shift to the numeric dominance of the second and third generations of migrants, events like the French riots and signifiers such as the headscarf confirm this continued, dangerous difference from the European mainstream and symbolize a "migration crisis" that in truth is a crisis caused by an ideology of political racelessness that seems incapable of addressing racialized inequality. This incapability permeates all sectors of society, from the continent-wide failure of school systems to address the needs of children from migrant and minority families to their overrepresentation in prisons and unemployment statistics (Crul and Vermeulen 2003; OECD 2006). And while the threat of Islam is decisively presented as coming from the outside *at* Europe, the cited incidents, as well as the debates surrounding them, primarily relate to Europe-born Muslims who are thus reframed as not belonging: parallel to older models of biological racism, the focus not on Islam as a religion but on the cultural values it supposedly brings with it cements the fundamental "foreignness" of Muslims born and raised in Europe.[17]

While this discourse follows familiar patterns, it is rarely framed in relation to the long history of racialization of religion in Europe. To do so would locate the source of current clash-of-civilization scenarios within an internal tradition rather than some inherent, fundamental otherness of the continent's Muslim population, expressed in its supposed religious intolerance, sexism, and homophobia, an otherness that thus prevents Muslims from ever becoming part of the European "We." Leo Lucassen (2005) challenged the contemporary discourse on "new" (i.e., non-European) immigrants as being "culturally" opposed to the European tradition of religious tolerance and gender equality by pointing out how Europeans conveniently seem to forget the continent's history of anti-Semitism. One could add that there is also a long history of racism and anti-Islamism traditionally directed against exactly those groups that are at the center of contemporary migration discourses, that is, Muslims and African migrants (while the numerical majority of contemporary migrants is provided by white, Christian southern and eastern European nations). In addition, Europe's history of anti-Semitism (and of gender inequality) might not be merely conveniently forgotten. Instead the image of the fundamentalist Muslim immigrant is instrumentalized to work through or rewrite and transfer this history: the supposed Judeo-Christian affinity and alliance against the lethal threat of radical Islam is naturalized and implied to be traditionally present, despite all historical evidence to the contrary (and despite the fact that in contemporary Europe, anti-Semitism is by no means a prerogative of Muslim mi-norities; on the contrary, it often coexists with Islamophobic and racist positions). The Muslim presence on the continent is thus acknowledged to define a new, unified Europe characterized by a tolerant secularism—a tol-erance, paradoxically, that is manifest not in the inclusion but the exclusion of Europe's largest religious minority.[18]

Recent debates, around the incompatibility of Islam with "modern" soci-eties, the French riots of 2005, or the "terrorist threat" posed by second-generation migrants, indicate that within dominant discourses on Europe it seems more feasible to continuously deny the existence of European racial and religious diversity than to adapt to a reality which would demand the end of the internalist narrative of European identity. The inability to ac-knowledge the continent's "impure" past and present indicates another as-pect of the rise of fundamentalism so often referenced in relation to the continent's Muslim minority: "if what we mean by "fundamentalism" is a defensive and exclusive retreat into a rigid and unchanging version of the past inhabited as Truth, then there is plenty of it about, not least in the so-called "modern West" (Hall 1991, 18).

"Unviable (Un)Subjects":
Methodological Challenges to Racelessness

In her *Excitable Speech* (1997), which aims to situate Althusser's concept of interpellation in concrete power relations through a discussion of legal regulations around hate speech, Judith Butler evokes a now-familiar situa-tion:

> Imagine the quite plausible scene in which one is called by a name and one turns around only to protest the name: "That is not me, you must be mistaken!" And then imagine that the name continues to force itself upon you, to delineate the space you occupy, to construct a social posi-tionality. Indifferent to your protests, the force of interpellation continues to work. One is still constituted by discourse, but at a distance from one-self. (J. Butler 1997a, 33)

The key problem in addressing and potentially deconstructing Europe's colorblindness might be that while the implicit, though not at all subtle, racialization of Europeanness as white and Christian and thus of racialized minorities as non-European seems undisputable, public discourse nonetheless rejects this observation as meaningless within a discursive framework shaped by an Enlightenment universalism that for centuries has managed to claim race as irrelevant while simultaneously treating it as all-important. How, then, can this system be effectively challenged? Naming it, verbalizing the unspoken mechanisms of exclusion seems an obvious first step but in itself is not necessarily sufficient. Too easily are these attempts at dismantling the system integrated into it, by defining the identification of racist structures as an act of racism (you are racist if you see race, and therefore you cannot be racist if you are colorblind), through the common claim that discourses on race are fundamentally tied to the U.S. experience and thus have no meaningful context in Europe, or by exclusively associating debates around race to a right-wing fringe without connection to the European mainstream.[19]

Thus, to develop methodological approaches that can successfully address the complicated question of race in Europe, one needs to look beyond the existing framework. I believe tools that might usefully be employed in naming the "unspeakable" existence of race in Europe can be found in fields that at first glance seem to have little connection to the topic at hand.[20] Creolizing theory, working on the intersections of concepts and disciplines, opens the potential of expressing exactly the positionality deemed impossible in dominant European discourses, that of Europeans of color, foregrounding their transgressive strategies of resistance, which are often downplayed in culturalist debates around Europe's so-called migration problem.

The foregoing Butler quote could be a case in point, as it seems to perfectly summarize a key condition shaping the situation of European minorities. Among the practical implications of the invisibility of racialized minorities is a Catch-22 leaving them with only two, impossible, options. The first is to identify as an insider of the national community, a position that inevitably clashes with the assigned status as other ("People will keep on asking: 'Where do you come from? . . . No, no, where do you *really* come from?'"). The second option is to accept the outsider status, the identification as "migrant." This move complies with the dominant discourse and offers a "legitimate" point of resistance through ethnic migrant organizing. It nevertheless creates its own set of problems: a movement built around ethnic solidarity and an identification with a homeland that is neither the place of residency nor of birth often clashes with the actual encounter with the imaginary home, in which the second-generation migrant is again perceived as an outsider:

> To say that we are French means a lot of different things; it's almost like saying that we are Christian, almost, because most of the time, French people are Christian. Maybe on the outside we're French and on the inside we're Arab. But really, our problem is that our parents are immigrants, and when we go to Algeria, we're still immigrants. So, we're somewhere in the middle. (Keaton 2006, 32)

Both positions create a conflict that cannot be successfully resolved within the system of colorblindness, which makes it impossible to name its root. In this context, Ming-Bao Yue's subway experience appears in a slightly different light: the German man's inquiry can be interpreted as not only a reaction to a situation that violates the European logic of externalizing race but an active attempt to reconfigure reality along acceptable lines while projecting the tension of otherness, of incompatible identities, onto the minority subject.

Far-fetched as it could seem, this process of silencing minority voices might best be explained by appropriating Butler again, namely, her "Imitation and Gender Insubordination," one of queer theory's key texts, and its conceptualization of lesbians as "unviable (un)subjects" of the economy of law (Butler 1991). Within her analysis of sexual power regimes, Butler differentiates between those who in discourses around gender and sexuality represent the opposite of the norm—and are thus indispensable for its definition and explicitly targeted by prohibitions, in this case male homosexuals—and those who do not even appear within the discourse, are an invisible aberration without discursive space. Not qualifying as "an object of prohibition" and instead relegated to a "domain of unthinkability and unnameability" (Butler 1991, 20), they thus remain without a place from where to resist their normative exclusion: "by being called a name, one is also, paradoxically, given a certain possibility for social existence, initiated into a temporal life of language that exceeds the prior purposes that animate that call" (Butler 1997a, 2). With necessary caution, one might transfer this analysis to the discourse around normative (ethnic) European identity in which only the seemingly unambiguous and opposing options of white Christian

European and migrant are presented as valid, "speakable" identities, while ambiguities and transgressions are discursively silenced.

The social existence of minorities is negated through silence but just as importantly through an active process of denial that reinforces the discursive rules of racelessness in everyday exchanges. In its most basic version, minority identity is policed by the endlessly repeated questioning of origin, at times elaborate, often reduced to the plain "Where do you come from?" This question is usually motivated not by curiosity but by a desire to affirm a preexisting knowledge: "You are not from here." The interrogation creates a discursive but very real paradox, since the true answer, "I am from here," is precisely the one that is not acceptable, as it falls outside of the logically possible, the thinkable. Because of this, the questioned minoritarian subject lacks the discursive power to shape the exchange to such an extent that it could cause a radical break by introducing a new option that would in effect destroy the existing paradigm: "To move outside of the domain of speakability is to risk one's status as a subject. To embody the norms that govern speakability in one's speech is to consummate one's status as a subject of speech" (Butler 1997a, 133). Minorities remain invisible and mute between the antagonism of "native" norm and "foreign" aberration, only able to become subjects of speech if they take on a fake but acceptable identity ("Oh, we've only been here about a year"). If one's existence depends partly on being addressed by another, the conditions of intelligibility become fundamental to hierarchies of power, so basic that they often go unnoticed, leaving minorities of color in Europe only the choice between being unintelligible or misinterpellated.

While Butler's model is useful in deconstructing how the seemingly individual, confusing, and repetitive process of interrogation that minority subjects constantly face is feeding into the larger framework of political racelessness, it is less helpful in addressing minoritarian responses to this alienating experience. The minority subject is not completely powerless in the exchange; while question and expected or accepted answer stay the same in an endless, almost compulsive process of repetition, minoritarian subjects can explore a variety of "false answers," all of which are acceptable if compatible with the "you are not from here" premise: within the clear limits of this discursive frame, it is possible to challenge, subvert, and parody its normative expectations ("I heard my brother saying with a smile: '. . . You know, German is such an easy language!'"). This strategy, frequently prac-

242 | *Fatima El-Tayeb*

ticed by minoritarian subjects in one form or another, can be gratifying and create an instant of disruption, momentarily throwing a wrench in the machinery of racelessness, but it does not yet change the discursive rules. In its uses as well as limits, it can also be linked to the tactic of "diversion" that Édouard Glissant develops for Caribbean narratives of identity (Glissant 1989, 18). Diversion is the reaction to an oppression that is total but at the same time diffuse, so that its source cannot be identified immediately and instead needs to be approached through dislocation, through experiencing the source of oppression as being elsewhere:

> Diversion is the ultimate resort of a population whose domination by an Other is concealed: it then must search *elsewhere* for the principle of domination, which is not evident in the country itself: because the system of domination . . . is not directly tangible. Diversion is the parallactic displacement of this strategy. (Glissant 1989, 20)

For our example, this would mean that the impossibility of minoritarian identity *within* the nation is so fundamental, so ingrained in the structure of society, that it cannot be initially addressed, in fact cannot be initially conceptualized by the minority subject itself. The conceptualization (for the subject) as well as the problematization (for society) is only possible through the detour of repetition-diversion: the "I am (not) from here, but . . ." Glissant cautions, however, that "diversion is not a useful ploy unless it is nurtured by reversion: not a return to the longing for origins, to some immutable state of Being, but a return to the point of entanglement, from where we were forcefully turned away; that is where we must ultimately put to work the forces of creolization, or perish" (Glissant 1989, 26). Not a return to an unconflicted origin or to the possibility of integration thus, but a return to the point of entanglement in which conflicting identity models clash before they are resolved into possible and impossible identities. This would be the point, then, from which resistance could be articulated, a position as subject of speech achieved. To arrive at this stage, however, a different archive needs to be accessed, one based on the experiences of marginalized, silenced communities, without presence in dominant discourses. In the chapter's final section, I highlight attempts at introducing such an archive into European public spaces, making visible and thus ineffective the mechanisms of color-blindness.

Creating Visibility: European Minority Activism

The Guyanese poet and filmmaker Meiling Jin writes:

> One day I learnt
> A secret art
> Invisible-Ness it was called.
> I think it worked . . .
> (Meiling Jin 1987, 126)

The disparity between the lived experience of minoritarian Europeans and their (non)perception by the majority creates an obvious alienation, a breakdown of communication. This, however, does not completely silence the misinterpellated subjects, who intervene in a discourse not meant to include them, creating not a legitimate positionality, discursive or otherwise, but a temporary disruption of a normative order that cannot recognize their existence. Verbal diversions in response to the normative "Where do you come from?" ritual, as well as spectacular incidents like the French riots, which seemed to confirm the self-fulfilling prophecy of migrant youths' threatening and invincible difference, can be read as part of a complicated and tense process of negotiating degrees of belonging. The strategy of claiming a space within the nation by moving beyond it, by "[opening] up a historical and experiential rift between the locations of residence and the locations of belonging," can be called fundamentally diasporic in drawing on identifications and models of identity that "[exist] outside of and sometimes in opposition to the political forms and codes of modern citizenship" (Gilroy 2000, 24).

Since their exclusion is framed in exactly these forms and codes of modern citizenship, going beyond the nation to enter it appears as a necessity for European minorities. In responding to the specific forms of exclusion and marginalization it faces, the current generation of Europeans of color increasingly draws on and transforms modes of resistance and analysis circulated in transnational discourses of diaspora, ranging from hip-hop culture to women-of-color feminism. This process necessarily transcends the limits of the national, as dialogue not only takes place in reaction to and addressed at a majoritarian audience refusing the minoritarian subjects' right to define their own subjectivity but becomes part of a collective move toward creating alternative modes of belonging: "These identities-in-difference emerge from a failed interpellation within the dominant public sphere. Their emergence is predicated on their ability to disidentify with the mass public and instead, through this disidentification, contribute to the function of a counterpublic sphere" (Muñoz 1999, 7). The process of disidentification described by José Esteban Muñoz in his U.S.-based study of "queers of color and the performance of politics"[21] seems easily applicable to a European minority tactic of "queering ethnicity," that is, strategies of resistance to racialization that work outside the logic of ethnicity and nation, using transgressive rather than affirmative models of identity (El-Tayeb 2006).

This move toward diasporic transnationality is not captured in the model of diaspora dominating European migration studies, however. This latter model revolves around the trope of the "lost home," in which the migrant's existence is seen as focusing entirely on his or her native land, the return to which is identified as the dominant life goal, and all activities in the temporary domicile of the host society appear focused on this central aim.[22] Understood in this way, diaspora indeed appears as a mere extension of the nation-state model, implying a "congruence between territory, culture, and identity" (Soysal 2000, 2) that suspends migrants and their descendants eternally between "home" and "host nation." Nonetheless the diaspora concept should not be discarded for the European context. While the term *migration* does not grasp the experience of a population that is born into one nation but never fully part of it, and *minority* does not quite encompass the transnational ties of that same population, *diaspora* can bring together both aspects, mirroring disidentification as "the third mode of dealing with dominant ideology, one that neither opts to assimilate within such a structure nor strictly opposes it . . . a strategy that works on and against dominant ideology" (Muñoz 1999, 11). It can thus offer a mode of resistance to the desire to resolve the tension that migrant and minority populations cause within the nation by placing them either firmly without or firmly within the state, suppressing what is central to these populations: their transnational affiliations, making them something different from either insiders or outsiders and thus a constant reminder of the limits of the nation model.

Diaspora is a concept that ideally, though far from automatically, can express this tension without the implicit need to resolve it and thus can become a useful concept in approaching European minority communities. When combined with new developments within queer theory, in particular queer-of-color critique (Muñoz 1999; Manalansan 2003; Ferguson 2004; Gopinath 2005), it allows us to describe a practice of identity (de)construction that results in a new type of diasporic consciousness neither grounded in ethnic identifications nor referencing a mythical homeland, but instead using the tension of living supposedly exclusive identities and transforming it into a creative potential, building a community based on the shared experience of multiple, contradictory positionalities. A process, in other words, in which "identity, too, becomes a noun of process" (Gilroy 2000, 252). The invisibility of minorities within the nation paradoxically also offers a certain freedom, namely, from prescriptive identity models. This makes possible eclectic and subversive appropriations that present multi-layered challenges to established notions of identity, opening up the potential of queering ethnicity as a nonessentialist, and often nonlinear, political strategy:

> Suturing "queer" to "diaspora" thus recuperates those desires, practices, and subjectivities that are rendered impossible and unimaginable within conventional diasporic and nationalist imaginaries. A consideration of queerness, in other words, becomes a way to challenge nationalist ideologies by restoring the impure, inauthentic, nonreproductive potential of the notion of diaspora. (Gopinath 2005, 11)

While Gayatri Gopinath's use of "queer" would not necessarily include the minority identity I am concerned with here, it seems possible to argue that Europeans of color are produced as "queer," "impossible" subjects in a heteronormative discourse of nation and diaspora. Without necessarily reflecting it theoretically, minority subjects use queer performance strategies in continuously rearranging the components of the supposedly stable but incompatible identities assigned to them, creating cracks in the circular logic of the system and pointing to a potential site of interaction of performativity and performance.[23] In doing so, they challenge the stubborn myth of the monoethnic European nation-state and the gender, racial, and sexual identities attached to it.

Migrant activism can be traced back to the beginning of labor migration, but over the last twenty years, European cities have witnessed the emergence of new minority networks based on the experiences of an increasingly younger, ethnically diverse urban population that is largely excluded from economic, political, and social participation in the community

"Raising Awareness When Dealing With Visible Minorities," Black Women Community, Arbeiten gegen Rassismen 2005.

of citizens. Denied membership in the nation, they built translocal structures that connect multiethnic metropolitan communities on the basis of a shared experience that is not primarily binational, as was the case with first-generation migrants, but multilocal, creating spaces that cross various national and ethnic borders. While this process is certainly not an organized mass movement, groups like Strange Fruit in the Netherlands, the Mouvement de l'Immigration et des Banlieus (MIB) in France, and Kanak Attak in Germany represent the first concerted efforts of racialized minorities to enter and define *as Europeans* the debate on what it means to be European (El-Tayeb 2006).

Visual culture is central to this translocal activism: it makes possible communication across language barriers, increasingly important as movements attempt to organize continent-wide; it allows immediate interventions into public spaces; and not the least important, it addresses a racialization that often operates on the visual, unspoken level. I will end my discussion of

Weißsein ist nichts
als das Produkt einer kollektiven
Imagination, das ausschließlich
durch die Existenz der „Anderen"
definiert werden kann.

"Being White," Anna Kowalska, Arbeiten gegen Rassismen 2005.

Europe and race with a brief illustration of this strategy, which returns us to the site at which the chapter began, the European public transport system. In the summer of 2005 in Vienna, and again in 2007 in Graz, a collective of artists and activists, organized under the slogan "Arbeiten gegen Rassismen" (Working against Racisms), staged an intervention into Austrian public spaces that can be read as a continuation of the performative self-defense practiced by Ming-Bao Yue and her brother on a Hamburg subway in the 1970s. Billboards in, on, and around the cities' streetcars addressed a number of "unmentionable" issues from the construction of whiteness and the invisibility of minorities in school curricula to the silence around the disappearance of the nation's Jewish population. The event, meant to "make visible the modes of operation of racisms and of resistance against them,"[24] created a situationist disruption, a gash in the seamless logic of political racelessness. At the same time, it used these moments of irritation to reconstruct an alternative European history, emphasizing suppressed con-

"Monument of 'Arianization,'" Martin Krenn, Arbeiten gegen Rassismen 2005.

nections, for example, those between racism and anti-Semitism, offering a reading of contemporary Europe that contextualizes excluded populations as well as the mechanisms of exclusion itself:

While campaigns like this obviously are not enough to change dominant attitudes, it is important to note that this is not all they are about. They can be read as practicing creolization by moving from interventions directed at, and using the terms of, an unresponsive majoritarian culture to an alternative model of identity, challenging dominant assumptions but at the same time fostering communication among formerly isolated minoritarian subjects, referencing a shared experience and thus shifting the source of the supposed problem that minority populations pose to European discourses of identity, from the marginalized individual to the marginalizing structures. In doing so, they lay open the workings of political racelessness and thus offer tools for its dismantling.

Notes

Many thanks to Shu-mei Shi, Françoise Lionnet, and the members of the UCLA Mellon Postdoctoral Program "Cultures in Transnational Perspective" for their helpful commentaries on an earlier draft of this chapter.

1 Thanks to Lisa Yoneyama for bringing Yue's article to my attention. For other national variants of the "Not looking European" experience, see, for example, Keaton 2006 and Ahmed's article "Nu even niet" on Web-log.nl (http://hoeiboei.weblog .nl/hoeiboei/fiza_ahmed/index.html).

2 While this regime is moderated by significant national and regional differences, comparative studies of minorities, that is, "second-generation migrants," in Europe indicate similarities despite different national rhetoric and policies (Crul and Vermeulen 2003). The presence of underlying common attitudes shaping the treatment of these groups makes it possible to talk about a *European* situation.

3 This chapter focuses on continental Europe, since the British discourse, while sharing some European tropes, addresses race in different, more explicit ways than the continental debate. Due to space constraints, I include in my discussion examples from Germany, the Netherlands, Switzerland, France, and Austria, hopefully making the case that European forms of racialization are indeed transnational. Eastern Europe unfortunately remains largely excluded, partly because its complicated position as not unambiguously European, that is, not fully integrated into the European Union, with a history of both providing racialized migrants to the West and aggressively marginalizing nonwhite minorities such as Jews, Roma, and Muslims, cannot be thoroughly addressed here.

4 The history of the racializations in Europe emphasizes race as a social rather than biological construct. My definition of Europeans of color does not claim any biological or scientific precision: while racializations claim to name natural, unchanging, obvious facts, they are always ambiguous, shifting, and unstable. *Europeans of color* thus is meant to reference populations defined as inherently non-European because of a racialized difference, while not meaning to imply that these groups are stable or face similar conditions.

5 Despite the Holocaust's central place in European rituals of remembrance, its lasting effects on European societies remain understudied. In an astonishing act of suppression, the ethnic homogeneity of postwar Europe upset by the beginning of large-scale labor migration often remains unrelated to the unprocessed disappearance of the Jewish minority population. See, for example, Amira Hass: "I found my answer years later, during the eighties, while studying in Amsterdam. Living there, I felt the true force of the void left after 1945, of how Europe, home to millions of Jews for hundreds of years, had simply spewed them out; how most people had collaborated with Nazi Germany's antipluralistic psychosis and accepted the gradual and final removal of the Jews with indifference. But more, I felt tormented by the ease with which Europe had accepted the emptiness that followed, had filled the void, and moved on" (2000, 8).

6 The billboard campaign was accompanied by an online game on the party's website where visitors could personally "kick out" black sheep (Haegler 2007).

7 The issue here is not at all to claim that Europe is worse (or better) than the United States, but merely to argue that the absence of particular forms of racialization—

for example, mandatory racial classifications in national censuses—does not necessarily equal the absence of race consciousness.

8 Other examples would be Brazil or the Dominican Republic, both nations that are both highly race-conscious and officially colorblind (see, e.g., Torres-Saillant 2000; Langfur 2006).

9 See the German Kanak Attak's manifesto on the Aktuell website: http://www.kanak-attak.de.

10 It has to be emphasized, however, that the narrative of Europe's ethnic and cultural homogeneity always corrected, rather than reflected, reality.

11 Likely the most striking illustration of this dynamic is the situation of the continent's Roma and Sinti populations, which, while being part of every European nation's reality and imaginary, remain more or less invisible in discourses on Europeanness. If Europe can afford to define itself as white and untouched by race matters despite the existence of a racialized native population numbering roughly ten million people, present in every European nation; if a history of racial subjugation that includes slavery and genocide remains severely understudied while the racist exclusion itself continues nearly unmitigated; if Roma and Sinti living in Europe since the early Middle Ages remain despised and marginalized foreigners in all their native nations, and recent UN and EU reports indicate that this is the case; then there seems to be little hope for Europe's ability to confront the dependency on whiteness at its core (European Commission Directorate-General for Employment and Social Affairs 2004; Ivanov et al. 2006; European Roma Rights Center 2007).

12 Also largely forgotten are the massive forced "repatriations" of minority populations in south and east Europe that took place between the end of World War I and the beginning of World War II, undertaken with the explicit aim to create national ethnic homogeneity where none existed before. See Aly 2003, 28–41.

13 For data on post–World War II migration to Europe (as well as individual European nations) see the Migration Policy Institute website, MigrationPolicy.org (http://www.migrationpolicy.org/research/europe.php).

14 Fiza Ahmed (2006), "Nu even niet," on Web-log.nl (http://hoeiboei.weblog.nl/hoeiboei/fiza_ahmed/index.html).

15 One example of this assimilation would be the French president Nicolas Sarkozy, son of a Hungarian immigrant, while his favorite opponents, the inhabitants of the banlieus, represent an example of the exclusion of Europeans of color from this process. Other illustrations are the Dutch word *allochton*, referencing those who are Dutch citizens by birth but not entirely of autochthonous Dutch parentage (in practice, the term applies exclusively to Dutch citizens of color) and the recent German category *Buerger mit migrantischem Hintergrund* (citizens with migrant background). See, e.g., Arts and Nabha 2001; Hoving 2005.

16 I do not mean to erase important differences between marginalized groups here. My point is that whoever is perceived as nonwhite is also, as a consequence, perceived as non-European, as an illegitimate presence. This perception does have material

consequences; at the same time, the situation of a European of color differs significantly from that of documented and undocumented migrants.

17 This perspective is also present in sympathetic representations. An article in the *Neue Zuericher Zeitung* in 2005 criticizing dominant French attitudes toward the country's Muslim minorities, for example, nonetheless uses the terms "'European' French" and "Muslim French" to separate the two groups (Ritte 2005).

18 According to a widely quoted poll in 2006, for example, 63 percent of the Dutch believe Islam to be incompatible with Europe—this despite an existing European Muslim population numbering at least fifteen million (Angus Reid Global Monitor 2006).

19 The example of the "black sheep" billboards and the official Dutch term *black schools* cited earlier is a case in point. The Swiss campaign generated some Europe-wide discussion, and it does provide a straightforward example of the almost schizophrenic European attitude veering between explicit racism and complete denial, but the Dutch term is as striking in its racial reference—more so since the term *black* is not generally used to refer to black citizens (or Dutch of color in general); for the former, the majority still favors the term *neger*, similar in meaning to the English term *Negro* but supposed to be without negative connotations in the liberal Dutch context. The racialized use of *black* to signify the link between underachievement and overrepresentation of minorities while rejecting it as an empowering term for people of color seems as clear an illustration of the European attitude while generating little controversy. See Arts and Nabha 2001; Haegler 2007.

20 In recent years, a growing number of younger authors join pioneers like Stuart Hall and Philomena Essed in challenging the notion that race has no place in the ideological framework shaping Europe. It seems far from coincidental that this literature, often written by members of racialized groups, draws on postcolonial and diaspora theories still largely ignored in mainstream European scholarship on migrants (Essed 1991; Steyerl and Guitiérez Rodríguez 2003; Ha 2004). While this new scholarship is slowly gaining ground, the consensus that Europe's others come from outside (to which they will ideally return) makes it especially hard for minority voices to enter public debates, including those of academia, leaving European migration studies a largely white field.

21 "Disidentification is meant to be descriptive of the survival strategies the minority subject practices in order to negotiate a phobic majoritarian public sphere that continuously elides or punishes the existence of subjects who do not conform to the phantasm of normative citizenship" (Muñoz 1999, 4).

22 This attitude, furthermore, is assumed to shape not only the life of the migrants themselves but also that of their children, whose identification with a "home" they often barely know is seen not as a reaction to their life in the here and now but as a shared nostalgia for the then and there. The prevailing notion of diaspora in migration studies accordingly has come under criticism for overestimating the role that the homeland plays for migrant populations of the first and later generations and

for underestimating the investment of those populations in their host societies. The sociologist Yasemin Soysal, one of the most prolific critics of the diaspora model, states: "The dominant conceptualization of diaspora presumptively accepts the formation of tightly bounded communities and solidarities (on the basis of common cultural and ethnic references) between places of origin and arrival. . . . Diasporas form when populations disperse from their homeland to foreign lands, engage in movements between the country of origin and destination, and carry out bidirectional transactions—economic, political and cultural. In this formulation, the primary orientation and attachment of diasporic populations is to their homelands and cultures; and their claims and citizenship practices arise from this home-bound, ethnic-based orientation" (Soysal 2000, 2).

23   In thus bridging the gap between performance and performativity, individual and community, these activists address a fundamental demand of queer of color critique (Johnson and Henderson 2005).

24   Arbeiten gegen Rassismen, press release, Vienna 2005, http://www.arbeitengegen rassismen.net (translation mine).

3

APPENDIX

A

✂

EUROPE AND THE ANTILLES
An Interview with Édouard Glissant

Andrea Schwieger Hiepko
Translated from the French by Julin Everett

The following text is the transcription of an interview of Édouard Glissant by Andrea Schwieger Hiepko in May 1998 in Berlin. On the occasion of his conference "Rethinking Europe: Electronic Media, Orality, and Identity," the author speaks of themes present in Caribbean literature, of his conception of creole, of the notion of rhizomic identity, and of his propositions for the future of European cultures.

ANDREA SCHWIEGER HIEPKO: The frontiers of Europe are closing themselves off from most non-European immigrants. Yet globalizing economic and cultural movements and vast transformations are accelerating everywhere. Which path should we follow to best adapt ourselves to the new structures taking shape in Europe as well as on other continents? Is this a problem that requires a poetic rather than a political response?

ÉDOUARD GLISSANT: I have several observations to make. As far as a method is concerned, I do not separate theoretical reflection from novelistic or artistic creation. For me these are two sides of the same coin. Where Europe is concerned, I think habits are hard to break, especially when one has conquered the world, governed the world, dominated the world. But I think that as long as there is no change, not only in consciousness, but also in the *imaginaire*, the imaginary or deep mentality of Europeans, nothing will happen.

I want to look back in order to explain this. I think that today, there is firstly a generalized conflict of cultures. That is obvious, isn't it? Conflict, but also attraction. Discord, but also harmony. And within these contact zones, I think there are two main types of cultures in the current *tout-monde*. I call these: atavistic cultures and composite cultures. In the case of Europe, we are manifestly in the presence of atavistic cultures. I call an atavistic culture a culture that has felt the need to create a myth related to the creation of the world, a genesis. And why? Because these cultures tend to link, in a rather distant and unconscious way, their present state to a creation of the world brought about by means of an uninterrupted filiation. And it is from this filiation that these cultures derive their legitimacy, their sense of ownership of their own land, and their right of expansion, which was the very foundation of colonization. I think that composite cultures, on the other hand, have not had the opportunity or the means to create a myth of the creation of the world because they are cultures born of history. Their birth is there, we can see it, and we don't need to go back to a distant and timeless past to try to understand what this birth was like. The problem is that today atavistic cultures tend to fall apart under the effects of contacts and migrations, whereas composite cultures become prone to a sort of nostalgia for atavistic origins. It is for this reason, for example, that in American countries there are so many religious sects. These sects represent a way of reclaiming whatever one can of the myths of the other, and of appropriating them.

If we carefully observe the situation in the world today, we can see that within most atavistic cultures, identity is an exclusionary concept, whereas in composite cultures, that possibility is almost nonexistent. In the Caribbean, for example, it is obvious that there is no possibility of ethnic massacres or ethnic purification because of the very notion of ethnicity to be found there. There are other problems, but not that one, because the Caribbean is an archipelago of countries born of creolization. The history of the Caribbean is a history of creolization, and such composite countries cannot embrace the adventures of the single root, of racial or linguistic purity, of the *racine unique*.

What is good now is that Europe is turning into an archipelago. That is to say that beyond national barriers, we see many islands taking shape in relation to one another. In France, for example, the Basque country, Catalonia, Brittany, Corsica, Alsace . . . Even in Germany, this tendency is very strong because it is part of history, and the political organization of Germany is a response to this. It seems, then, in my opinion, that to unify Europe means to develop these islands, perhaps to the detriment of the notion of the nation and, beyond that, of national borders. To me this seems to be a very strong trend right now. I feel it acutely in European life, which is becoming a sort of archipelago with islands maintaining relations among themselves. Official, administrative life still takes place through nation-states. But quotidian and cultural life has already gone beyond this stage and has put regions in contact with one another.

ASH: Do you not see a sort of provincialization of Europe? Autonomist movements, such as Catalonia's: don't they imply a competition among the different regions? Aren't they developing a new patriotism that could endanger peace?

EG: This is the difficulty: to develop an island-region, must this island-region become nationalistic? This would be the worst possible thing. When the Basques fall into extremism, we see a form of exclusion of the other, which, for me, is not favorable to the evolution of an island-region. Also we notice that in Europe, which is a region of atavistic cultures, every attempt at creolization—as in the regions around the Mediterranean basin—every attempt not at synthesis but at contact has produced unexpected and unforeseeable results. There has been a violent return or backwash of identity which has systematically taken these places as targets. Cities of creolization like Beirut in Lebanon or Sarajevo in Yugoslavia are good examples because there the return to atavistic drives leads to the clamor for that which had provoked so many catastrophes, everywhere in the world: ethnic purity, racial purity, the strength of the nation. No military, social, or economic program can solve this problem so long as the imaginary of the populations has not changed, that is to say, so long as people are not convinced that contact with, and tolerance of, the other is not automatically the cause of dilution and disappearance; better yet, that we can change, no longer be the same, and exchange something with the other without losing or diluting oneself, without vanishing into a kind of nonspace. That's what's at stake in our time. Is it possible to change the imaginary? That is, not only the conscious but also the unconscious, the imaginary of a people in order to curb once and for all the drive to return to ancient exclusions.

It seems to me that in the world, all conflicts are related to this partition. India and Pakistan, each trying to impose their truth or faith on the other. The Indians of Chiapas, who are an atavistic culture, up against the rest of Creole society in Mexico. The Amerindians of the United States are in the same situation with regard to American settlements. . . . In all these conflicts—but also with the Serbs, the Croats, and the Muslims in Yugoslavia—that is the fundamental issue. One can easily give economic reasons. That would be partially true, but not fundamentally so. The reality, rather, consists in what's at stake for cultures that are similar, meaning that they are atavistic but had also succeeded in creating islands of creolization.

I've read horrible stories about Yugoslavia. About villages connected by a bridge and populations that had intermarried. But when unitary forms of identity surfaced again, the bridge was destroyed with dynamite; women returned to their families; and children, well, no one really knew where to put them. *That* is the return to the forms of exclusionary identity that are linked to the very nature of atavistic cultures. In addition, the advantage of an atavistic culture is a certain familiarity and intimacy with one's God, the fact of being able to hear his voice. But in the present state of the tout-monde, where creolization happens so much more strikingly and rapidly, to have such a point of view is, of course, a terrible handicap, one that burdens all the migrants of Europe.

And I don't think unemployment is the driving force of intolerance and of racism. It is rather that people have not yet changed their imaginary. They still believe that in order to live, one must enjoy a form of legitimacy established by one's own territory, a space devoid of the other. But the relationship to one's territory, to the earth, seems much more complex to me. I very much like Amerindian cultures, which, even though they are atavistic cultures, still say: "We are not the owners of the earth, we are the custodians of the earth." That does not prevent them from fighting for their land. The proof is that they resisted the Americans. But theirs is an attitude of inclusion rather than exclusion. And I think that if we do not have an open debate about this issue, problems will continue to surface in Europe as elsewhere.

ASH: Your theory of the *chaos-monde* (chaos-world) has found a large echo within the philosophical community in France. I see in it the notion of the unexpected, the opposition between composite forms and monolithic ones, dispersion, alienation, et cetera. How does your theory relate to the notion of the rhizome versus that of the single root?

EG: What I call chaos-monde is not the world in disorder. Disorder can be a part of it, but that's not essential. It is rather the world of the unexpected, which is difficult to accept because we fear the uncertain. All of Occidental thought was based on foreseeability, knowability. One could change the world because one knew it in the way that one knows a physical phenomenon. And this way of thinking has permitted the Occident to conquer the world. But today the world is realized, known, in its totality. In practice, the physical conquest of space is no longer possible. We no longer have the kind of legitimacy that Christopher Columbus, for one, enjoyed. He left with the cross and the sword and imposed both of them. Today we have religious wars but no more conquests. We have no more open spaces into which we can surge with our own emblems. Therefore we can no longer disentangle the inextricable mass of elements that come into contact with one another in the *totalité-monde*. We can no longer think in a systematic way about the state of the world. We can no longer predict the outcome of our plans. This frightens us because we tell ourselves unconsciously: "If I cannot see the future, make projections, what do I do?" That is also the imaginary that needs to be changed. Getting rid of the fear of the unforeseeable.

ASH: In the era of globalization, it seems that the concept of the nation is no longer suitable for the network of interdependent and diverse identity formations. That being the case, how do you view the possibility of a renewal or reformulation of Caribbean identity in what you call the tout-monde?

EG: All of this is linked to the fact that we have moved from the single root to the rhizome—and I return here to Deleuze and Guattari's image. They use it to speak of the processes of thought. But I use it to speak of questions of identity. We have shifted from believing in identity as a single root to hoping for identity as a rhizome. We must have the courage to admit that identity conceived as a rhizome or as a form of relation is neither an absence of identity, a lack of identity, nor a weakness. It is a vertiginous inversion of the nature of identity. But there again, people are afraid of this.

Once I did a television program on Kanak television—they were inaugurating a university of communication in Nouméa. We were having an intense discussion, and a gentleman said to me suddenly: "I'd like to ask you a provocative question. Don't you think that the reason you have such ideas is because you have no identity?" He thought that the fact of spreading oneself out in the world would mean that one loses one's identity. For him, having an identity meant being rooted in one's soil. And this thought is very symptomatic of the fear of becoming stateless, of being like a multitude without a homeland, roaming the earth. But that's not what this is all about. My own place which is inexorable, *incontournable*, I relate it to all the places of the world, without exception, and it is by doing so that I leave behind single-root identity and begin to enter into the mode of rhizomic identity, that is to say, identity-as-relation.

Such a change in people's imaginary would allow us to tolerate better the fact that any place or location is a chaos-monde, because that idea does scare us. Conversely, to imagine the world as a chaos-monde allows us direct access to dimensions of thought that have not yet received due recognition, namely, errantry, nomadic thought, and the abandonment of linearity and causality. So long as we do not collectively resolve these issues, we will continue to fall back into our old aberrations and ancient forms of oppression.

ASH: Do you think that the media will keep pushing us to abandon old concepts of identity in order to find ones more suitable to our epoch?

EG: It is very difficult to change one's imaginary, and thus one's identity, when one is caught up in a system of thought which is continental in nature. Electronic technologies are first and foremost techniques of written communication. But the fact is that orality, which is also a technique, is quite comparable to what we see on the Internet. Both show wild forms of accumulation, the excessiveness of an unexpected and unstoppable flow. What are the signs of oral culture? It is exactly this sense of relation, of the unexpected, the excessive, and the cumulative. That is why I think that a poetics of relation is akin to electronic technologies. All the concepts of the poetics of relation are present in information technology. The Internet, like poetics, has no moral. The Internet is a risk and so is the poetics of relation. What I think is that the two can change our imagination and our relationship to the unforeseeable, something which is essential if we are to find a new identity, a rhizomic identity.

Note

This interview was first published as "L'Europe et les Antilles: Une interview d'Édouard Glissant," in *Mots Pluriels*, no 8. (October 1998), and has been translated and reprinted by permission of Andrea Schwieger Hiepko. It has also been published in German as "Europa und die Antillen: Vom Handicap, Gott im Zeitalter der Kreolisierung zu duzen; Interview mit dem martinikanischen Autor und Wissenschaftler Édouard Glissant," *Lettre International* (Berlin) 42, no. 3 (1998): 88–91.

B

❧

CREOLIZATION
Definition and Critique

Dominique Chancé
Translated from the French by Julin Everett

The term *creolization* has grown increasingly prominent in the fields of literary criticism and anthropology in the last few years, taking the place of terms such as *métissage, transculturation*, and *acculturation* in Francophone areas, but also in Hispanophone and Anglophone Caribbean studies in general. Numerous intellectuals have adopted the term, following the lead of the Martinican author Édouard Glissant, who, since the 1990s, has consistently vaunted the merits of creolization in his writings. Numerous works have been devoted to creolization, and the term has been used to describe both Caribbean sociocultural phenomena and the literary characteristics of authors such as Alejo Carpentier (Cuba), Wilson Harris (Guyana), and Edward Kamau Brathwaite (Jamaica).

But the fate of the word *creolization* can be explained only through paradox. Borrowed from the language of linguists who have defined scientifically the formation of specific creoles while progressively extending the term to the domain of cultural phenomena, *creolization* eventually detached itself from these linguistic approaches and came to designate broad sociocultural processes, without regard for the specificities brought to light by linguists.

Antillanité and Creolization

In the work of Édouard Glissant, the word *creolization* first appears in 1981, in *Le discours antillais* (Caribbean Discourse), but it is not yet one of the author's central concepts. This term occurs in the context of a definition of

Antillanité, as opposed to *Creolité* (creoleness), which was then linked primarily to the linguistic militancy Glissant denounces as confining:

> *Creolité* takes up what our language suffers from (a discriminating monolingualism), and it ignores Antillean histories, namely, what links us to Jamaicans and Puerto Ricans beyond the language barrier. (Glissant 1981/1989, 497; 263)

In contrast to this identity-based defense of a homogenized creole (unknown to Hispanophone islands), Édouard Glissant proposes a definition of *Antillanité* in which linguistic formations are but one of the many results of the colonial encounter that can be extrapolated to other cultural realities more suited for grounding Caribbean unity, namely,

> cultures derived from plantations; insular civilizations . . . ; social pyramids with an African or East Indian base and a European peak; languages of compromise; the general cultural phenomenon of creolization; patterns of encounter and synthesis. (Glissant 1981/1989, 422; 222)

From the outset, Glissant emphasizes a process that unifies rather than focusing on specific entities:

> If we speak of *cultures métissées*, or creolized cultures (like the Antillean one, for example), it is not to define a category in-itself that will by its very nature be opposed to other categories ("pure" cultures), but in order to assert that today an infinite number of approaches to *Relation* or creolization are available, on the levels both of thought and undertaking: in theory and in practice. (Glissant 1981/1989, 250; 140)

By becoming a universalizable human endeavor, creolization understood as the mode of realization of *la Relation* is, starting in the 1990s, a worldwide phenomenon of which the Caribbean is only a specific, exemplary case.

Creolization and Creoleness

To be sure, *Créolité*, or creoleness, evolved during that decade, moving from a purely linguistic definition to a multidimensional and cultural approach, so much so that creoleness can now be expressed in French: "*We did conquer it, this French language* . . . [and] in it we built our language," write the authors of *Éloge de la créolité* (In praise of Creoleness), even adding, as a form of paradox, that the "creole novelist" will have to turn into "the discoverer of the creoleness of Creole" (Bernabé, Chamoiseau, and Confiant 1989, 46; 1990, 900).

Nevertheless Édouard Glissant did not stop reaffirming the distinction between creoleness and creolization. For him, the authors of *In Praise of Creoleness* seem to have privileged the outcome at the expense of the process: "My friends Raphaël Confiant and Chamoiseau were in a bit too much of a hurry," Glissant declared in an interview. "Creoleness only works in the Caribbean. Creolization, on the other hand, is not an essence, but a universal process" (Anquetil 1992, 54). For his part, Patrick Chamoiseau believes that Glissant's position is nothing but "artifice":

> Creolization is the process. There is a process of creolization in the Caribbean which has brought about different outcomes on each island, and these outcomes are *creolenesses*, which themselves obey the movement of creolization. He accuses us of wanting to create a new identity-based essence. . . . I don't see how one could recreate an identity-based essence, like Negritude or such. (interview in Chancé 2000, 209)

What is at stake in this polemic is the need to avoid fixing identities as if they were essences, as entities in a series or sequence: Negritude, *Antillanité*, *Créolité*. Negritude was first experienced as a simplified métissage essentially turned toward African origins and traces; creoleness, as a diversity somewhat too constrained by a location and, in its related themes, a composite that would tend to reconstitute a singular identity. Creolization, by contrast, presents itself as a worldwide process of contacts, encounters, and relations that have neither a specific content nor specific modalities. To be sure, starting with *Poétique de la Relation* (Poetics of Relation), Glissant privileges not the concept of identitarian specificities but that of the living process, with its unforeseeable consequences:

> If we posit *métissage* as, generally speaking, the meeting and synthesis of two differences, creolization seems to be a limitless *métissage*, its elements diffracted and its consequences unforeseeable. Creolization diffracts, whereas certain forms of *métissage* can concentrate [essentialize] one more time. (Glissant 1990, 46; 1997a, 34 [trans.])

Creolization and Globalization

Édouard Glissant has given many definitions of creolization, insisting on the one hand on the contradictions that the term can generate, on the violence that cannot be eluded within this process, and on the other hand, privileging its planetary dimension:

> I call creolization the encounter, the interference, the shock, the harmonies and the disharmonies among cultures, in the achieved totality of the *monde-terre* [earth-world]. . . . My proposition is that today the entire world is becoming archipelized and creolized. (Glissant 1997b, 194)

Subsequently for him, the concept of creolization encompasses and exceeds the concepts of métissage or acculturation, and it responds to the phenomenon of globalization, which should be combated as a forced "mise en relation" or encounter, a mode of standardization and domination that produces "a standardized dilution." Conversely, "creolization is not a fusion, it requires that each component persist, even if it is already changing" (1997b, 210). Finally, the world of creolization is a "baroque" world where "all things change within a process of exchange." Here "the imaginary" is privileged as a mode of apprehension because

> creolization is unpredictable: one cannot calculate its consequences. That is the difference, in my opinion, between creolization and *métissage*, on the one hand, and creolization and transculture, on the other. It is possible to tackle transculturation as a concept, but creolization can only be grasped by the imaginary. (Glissant 1997b, 126)

Creolization and *Chaos-Monde*

By generalizing the term to avoid specifying its categories, Glissant makes *creolization* more open but also much vaguer. Those who use it are often unaware of the most basic scientific principles of linguistic theories, favoring instead a phantasmatic or mythic vision. "The general process of creolization," for René Depestre, appears to be a "mode of synergy and of eminently syncretic creativity" that has "produced a society and a civilization out of the aggregates of biological fuel that were thrown pell-mell from the slave ship into the closed system of the colonial plantation" (1994, 163). Glissant remains deliberately elliptical:

> Creolization is one of the modes of entanglement—and not merely a linguistic outcome. It is characterized by its processes and certainly not by the "contents" that influence its operations. This is where we depart from the concept of creoleness. (1990, 103; 1997, 89 [trans.])

An "imaginary" without a precise content, rather than a concept, is what would account for the most common and the most crucial of contemporary phenomena, without allowing for a more precise definition than that of a contact, an "entanglement," a combustion, or that *chaos-monde* that Glissant describes in his latest essays and novels, *Tout Monde, Traité du Tout-Monde,* and *Le Monde incréé.*

However, the fact is that linguists have articulated specific contents for the concept of creolization; above all, they have described the process in its different phases, according to a sociohistorical evolution that goes from the colonial habitation to the plantation. Struggling against ideological presuppositions, linguists have rejected quite a few myths. For example, the idea of contact or of a "language of compromise" is insufficient for understanding the development of creole languages. On this topic, Robert Chaudenson writes in *Des îles, des hommes, des langues* (Creolization of Language and Culture):

> The theory that views linguistic creolization as simply a "mix" of coexistent linguistic systems is not consistent with the most common linguistic reality. The constant outcome of the contact of two languages in the same community is much more the domination of one by the other than a harmonious mix! This is even more so in the colonial societies where creoles developed. (Chaudenson 1992/2001, 281; 305)

It is by means of an analysis that involves first the linguistic followed by a careful expansion to other cultural domains that one can begin to ask why Spanish has not produced a creole; to show that the least verbal arts and customs are those that are more largely composed of non-European elements, and to examine the interweavings of both linguistic practices and cultural realities. One could wonder about the meaning of the Glissantian expression "each component persists, even if it is already changing." At what cost and under what conditions does a particular "interference" happen between two religions, two musical systems, two storytelling traditions, or two cuisines? Doesn't a particular "mode of synergy and of eminently syncretic creativity," as evoked earlier by René Depestre, imply both some inertia and the destruction of certain components? Are we not justified in wondering why Édouard Glissant has a tendency to refer to the laws of quantum physics or to chaos theories rather than to linguistics to explain the realities of language and culture, which are intimately linked in any case?

It would be surprising if creolization, a phenomenon that is increasingly universal according to critics and sociologists, were to remain unexplained, and if the laws that regulate the interaction of its components were to continue to be mysterious. To be sure, linguists destroy certain fantasies that utopians take pleasure in cultivating. However, the technical description of the realities of creolization, from either the sociopolitical or the literary point of view, would make it a more effective concept or imaginary the effects of which are being felt in the Caribbean as well as in countries of the Old World whose creolized metropolises are in some cases the capitals of islands such as Puerto Rico, Haiti, or Martinique. If the whole world is on its way to creolization, then it is all the more useful to understand with precision the processes and the conditions that underwrite such a movement.

Note

This overview was first published as "Creólisation" in *Vocabulaire des études francophones: Les concepts de base*, ed. Michel Beniamino and Lise Gauvin (Paris: Pulim, 2005), 49–53.

REFERENCES

Abbate, Carolyn. 2001. *In Search of Opera*. Princeton: Princeton University Press.

Agamben, Giorgio. 1998. *Homo Sacer: Sovereign Power and Bare Life*. Stanford: Stanford University Press.

———. 2000. *Means without End: Notes on Politics*. Minneapolis: University of Minnesota Press.

Ahmad, Aijaz. 1992. "Jameson's Rhetoric of Otherness and the 'National Allegory.'" In *In Theory: Classes, Nations, Literatures*, 95–122. London: Verso.

Aly, Götz. 2003. *Rasse und Klasse: Nachforschungen zum deutschen Wesen*. Frankfurt am Main: S. Fischer.

al-Zuhili, Sheikh Wahbeh M. 2005. "Islam and International Law." *International Review of the Red Cross* 858: 269–83.

Amenda, Lars. 2006. *Fremde, Hafen, Stadt: Chinesische Migration und ihre Wahrnehmung in Hamburg, 1897–1972*. München: Dölling und Galitz.

Amin, Samir. 2003. *Obsolescent Capitalism: Contemporary Politics and Global Disorder*. Trans. Patrick Camiller. London: Zed.

Ampadu, Lena. 2004–5. "Racial, Gendered, and Geographical Spaces in Octavia Butler's *Kindred*." *CEA Magazine* 17:70–78.

Anghie, Antony. 2005. *Imperialism, Sovereignty, and the Making of International Law*. Cambridge: Cambridge University Press.

Angus Reid Global Monitor. 2006. "Islam Incompatible with Europe, Say Dutch." June 7.

Anquetil, Gilles. 1992. "L'Utopie créole de Patrick Chamoiseau." *Le Nouvel Observateur* 27:54–55.

Anzaldúa, Gloria. 1990. *Making Face, Making Soul/Haciendo Caras: Creative and Critical Perspectives by Feminists of Color*. San Francisco: Aunt Lute.

———. 1999. *Borderlands/La Frontera: The New Mestiza*. San Francisco: Aunt Lute.

Appiah, K. Anthony. 2005. *The Ethics of Identity*. Princeton: Princeton University Press.

Armel, Aliette. 2002. "Assia Djebar: La mémoire des femmes." *Magazine Littéraire* 410:98–103.

Arts, Hiske, and Anita Nabha. 2001. "Education in the Netherlands: Segregation in a 'Tolerant' Society." *Humanity in Action Research Report* (New York).

Asad, Talal. 2003. *Formations of the Secular: Christianity, Islam, Modernity*. Stanford: Stanford University Press.

Bacholle-Boskovic, Michèle. 2003. "*La femme sans sépulture* d'Assia Djebar ou une histoire pas enterrée." *Expressions Maghrébines* 2 (1): 79–90.

Badiou, Alain. 1999. *Manifesto for Philosophy*. Ed. and trans. Norman Madarasz. New York: State University of New York Press.

———. 2005. *Metapolitics*. London: Verso.

———. 2006. "Daily Humiliation." In *Polemics*, trans. Steve Corcoran, 111–14. London: Verso.

Balibar, Étienne. 2004. *We, the People of Europe? Reflections on Transnational Citizenship*. Princeton: Princeton University Press.

Balibar, Étienne, and Immanuel Wallerstein. 1992. *Race, Nation, Class: Ambiguous Identities*. London: Verso.

Barkat, Sidi Mohammed. 2005. *Le corps d'exception*. Paris: Editions Amsterdam.

Baudrillard, Jean. 2006. "The Pyres of Autumn." *New Left Review* 37:5–8.

Beauvoir, Simone de. 1960. *La force de l'âge*. Paris: Gallimard.

Beckles, Hilary, and Verene Shepherd, eds. 1991. *Caribbean Slave Society and Economy*. New York: New Press.

Benhabib, Seyla. 2004. *The Rights of Others: Aliens, Residents, and Citizens*. Cambridge: Cambridge University Press.

Benlahcene, Badrane. 2004. *A Metatheoretical Study of Malek Bennabi's Approach to Civilization*. Ph.D. thesis, School of Graduate Studies, Universiti Putra Malaysia.

Bennabi, Malik. 2003a. *The Question of Culture*. Trans. Abdul Wahid Lu'lu'a. Kuala Lumpur: International Institute of Islamic Thought. (Orig. pub. 1971.)

———. 2003b. *The Question of Ideas in the Muslim World*. Trans. Mohamed El-Tahir El Mesawi. Kuala Lumpur: International Institute of Islamic Thought. (Orig. pub. 1970.)

Berio, Luciano. 2006. *Remembering the Future*. Cambridge: Harvard University Press.

Bernabé, Jean, Patrick Chamoiseau, and Raphaël Confiant. 1989. *Éloge de la créolité*. Paris: Gallimard.

Berson, Misha. 1990. *Between Worlds: Contemporary Asian-American Plays*. New York: Theater Communications Group.

Best, Lloyd. 1967. "Independent Thought and Caribbean Freedom." *New World Quarterly* 3 (4): 3–19.

———. 1996. "Independence and Responsibility." In *The Critical Tradition of Caribbean Political Economy: The Legacy of George Beckford*, ed. Kari Levitt and Michael Witter. Kingston: Ian Randle.

Bhabha, Homi. 1994. *The Location of Culture*. London: Routledge.

Bhabha, Homi K., and John Comaroff. 2002. "Speaking of Postcoloniality in the Continuous Present: A Conversation." In *Relocating Postcolonialism*, ed. David Theo Goldberg and Ato Quayson, 15–46. Oxford: Blackwell.

Blaut, J. M. 1993. *The Colonizer's Model of the World: Geographical Diffusionism and Eurocentric History*. New York: Guilford Press.

Bockenforde, Ernst-Wolfgang. 1998. "The Concept of the Political: A Key to Understanding Carl Schmitt's Constitutional Theory." In *Law as Politics: Carl Schmitt's Critique of Liberalism*, ed. David Dyzenhaus. Durham: Duke University Press.

Bojadzije, Manuela, and Isabelle Saint-Saëns. 2006. "Borders, Citizenship, War, Class: A Discussion with Etienne Balibar and Sandro Mezzadra." In "Of Borders and Discos," special issue, *New Formations* 58:10–30.

Bourriaud, Nicolas. 1998. *Esthétique relationnelle*. Dijon: Les Presses du Réel.

———. 2002. *Relational Aesthetics*. Trans. Simon Pleasance and Fronza Woods with Mathieu Copeland. Dijon: Les Presses du Réel.

Boussalah, Zarha. 2005. "Malek Bennabi: An Analytical Study of His Theory of Civilization." Paper Presented at the AMSS 34th Annual Conference (http://i-epistemology.net/history/668-malek-bennabi-an-analytical-study-of-his-theory-of-civilization.html).

Bradley, Patricia. 1998. *Slavery, Propaganda and the American Revolution*. Jackson: University Press of Mississippi.

Braidotti, Rosi. 2009. *La philosophie . . . là où on ne l'attend pas*. Paris: Larousse.

Brantlinger, Patrick. 2003. *Dark Vanishings: Discourse on the Extinction of Primitive Races, 1800–1930*. Ithaca: Cornell University Press.

Brennan, Teresa. 2004. *The Transmission of Affect*. Ithaca: Cornell University Press.

Breuer, Josef, and Sigmund Freud. 1893. "On the Psychical Mechanism of Hysterical Phenomena: Preliminary Communication." In *The Standard Edition of the Complete Psychological Works of Sigmund Freud*, vol. II, 8–11.

———. 1940/1957. "Über den psychischen Mechanismus hysterischer Phänomene: Vorläufige Mitteilung (1893)." In *Studien über Hysterie*, vol. 1 of Sigmund Freud, *Gesammelte Werke*. Frankfurt am Main: Fischer Verlag, 1940. Trans. James Strachey and Anna Freud as "On the Psychical Mechanism of Hysterical Phenomena: Preliminary Communication," in *Studies in Hysteria*, vol. 2 of *The Standard Edition of the Complete Psychological Works of Sigmund Freud* (New York: Basic Books, 1957).

Brown, Michael K., et al. 2003. *Whitewashing Race: The Myth of a Color-Blind Society*. Berkeley: University of California Press.

Brown, Wendy. 2002. "Resisting Left Melancholia." In *Loss: The Politics of Mourning*, ed. David Eng and David Kazanjian, 458–65. Berkeley: University of California Press.

Bruckner, Pascal. 2007. "Enlightenment Fundamentalism or Racism of the Anti-Racists?" Perlentaucher.de.

Butler, Judith. 1991. "Imitation and Gender Insubordination." In *Inside/Out: Lesbian Theories, Gay Theories*, ed. Diana Fuss, 13–31. New York: Routledge.

——. 1997a. *Excitable Speech: A Politics of the Performative*. New York: Routledge.

——. 1997b. *The Psychic Life of Power: Theories in Subjection*. Stanford: Stanford University Press.

Butler, Octavia E. 1979/1988. *Kindred*. Boston: Beacon Press.

Byrd, Jodi. 2002. "Colonialism's Cacophony: Natives and Arrivants at the Limits of Postcolonial Theory." Ph.D. diss., University of Iowa.

Calle-Gruber, Mireille. 2005. "L'Ecrire nomade—ici ailleurs à une passante." In *Assia Djebar, nomade entre les murs . . . Pour une poétique transfrontalière*, ed. Mireille Calle-Gruber, 67–80. Paris: Maisonneuve et Larose.

Carens, Joseph. 1987. "Aliens and Citizens: The Case for Open Borders." *Review of Politics* 49 (2): 251–73.

Caruth, Cathy, ed. 1995. *Trauma: Explorations in Memory*. Baltimore: Johns Hopkins University Press.

——. 1996. *Unclaimed Experience*. Baltimore: Johns Hopkins University Press.

Castro-Gómez, Santiago. 2005. *La hybris del punto cero: Ciencia, raza e ilustración en la Nueva Granada (1750–1816)*. Bogotá: Editorial Pontificia Universidad Javeriana.

——. 2007. "The Missing Chapter of Empire: Postmodern Reorganization of Coloniality and Post-Fordist Capitalism." In "Globalization and the Decolonial Option," special issue, *Cultural Studies* 21 (2–3): 428–48.

Césaire, Aimé. 1955/1972. *Discourse on Colonialism*. Trans. Joan Pinkham. New York: Monthly Review Press.

Chakrabarty, Dipesh. 2000. *Provincializing Europe: Postcolonial Thought and Historical Difference*. Princeton: Princeton University Press.

Chancé, Dominique. 2000. *L'auteur en souffrance: Essai sur la position et la représentation de l'auteur dans le roman antillais contemporain, 1981–1992*. Paris: Presses Universitaires de France.

Chanda, Tirthankar. 2000. "The Cultural Creolization of the World: An Interview with Edouard Glissant." *France Diplomatie* 38 (http://www.diplomatie.gouv.fr/en/article_imprim.php3?id_article=6589).

Chandrasekhar, C. P., and Jayati Ghosh. 1998. "Hubris, Hysteria, Hope: The Political Economy of Crisis and Response in Southeast Asia." In *Tigers in Trouble: Financial Governance, Liberalisation, and Crises in East Asia*, ed. K. S. Jomo, 63–84. London: Zed.

Chang, Hsiao-hung. 1997. *Gender and Cross-Dressing* (in Chinese). Taipei: Hung-fan.

Chatterjee, Partha. 1986. *Nationalist Thought and the Colonial World: A Derivative Discourse*. Minneapolis: University of Minnesota Press.

Chaudenson, Robert. 1992/2001. *Des îles, des hommes, des langues: Essai sur la créolisation linguistique et culturelle*. Paris: L'Harmattan, 1992. Reprinted as *Creolization of Language and Culture*, ed. and trans. Salikoko S. Mufwene et al. London: Routledge.

Cheah, Pheng. 2003. *Spectral Nationality: Passages of Freedom from Kant to Postcolonial Literatures of Liberation*. New York: Columbia University Press.

———. 2007. "Biopower and the New International Division of Reproductive Labor." *boundary 2* 34 (1): 79–113.

Cheng, Anne Anlin. 2001. *The Melancholy of Race: Psychoanalysis, Assimilation, and Hidden Grief*. New York: Oxford University Press.

Chikhi, Beïda. 1997. *Littérature algérienne: Désir d'histoire et esthétique*. Paris: L'Harmattan.

Ching, Leo T. S. 2001. *Becoming "Japanese": Colonial Taiwan and the Politics of Identity Formation*. Berkeley: University of California Press.

Chossudovsky, Michel. 1998. "'Financial Warfare' Triggers Global Economic Crisis." In *And Our Rice Pots Are Empty: The Social Cost of the Economic Crisis*, 40–51. Penang, Malaysia: Consumers International.

Chow, Rey. 1992. "Postmodern Automatons." In *Feminists Theorize the Political*, ed. Judith Butler and Joan W. Scott, 101–17. New York: Routledge.

———. 2006. *The Age of the World Target: Self-Referentiality in War, Theory, and Comparative Work*. Durham: Duke University Press.

Christian, Barbara. 1990. "The Race for Theory." In *Making Face, Making Soul/Haciendo Caras: Creative and Critical Perspectives by Feminists of Color*, ed. Gloria Anzaldúa, 335–45. San Francisco: Aunt Lute.

Clark, VèVè A. 1990/1994. "Developing Diaspora Literacy: Allusion in Maryse Condé's *Heremakhonon*." In *Out of the Kumbla: Caribbean Women and Literature*, ed. Carole Boyce Davies and Elaine Savory Fido, 303–19. Trenton, N.J.: Africa World Press.

Crenshaw, Kimberlé W. 1989. "Demarginalizing the Intersection of Race and Sex: A Black Feminist Critique of Antidiscrimination Doctrine, Feminist Theory, and Antiracist Politics." In *Feminist Legal Theory: Readings in Law and Gender*, ed. Katharine Bartlett and Roseanne Kennedy, 57–80. Boulder: Westview Press.

Crossley, Robert. 1988. Introduction to *Kindred*, by Octavia Butler, ix–xxvii. Boston: Beacon Press.

Crul, Maurice, and Hans Vermeulen. 2003. "The Second Generation in Europe." *International Migration Review* 37 (4): 965–86.

Cvetkovich, Ann. 2003. *An Archive of Feelings: Trauma, Sexuality, and Lesbian Public Cultures*. Durham: Duke University Press.

Damrosch, David. 1995. "Literary Study in an Elliptical Age." In *Comparative Literature in the Age of Multiculturalism*, ed. Charles Bernheimer, 122–33. Baltimore: Johns Hopkins University Press.

Dash, J. Michael. 1998. *The Other America: Caribbean Literature in a New World Context*. Charlottesville: University Press of Virginia.

Davis, David B. 1966. *The Problem of Slavery in Western Culture*. New York: Oxford University Press.

Dayan, Joan. 1995. *Haiti, History, and the Gods*. Berkeley: University of California Press.

Deeney, John J. 1993. "Of Monkeys and Butterflies: Transformation in M. H. Kingston's *Tripmaster Monkey* and D. H. Hwang's *M. Butterfly*." *MELUS* 18 (4): 21–39.

Deleuze, Gilles. 1988. *Foucault*. Trans. Seán Hand. Minneapolis: University of Minnesota Press.

de Moor, Margriet. 2007. "Alarm Bells in Muslim Hearts." *Süddeutsche Zeitung*, April 17.

Depestre, René. 1994. "Les aventures de la créolité." In *Écrire la parole de nuit: La nouvelle littérature antillaise*, ed. Ralph Ludwig, 159–70. Paris: Gallimard.

Derrida, Jacques. 1998. "Faith and Knowledge: The Two Sources of 'Religion' at the Limits of Reason Alone." In *Religion*, ed. Jacques Derrida and Gianni Vattimo, 1–78. Stanford: Stanford University Press.

———. 2003. "Autoimmunity: Real and Symbolic Suicides." In *Philosophy in a Time of Terror: Dialogues with Jürgen Habermas and Jacques Derrida*, ed. Giovanna Borradori, 85–136. Chicago: University of Chicago Press.

———. 2005a. *The Politics of Friendship*. Trans. George Collins. London: Verso.

———. 2005b. *Rogues: Two Essays on Reason*. Trans. Pascale-Anne Brault and Michael Naas. Stanford: Stanford University Press.

Dirlik, Arif. 1997. *The Postcolonial Aura: Third World Criticism in the Age of Global Capitalism*. Boulder: Westview Press.

———. 2007. "Contemporary Challenges to Marxism: Postmodernism, Postcolonialism, Globalization." *Amerasia* 33 (3): 1–18.

Djebar, Assia, dir. 1978. *La nouba des femmes du Mont Chenoua*.

———. 1985. *L'amour, la fantasia*. Paris: J.-C. Lattès.

———. 1995. *Vaste est la prison*. Paris: Albin Michel.

———. 2002. *La femme sans sépulture*. Paris: Albin Michel.

Donadey, Anne. 2000a. "The Multilingual Strategies of Postcolonial Literature: Assia Djebar's Algerian Palimpsest." *World Literature Today* 74 (1): 27–36.

———. 2000b. "Portrait of a Maghrebian Feminist as a Young Girl: Fatima Mernissi's *Dreams of Trespass*." *Edebiyât: The Journal of Middle Eastern Literatures* 11 (1): 85–103.

———. 2001. *Recasting Postcolonialism: Women Writing between Worlds*. Portsmouth, N.H.: Heinemann.

———. 2007. "Overlapping and Interlocking Frames for Humanities Literary Studies: Assia Djebar, Tsitsi Dangarembga, Gloria Anzaldúa." *College Literature* 34 (4): 22–42.

———. 2008. "African American and Francophone Postcolonial Memory: Octavia Butler's *Kindred* and Assia Djebar's *La femme sans sépulture*." *Research in African Literatures* 39 (3): 65–81.

Dong, Harvey. 2001. "Transforming Student Elites into Community Activists: A Legacy of Asian American Activism." In *Asian Americans: The Movement and the Moment*, ed. Steve Louie and Glenn Omatsu, 187–205. Los Angeles: UCLA Asian American Studies Center Press.

Dosse, François. 1998. *History of Structuralism*. Vol. 1, *The Rising Sign, 1945–1966*. Trans. Deborah Glassman. Minneapolis: University of Minnesota Press.

Du Bois, W. E. B. 1903/1995. *The Souls of Black Folk*. New York: Signet Classic.

————. 1935/1962. *Black Reconstruction in America, 1860–1880*. Cleveland: World Publishing.

DuCille, Ann. 1994. "Postcolonialism and Afrocentricity: Discourse and Dat Course." In *The Black Columbiad: Defining Moments in African American Literature and Culture*, ed. Werner Sollors and Maria Diedrich, 28–41. Cambridge: Harvard University Press.

Dussel, Enrique. 1993. "Eurocentrism and Modernity (Introduction to the Frankfurt Lectures)." *boundary 2* 20 (3): 65–76.

————. 2002. "World System and 'Transmodernity.'" *Nepantla: Views from South* 3 (2): 221–44.

Dyzenhaus, David, ed. 1998. *Law as Politics: Carl Schmitt's Critique of Liberalism*. Durham: Duke University Press.

Eagleton, Terry. 2003. *After Theory*. New York: Basic Books.

Edwards, Brent Hayes. 2003. *The Practice of Diaspora: Literature, Translation, and the Rise of Black Internationalism*. Cambridge: Harvard University Press.

Edwin, Steve, and Kelly Oliver. 2002. "Psychic and Social Engagements." In *Between the Psyche and the Social*, ed. Oliver and Edwin, vii–xiii. Lanham, Md.: Rowman and Littlefield.

Ellen, Roy, and Holly Harris. 2000. Introduction to *Indigenous Environmental Knowledge and Its Transformations: Critical Anthropological Perspectives*, ed. Roy Ellen, Peter Parks, and Alan Baker, 1–33. Amsterdam: Harwood Academic.

El-Tayeb, Fatima. 2006. "Urban Diasporas: Race, Identity, and Popular Culture in a Post-ethnic Europe." In *Motion in Place / Place in Motion: 21st Century Migration*, JCAS Symposium Series 22, Population Movement in the Modern World 10.

Eng, David L. 1994. "In the Shadows of a Diva: Committing Homosexuality in David Henry Hwang's *M. Butterfly*." *Amerasia Journal* 20 (1): 93–116.

Eng, David, and David Kazanjian, eds. 2002. *Loss: The Politics of Mourning*. Berkeley: University of California Press.

Enwezor, Okwui, et al., eds. 2003. *Créolité and Creolization*. Ostfildern-Ruit: Hatje Cabtze.

Eriksen, Thomas Hylland. 1999. "*Tu dimunn pu vini kreol*: The Mauritian Creole and the Concept of Creolization." Lecture, Oxford University, December 1999. Working paper from the programme in Transnational Connections, WPTC-99-13 (http://www.potomitan.info/ki_nov/moris/creolization.html).

Erikson, Kai. 1994. *A New Species of Trouble: The Human Experience of Modern Disasters*. New York: W. W. Norton.

Essed, Philomena. 1991. *Understanding Everyday Racism: An Interdisciplinary Theory*. London: Sage.

European Commission Directorate-General for Employment and Social Affairs. 2004.

The Situation of Roma in an Enlarged European Union. Luxembourg: Office for Official Publications of the European Communities.

European Roma Rights Center. 2007. *The Glass Box: Exclusion of Roma from Employment*. Budapest.

Fanon, Frantz. 1952/1967. *Peau noire, masques blancs*. Paris: Seuil. *Black Skin, White Masks*. Trans. Charles Lam Markham. New York: Grove.

———. 1959/1968. "L'Algérie se dévoile." In *Sociologie d'une révolution: L'An V de la révolution algérienne*, 16–50. Paris: Maspéro. "Algeria Unveiled." In *A Dying Colonialism*. Trans. Haakon Chevalier. New York: Grove.

———. 1961/1963. *Les damnés de la Terre*. Paris: Maspéro. *The Wretched of the Earth*. Trans. Constance Farrington, New York: Grove.

———. 2004. *The Wretched of the Earth*. Trans. Richard Philcox. New York: Grove.

———. 2008. *Black Skin, White Masks*. Trans. Richard Philcox. New York: Grove.

Ferguson, Roderick A. 2004. *Aberrations in Black: Toward a Queer of Color Critique*. Minneapolis: University of Minnesota Press.

Fischer, Sibylle. 2004. *Modernity Disavowed: Haiti and the Cultures of Slavery in the Age of Revolution*. Durham: Duke University Press.

Fisher, Dominique. 2003. "L'Anamnèse, histoire ou littérature en état d'urgence." *Expressions Maghrébines* 2 (1): 113–23.

Foster, Guy Mark. 2007. "'Do I Look like Someone You Can Come Home to from Where You May Be Going?': Re-mapping Interracial Anxiety in Octavia Butler's *Kindred*." *African American Review* 41 (1): 143–64.

Foucault, Michel. 1977. *Language, Counter-memory, Practice: Selected Essays and Interviews*. Trans. Donald F. Bouchard and Sherry Simon. Ithaca: Cornell University Press.

———. 1980. *Power/Knowledge: Selected Interviews and Other Writings, 1972–1977*. Ed. Colin Gordon. Trans. Colin Gordon, Leo Marshall, and John Mepham. Brighton: Harvester Wheatsheaf.

———. 1995. *Discipline and Punish*. Trans. Alan Sheridan. New York: Vintage.

———. 1997. "Security, Territory, Population." In *Ethics, Subjectivity, and Truth: Essential Works of Foucault, 1954–1984*, vol. 1, ed. Paul Rabinow, trans. Robert Hurley et al. New York: New Press.

Freire, Paulo. 1967/2008. *Pedagogy of the Oppressed*. New York: Continuum.

Freud, Sigmund. 1917. "Mourning and Melancholia." In *The Standard Edition of the Complete Psychological Works of Sigmund Freud*, vol. XXIV, 239–60. London: Hogarth.

———. 1923. "The Ego and the Id." In *The Standard Edition of the Complete Psychological Works of Sigmund Freud*, vol. XIX, 3–66. London: Hogarth.

———. 1940. *Jenseits des Lustprinzips. Gesammelte Werke*, Band XIII. Frankfurt am Main: Fischer. Reprinted as *Beyond the Pleasure Principle*, in *On Metapsychology: The Theory of Psychoanalysis*, vol. 11 of *The Pelican Freud Library*, trans. James Strachey (Harmondsworth: Penguin, 1984).

———. 1943. *Über Psychoanalyse: Fünf Vorlesungen* (1909). *Gesammelte Werke*,

Band VIII. Frankfurt am Main: Fischer. Reprinted as *Five Lectures on Psycho-Analysis*, in *The Standard Edition of the Complete Psychological Works of Sigmund Freud*, vol. IX, trans. James Strachey and Anna Freud (London: Hogarth, 1957).

———. 1955. "Extracts from Freud's Footnotes to His Translation of Charcot's *Tuesday Lectures*." In *The Standard Edition of the Complete Psychological Works of Sigmund Freud*, vol. I, *Pre-psychoanalytic Publications and Unpublished Drafts (1886–1899)*, trans. James Strachey and Anna Freud. London: Hogarth.

———. 1940/1957a. "Frau Emmy von N." In *Studien über Hysterie. Gesammelte Werke*, Band I. Reprinted as "Case 2. Frau Emmy von N," in *The Standard Edition of the Complete Psychological Works of Sigmund Freud*, vol. II, *Studies in Hysteria*, trans. James Strachey and Anna Freud (London: Hogarth).

———. 1940/1957b. "Miß Lucy R." *Studien über Hysterie. Gesammelte Werke*, Band I. Reprinted as "Case 3. Miss Lucy R.," in *The Standard Edition of the Complete Psychological Works of Sigmund Freud*, vol. II, *Studies in Hysteria*, trans. James Strachey and Anna Freud (London: Hogarth).

Fukuzawa, Yukichi. 1997. "On Leaving Asia." In *Japan: A Documentary History*, ed. David Lu. Armonk, N.Y.: M. E. Sharpe.

Gallagher, Mary. 2002. *Soundings in French Caribbean Writing since 1950: The Shock of Space and Time*. Oxford: Oxford University Press.

Galli, Carlo. 2001. *Spazi politic: L'età moderna e l'età globale*. Bologne: Il Mulino.

Garraway, Doris Lorraine. 2005. *The Libertine Colony: Creolization in the Early French Caribbean*. Durham: Duke University Press.

Gates, Henry Louis, Jr., ed. 1984. *Black Literature and Literary Theory*. New York: Methuen.

———. 1986. "Editor's Introduction: Writing 'Race' and the Difference It Makes." In *"Race," Writing, and Difference*, ed. Henry Louis Gates Jr. and K. Anthony Appiah, 1–20. Chicago: University of Chicago Press.

———. 1988. *The Signifying Monkey: A Theory of African-American Literary Criticism*. New York: Oxford University Press.

Geggus, David, ed. 2001. *The Impact of the Haitian Revolution in the Atlantic World*. Columbia: University of South Carolina Press.

Gikandi, Simon. 2004. "Poststructuralism and Postcolonial Discourse." In *The Cambridge Companion to Postcolonial Literary Studies*, ed. Neil Lazarus, 97–119. Cambridge: Cambridge University Press.

Gill, Ranjit. 1997. *Black September: Nationalistic Ego, Indifference, and Greed Throw Southeast Asia's Equity and Financial Markets into Turmoil*. Singapore: Epic Management Services.

———. 1998. *Asia under Siege: How the Asian Miracle Went Wrong*. Singapore: Epic Management Services.

Gilroy, Paul. 1993. *The Black Atlantic: Modernity and Double Consciousness*. Cambridge: Harvard University Press.

———. 2000. *Against Race: Imagining Political Culture beyond the Color Line*. Cambridge: Harvard University Press.

Glissant, Édouard. 1981/1989. *Le discours antillais*. Paris: Editions du Seuil, 1981. *Caribbean Discourse*. Reprinted as *Caribbean Discourse: Selected Essays*, trans. J. Michael Dash (Charlottesville: University Press of Virginia, 1989).

———. 1989. *Caribbean Discourse: Selected Essays*. Trans. J. Michael Dash. Charlottesville: University Press of Virginia.

———. 1990. *Poétique de la relation*. Paris: Gallimard.

———. 1995. "L'imaginaire des langues." In *Introduction à une poétique du divers*. Montreal: Presses de l'Université de Montréal.

———. 1996. *Introduction à une poétique du divers*. Paris: Gallimard.

———. 1997a. *Poetics of Relation*. Trans. Betsey Wing. Ann Arbor: University of Michigan Press.

———. 1997b. *Traité du Tout-Monde, Poétique IV*. Paris: Gallimard.

———. 1998. "L'Europe et les Antilles." Interview with Andrea S. Hiepko. *Mots pluriels*, 8 October (http://www.arts.uwa.edu.au/MotsPluriels/MP898ash.html).

Goldberg, David Theo. 2002. *The Racial State*. Malden, Mass.: Blackwell.

———. 2006. "Racial Europeanization." *Ethnic and Racial Studies* 29 (2): 331–64.

Gopinath, Gayatri. 2005. *Impossible Desires: Queer Diasporas and South Asian Public Cultures*. Durham: Duke University Press.

Gordon, Lewis. 2000. *Existentia Africana: Understanding Africana Existential Thought*. London: Routledge.

Govan, Sandra Y. 1986. "Homage to Tradition: Octavia Butler Renovates the Historical Novel." *MELUS* 13 (2): 79–96.

Grande, Sandy. 2004. *Red Pedagogy: Native American Social and Political Thought*. Lanham, Md.: Rowman and Littlefield.

Grovogui, Siba N'Zatioula. 1996. *Sovereigns, Quasi Sovereigns and Africans: Race and Self Determination in International Law*. Minneapolis: Minnesota University Press.

Gruesser, John Cullen. 2005. *Confluences: Postcolonialism, African American Literary Studies, and the Black Atlantic*. Athens: University of Georgia Press.

Ha, Kien Nghi. 2004. *Ethinizitaet und Migration Reloaded: Kulturelle Identitaet, Differenz und Hybriditaet im postkolonialen Diskurs*. Berlin: Wissenschaftlicher Verlag.

Ha, Marie-Paule. 2009. "Double Trouble: Doing Gender in Hong Kong." *Signs: Journal of Women in Culture and Society* 34 (2): 423–49.

Habermas, Jürgen. 1998. *The Inclusion of the Other: Studies in Political Theory*. Ed. Ciaran Cronin and Pablo De Greiff. Cambridge: MIT Press.

Habermas, Jürgen, and Jacques Derrida. 2003. "Unsere Erneuerung: Nach dem Krieg: Europas Wiedergeburt." *Frankfurter Allgemeine Zeitung*, May 31.

Haegler, Max. 2007. "Mit Internetspielen gegen Auslaender." *Die Tageszeitung*. September 17.

Hall, Stuart. 1991. "Europe's Other Self." *Marxism Today*, August, 18.

———. 2003a. "Créolité and the Power of Creolization." In *Créolité and Creolization*, ed. Okwui Enwezor et al., 27–41. Ostfildern-Ruit: Hatje Cabtze.

———. 2003b. "Creolization, Diaspora, and Hybridity in the Context of Globalization." In *Créolité and Creolization*, ed. Okwui Enwezor et al., 185–98. Ostfildern-Ruit: Hatje Cabtze.

Hanchard, Michael. 2006. *Party/Politics: Horizons in Black Political Thought*. Oxford: Oxford University Press.

Hansen, Mogens Herman. 1991. *The Athenian Democracy in the Age of Demosthenes: Structure, Principles, and Ideology*. Oxford: Blackwell.

Harding, Sandra. 1998. *Is Science Multicultural? Postcolonialisms, Feminisms, and Epistemologies*. Bloomington: Indiana University Press.

Hardt, Michael, and Antonio Negri. 2000. *Empire*. Cambridge: Harvard University Press.

Haring, Lee. 2003. "Techniques of Creolization." *Journal of American Folklore* 116 (459): 19–35.

———. 2004. "Cultural Creolization." *Acta Ethnographica Hungarica* 49 (1–2): 1–38.

———. 2005. "Eastward to the Islands: The Other Diaspora." *Journal of American Folklore* 118 (469): 290–307.

Harvey, David. 2005. *A Brief History of Neoliberalism*. Oxford: Oxford University Press.

Hass, Amira. 2000. *Drinking the Sea at Gaza: Days and Nights in a Land under Siege*. New York: Metropolitan Books.

Hegel, Georg Wilhelm Friedrich. 1975. *Lectures on the Philosophy of World History, Introduction*. Trans. H. B. Nisbet. Cambridge: Cambridge University Press.

Heidegger, Martin. 1971. "The Origin of the Work of Art." In *Poetry, Language, Thought*, trans. Albert Hofstadter, 15–86. New York: Harper and Row.

———. 1982. "A Dialogue on Language between a Japanese and an Inquirer." In *On the Way to Language*, trans. Peter D. Hertz, 1–56. New York: Harper One.

Henderson, Jeffrey. 1993. "Against the Economic Orthodoxy: On the Making of the East Asian Miracle." *Economy and Society* 22 (2): 200–217.

———. 1999. "Uneven Crises: Institutional Foundations of East Asian Economic Turmoil." *Economy and Society* 28 (3): 327–68.

Henderson, Mae G. 1996. "'Where, by the Way, Is This Train Going?' A Case for (Black) Cultural Studies." *Callaloo* 19 (1): 60–67.

Hesse, Barnor. 2007. "Racialized Modernity: An Analytics of White Mythologies." *Ethnic and Racial Studies* 30 (4): 643–63.

———. Forthcoming. *Creolizing the Political: A Genealogy of the African Diaspora*. Durham: Duke University Press.

Hesse, Barnor, and S. Sayyid. 2006. "Narrating the Postcolonial Political and the Immigrant Imaginary." In *A Postcolonial People: South Asians in Britain*, ed. N. Ali, V. S. Kalra, and S. Sayyid. London: Hurst.

Hirschkind, Charles. 2006. *The Ethical Soundscape: Cassette Sermons and Islamic Counterpublics*. New York: Columbia University Press.

Ho, Fred, and Bill V. Mullen, eds. 2008. *Afro Asia: Revolutionary Political and Cultural Connections between African Americans and Asian Americans*. Durham: Duke University Press.

Holland, Sharon P. 2000. "The Revolution, 'In Theory.'" *American Literary History* 12 (1–2): 327–36.

Homans, Peter. 2000. *Symbolic Loss: The Ambiguity of Mourning and Memory at Century's End*. Charlottesville: University of Virginia Press.

Honig, Bonnie. 1993. *Political Theory and the Displacement of Politics*. Ithaca: Cornell University Press.

Horváth, Miléna. 2004. "La médiation par l'écriture: Entre-deux et interculturalité chez Assia Djebar." *Dalhousie French Studies* 68:37–44.

Hoving, Isabel. 2005. "Circumventing Openness: Creating New Senses of Dutchness." *Transit* 1:1–9.

Hunt, Alfred N. 1988. *Haiti's Influence on Antebellum America: Slumbering Volcano in the Caribbean*. Baton Rouge: Louisiana State University Press.

Huntington, Samuel. 1996. *The Clash of Civilizations and the Remaking of the World Order*. New York: Simon and Schuster.

Hutcheon, Linda. 1988. *A Poetics of Postmodernism: History, Theory, Fiction*. New York: Routledge.

Hwang, David Henry. 1986. *M. Butterfly*. New York: Penguin.

———. 1989–1990. "Evolving a Multicutural Tradition." MELUS 16:16–19.

———. 1990. *FOB and Other Plays*. New York: Penguin.

———. 1992. *The Voyage*. New York: Metropolitan Opera House.

———. 2003. *Flower Drum Song*. New York: Theatre Communications Group.

Ivanov, Andrey, et al. 2006. *At Risk: Roma and the Displaced in Southeast Europe*. Bratislava: United Nations Development Programme, Regional Bureau for Europe and the Commonwealth of Independent States.

James, C. L. R. 1938. *A History of Negro Revolt*. New York: Haskell House.

———. 1980a. *The Black Jacobins: Toussaint L'Ouverture and the San Domingo Revolution*. London: Allison and Busby.

———. 1980b. *Spheres of Existence: Selected Writings*. London: Allison and Busby.

Jameson, Fredric. 1986. "Third-World Literature in the Era of Multinational Capital." *Social Text* 15:65–88.

———. 1988. "Periodizing the 60s." In *The Ideologies of Theory: Essays, 1971–1986*, vol. 2, *The Syntax of History*, 178–208. Minneapolis: University of Minnesota Press.

———. 1990. "Modernism and Imperialism." In *Nationalism, Colonialism, and Literature*, ed. Fredric Jameson, Edward Said, and Terry Eagleton, 43–66. Minneapolis: University of Minnesota Press.

Johnson, E. Patrick, and May G. Henderson, eds. 2005. *Black Queer Studies: A Critical Anthology*. Durham: Duke University Press.

Jomo, K. S. 1998. "Introduction: Financial Governance, Liberalisation, and Crises in East Asia." In *Tigers in Trouble: Financial Governance, Liberalisation, and Crises in East Asia*, ed. K. S. Jomo, 1–32. London: Zed.

Kagan, Robert. "Power and Weakness. 2002. Why the United States and Europe See the World Differently." *Policy Review* 113 (June/July) (http://www.hoover. org/ publications/policyreview/3460246.html).

Kassir, Samir. 2006/2004. *Being Arab.* Trans. Will Hobson, with an introduction by Robert Fisk. London: Verso. [*Considerations sur le malheur arabe.* Paris: Actes Sud Sindbad]

Keaton, Trica. 2006. *Muslim Girls and the Other France: Race, Identity Politics, and Social Exclusion.* Bloomington: Indiana University Press.

Keenan, Alan. 2003. *Democracy in Question: Democratic Openness in a Time of Political Closure.* Stanford: Stanford University Press.

Kehde, Suzanne. 1994. "Engendering the Imperial Subject: The (De)construction of (Western) Masculinity in David Henry Hwang's *M. Butterfly* and Graham Greene's *The Quiet American.*" In *Fictions of Masculinity: Crossing Cultures, Crossing Sexualities*, ed. Peter F. Murphy, 241–54. New York: New York University Press.

Kerr, Douglas. 1991. "David Henry Hwang and the Revenge of Madame Butterfly." In *The Asian Voices in English*, ed. Mimi Chan and Roy Harris, 119–30. Hong Kong: Hong Kong University Press.

Khatibi, Abdelkebir. 1983. *Maghreb pluriel.* Paris: Denoël.

Kimmelman, Michael. 2009. "In France, a War of Memories over Memories of War." *New York Times*, March 5.

King, C. Richard, ed. 2000. *Postcolonial America.* Urbana: University of Illinois Press.

King, Deborah K. 1988. "Multiple Jeopardy, Multiple Consciousness: The Context of a Black Feminist Ideology." In *Feminist Theory in Practice and Process*, ed. Micheline R. Malson, Jean F. O'Barr, Sarah Westphal-Wihl, and Mary Wyer, 75–105. Chicago: University of Chicago Press.

Klausen, Jytte. 2006. "Rotten Judgment in the State of Denmark." Salon.com, February 8.

Koh, Adeline, and Frieda Ekotto. 2007. "Frantz Fanon in Malaysia: Reconfiguring the Ideological Landscape of *Negritude* in *Sepet.*" In *Land and Landscape in Francographic Literature: Remapping Uncertain Territories*, ed. Magali Compan and Katarzyna Pieprzak, 121–41. Newcastle, UK: Cambridge Scholars.

Kostelanetz, Richard, ed. 1997. *Writings on Glass: Essays, Interviews, Criticism.* New York: Schirmer.

Kristeva, Julia. 2008. "French Theory." In *World Writing: Poetics, Ethics, Globalization*, ed. Mary Gallagher, 122–37. Toronto: University of Toronto Press.

Kubitschek, Missy Dehn. 1991. *Claiming the Heritage: African-American Women Novelists and History.* Jackson: University Press of Mississippi.

Kusch, Rodolfo. 2000. *Obras Completas.* Rosario, Argentina: Editorial Fundación Ross.

Kymlicka, Will. 1991. *Liberalism, Community, and Culture.* Oxford: Oxford University Press.

Lacan, Jacques. 1977. "Aggressivity in Psychoanalysis." In *Écrits: A Selection*, trans. Alan Sheridan, 8–29. London: Tavistock.

———. 1992. *The Seminar of Jacques Lacan. Book VII. The Ethics of Psychoanalysis, 1959-60.* Trans. Dennis Porter. London: Routledge.

LaCapra, Dominick. 1999. "Trauma, Absence, Loss." *Critical Inquiry* 25 (4): 696–727.

Laclau, Ernesto. 1979. *Politics and Ideology in Marxist Theory,* London: Verso Books.

———. 1990. *New Reflections on the Revolution of Our Time.* New York: Verso.

———. 2005. *On Populist Reason.* New York: Verso.

Lacoue-Labarthe, Philippe, and Jean-Luc Nancy. 1997. *Retreating the Political.* London: Routledge.

Lamming, George. 1992. "The Occasion for Speaking." In *The Pleasures of Exile,* 23–50. Ann Arbor: University of Michigan Press. (Orig. pub. 1960.)

Lang, George. 2000. *Entwisted Tongues: Comparative Creole Literatures.* Amsterdam: Ro dopi.

Langfur, Hal. 2006. "Could This Be Heaven or Could This Be Hell? Reconsidering the Myth of Racial Democracy in Brazil." *Ethnohistory* 53 (3): 603–13.

Lawrence, Philip. 1997. *Modernity and War: The Creed of Absolute Violence.* New York: St. Martin's Press.

Lefort, Claude. 1988. *Democracy and Political Theory.* Cambridge: Polity in association with Basil Blackwell.

LeSueur, James D. 2001. *Uncivil War: Intellectuals and Identity Politics during the Decolonization of Algeria.* Philadelphia: University of Pennsylvania Press.

Levecq, Christine. 2000. "Power and Repetition: Philosophies of (Literary) History in Octavia E. Butler's *Kindred.*" *Contemporary Literature* 41 (3): 525–53.

Lewis, David H. 2006. *Flower Drum Songs: The Story of Two Musicals.* Jefferson, N.C.: McFarland.

Lindqvist, Sven. 1997. *Exterminate All the Brutes.* London: Granta.

Lionnet, Françoise. 1989. *Autobiographical Voices: Race, Gender, Self-Portraiture.* Ithaca: Cornell University Press.

———. 1993. "*Créolité* in the Indian Ocean: Two Models of Cultural Diversity." *Yale French Studies* 82:101–12.

———. 1995. "Spaces of Comparison." In *Comparative Literature in the Age of Multiculturalism,* ed. Charles Bernheimer, 165–74. Baltimore: John Hopkins University Press.

———. 1998a. "Performative Universalism and Cultural Diversity: French Thought and American Contexts." In *Terror and Consensus: Vicissitudes of French Thought,* ed. Jean-Joseph Goux and Philip R. Wood, 119–32. Stanford: Stanford University Press.

———. 1998b. "Questions de méthode: Itinéraires ourlés de l'autoportrait et de la critique." In *Postcolonialisme et autobiographie: Albert Memmi, Assia Djebar, Daniel Maximin,* ed. Alfred Hornung and Ernstpeter Ruhe, 5–20. Amsterdam: Rodopi.

———. 2006. "Cultivating Mere Gardens? Comparative Francophonies, Postcolonial Studies, and Transnational Feminisms." In *Comparative Literature in an Age of Globalization,* ed. Haun Saussy, 100–113. Baltimore: Johns Hopkins University Press.

————. 2008. "Continents and Archipelagoes: From *E Pluribus Unum* to Creole Solidarities." *PMLA* 123 (5): 1503–15.

————. 2009. "Matière à photographie: cosmopolitique et modernité créoles à l'Ile Maurice." *French Forum* 34 (3): 75–99.

————. Forthcoming. "Counterpoint and Double Critique in Edward Said and Abdelkebir Khatibi: A Transcolonial Comparison." In *A Companion to Comparative Literature*, ed. Ali Behdad and Dominic Thomas. Oxford: Blackwell.

Lionnet, Françoise, and Ronnie Scharfman, eds. 1993. *Post/Colonial Conditions: Exiles, Migrations, and Nomadisms*. New Haven: Yale University Press.

Lionnet, Françoise, and Shu-mei Shih, eds. 2005. *Minor Transnationalism*. Durham: Duke University Press.

Lionnet Françoise, and Thomas C. Spear, eds. Forthcoming. "Mauritius in/and Global Culture: Politics, Literature, Visual Arts." *International Journal of Francophone Studies*.

Long, Lisa A. 2002. "A Relative Pain: The Rape of History in Octavia Butler's *Kindred* and Phyllis Alesia Perry's *Stigmata*." *College English* 64 (4): 459–83.

Lowe, Lisa. 1996. *Immigrant Acts: On Asian American Cultural Politics*. Durham: Duke University Press.

————. 2005. "The Intimacies of Four Continents." In *Haunted by Empire: Geographies of Intimacy in North American History*, ed. Ann Laura Stoler. Durham: Duke University Press.

Lubiano, Wahneema. 1991. "Shuckin' Off the African-American Native Other: What's 'Po-Mo' Got to Do with It?" *Cultural Critique* 11:149–87.

————. 1996. "Mapping the Interstices between Afro-American Cultural Discourse and Cultural Studies: A Prolegomenon." *Callaloo* 19 (1): 68–77.

Lucassen, Leo. 2005. *The Immigrant Threat: The Integration of Old and New Migrants in Western Europe since 1850*. Urbana: University of Illinois Press.

Lyotard, Jean-François, and Jean-Loup Thébaud. 1985. *Just Gaming*. Trans. Wlad Godzich. Minneapolis: University of Minnesota Press.

Macey, David. 1999. "The Recall of the Real: Fanon and Psychoanalysis." *Constellations* 6 (1): 97–107.

————. 2002. *Frantz Fanon: A Biography*. New York: Picador.

MacLeod, Christine. 1997. "Black American Literature and the Postcolonial Debate." Special issue, *Yearbook of English Studies* 27:51–65.

Mahbubani, Kishore. 2008. *The New Asian Hemisphere: The Irresistible Shift of Global Power to the East*. New York: Public Affairs.

Maida, Patricia. 1991. "*Kindred* and *Dessa Rose*: Two Novels That Reinvent Slavery." *CEA Magazine* 4 (1): 43–52.

Maldonado-Torres, Nelson. 2007. "On the Coloniality of Being: Contributions to the Development of a Concept." *Cultural Studies* 21 (2–3): 240–71.

Manalansan, Martin F., IV. 2003. *Global Divas: Filipino Gay Men in the Diaspora*. Durham: Duke University Press.

Mann, Michael. 2005. *The Dark Side of Democracy: Explaining Ethnic Cleansing*. Cambridge: Cambridge University Press.

Marsaud, Olivia. 2007. "*Viva Laldjérie!* Nadir Moknèche film l'Algérie de l'après-terrorisme." *Afik-com*, April 9.

Marx, Karl, and Friedrich Engels. 1932/1970. *Die Deutsche Ideologie. Marx/Engels Gesamtausgabe*, vol. 1:5, ed. V. Adoratskij. Berlin: Marx-Engels Verlag, 1932. Reprinted as *The German Ideology: Part One, with Selections from Parts Two and Three*, trans. C. J. Arthur (New York: International Publishers, 1970).

Mbembe, Achille. 2001. *On the Postcolony*. Berkeley: University of California Press.

McClintock, Anne. 1995. *Imperial Leather: Race, Gender, and Sexuality in the Colonial Conquest*. New York: Routledge.

McCormick, John. 1999. *Carl Schmitt's Critique of Liberalism: Against Politics as Technology*. Cambridge: Cambridge University Press.

McCumber, John. 2009. "Philosophy vs. Theory: Reshaping the Debate." *Mondes Francophones*, August (http://mondesfrancophones.com).

Mehta, Uday Singh. 1999. *Liberalism and Empire: A Study in Nineteenth-Century British Liberal Thought*. Chicago: University of Chicago Press.

Meiling Jin. 1987. "Strangers in a Hostile Landscape." In *Watchers and Seekers: Creative Writing by Black Women in Britain*, ed. Rhonda Cobham and Merle Collins. London: The Women's Press.

Melas, Natalie. 2007. *All the Difference in the World: Postcoloniality and the Ends of Comparison*. Stanford: Stanford University Press.

Mernissi, Fatima. 1994. *Dreams of Trespass: Tales of a Harem Girlhood*. Reading, Mass.: Addison-Wesley.

Mezzadra, Sandro. 2001/2004. *Diritto di fuga: Migrazioni, cittadinanza, globalizzazione*. Verona: Ombre Corte. "The Right to Escape." *Ephemera* 4(3): 267–75.

Mignolo, Walter. 2000a. "Dussel's Philosophy of Liberation: Ethics and the Geopolitics of Knowledge." In *Thinking from the Underside of History: Enrique Dussel's Philosophy of Liberation*, ed. Linda Alcoff and Eduardo Mendieta, 27–51. Boulder: Rowman and Littlefield.

———. 2000b. *Local Histories/Global Designs: Coloniality, Subaltern Knowledges, and Border Thinking*. Princeton: Princeton University Press.

———. 2002. "The Geopolitics of Knowledge and the Colonial Difference." *South Atlantic Quarterly* 101 (1): 57–96.

———. 2007. "Delinking: The Rhetoric of Modernity, the Logic of Coloniality, and the Grammar of Decoloniality." *Cultural Studies* 21 (2–3): 449–514.

Mills, Charles. 1997. *The Racial Contract*. Ithaca: Cornell University Press.

Mitchell, Angelyn. 2002. *The Freedom to Remember: Narrative, Slavery, and Gender in Contemporary Black Women's Fiction*. New Brunswick, N.J.: Rutgers University Press.

Mitscherlich, Alexander, and Margarete Mitscherlich. 1967/1975. *The Inability to Mourn: Principles of Collective Behavior*. New York: Grove.

Mokeddem, Malika. 1998/1993. *The Forbidden Woman*. Trans. K. Melissa Marcus. Lincoln: University of Nebraska Press. [*L'interdite*. Paris: Editions Grasset & Fasquelle]

Morrison, Toni. 1987. *Beloved: A Novel*. New York: Knopf.

———. 1989. "Unspeakable Things Unspoken: The Afro-American Presence in American Literature." *Michigan Quarterly Review* 28:1–34.

———. 1990. "The Site of Memory." In *Out There: Marginalization and Contemporary Cultures*, ed. Russell Ferguson, Martha Gever, Trinh T. Minh-ha, and Cornel West, 299–305. New York: New York Museum of Contemporary Art.

Mostern, Kenneth. 2000. "Postcolonialism after W. E. B. Du Bois." In *Postcolonial Theory and the United States: Race, Ethnicity, and Literature*, ed. Amritjit Singh and Peter Schmidt, 258–76. Jackson: University Press of Mississippi.

Moten, Fred. 2003. *In the Break: The Aesthetics of the Black Radical Tradition*. Minneapolis: University of Minnesota Press.

Mouffe, Chantal. 1998. "Carl Schmitt and the Paradox of Liberal Democracy." In *Law as Politics: Carl Schmitt's Critique of Liberalism*, ed. David Dyzenhaus. Durham: Duke University Press.

———. 2005. *On the Political*. London: Routledge.

Moya, Paula, and M. Hames-Garcia, eds. 2000. *Reclaiming Identity: Realist Theory and the Predicament of Postmodernism*. Berkeley: University of California Press.

Muñoz, José Esteban. 1999. *Disidentifications: Queers of Color and the Performance of Politics*. Minneapolis: University of Minnesota Press.

Murdoch, H. Adlai, and Anne Donadey, eds. 2005. *Postcolonial Theory and Francophone Literary Studies*. Gainesville: University Press of Florida.

Najita, Tetsuo, and H. D. Harootunian. 1998. "Japan's Revolt against the West." In *Modern Japanese Thought*, ed. Bob T. Wakabayashi. Cambridge: Cambridge University Press.

Nandy, Ashis. 1989. *The Intimate Enemy: Loss and Recovery of Self under Colonialism*. Delhi: Oxford University Press.

Nesbitt, Nick. 2003. *Voicing Memory: History and Subjectivity in French Caribbean Literature*. Charlottesville: University of Virginia Press.

Nnaemeka, Obioma. 2004. "Nego-Feminism: Theorizing, Practicing, and Pruning Africa's Way." *Signs: Journal of Women in Culture and Society* 29 (2): 357–86.

Noblet, Pascal. 1993. *L'Amérique des minorités: Les politiques d'intégration*. Paris: L'Harmattan.

Nora, Pierre. 1984. "Entre mémoire et histoire: La problématique des lieux." In *Les lieux de mémoire*, vol. 1, xv–xlii. Paris: Gallimard.

Norindr, Panivong. 1999. "Mourning, Memorials, and Filmic Traces: Remembering the *Corps étrangers* and Unknown Soldiers in Bertrand Tavernier's Films." *Studies in Twentieth Century Literature* 23 (1): 117–41.

Nwankwo, Ifeoma Kiddoe. 2005. *Black Cosmopolitanism: Racial Consciousness and Transnational Identity in the Nineteenth-Century Americas*. Philadelphia: University of Pennsylvania Press.

OECD Directorate for Education. 2006. Organization for Economic Co-operation and Development Report. "Where Immigrant Students Succeed: A Comparative Review of Performance and Engagement in PISA." OECD.org (http://www.oecd .org/dataoecd/2/38/36664934.pdf).

Oestreich, James R. 1992. "A Persistent Voyager Lands at the Met." *New York Times Magazine*, October 11, 22–28.

Okakura, Kakuzo. 1903. *The Ideals of the East with Special Reference to the Art of Japan.* London: J. Murray.

Oliver, Kelly. 2001. *Witnessing: Beyond Recognition.* Minnesota: University of Minneapolis Press.

———. 2002 "Psychic Space and Social Melancholy." In *Between the Psyche and the Social,* ed. Oliver and Edwin, 49–65. Lanham, Md.: Rowman and Littlefield.

———. 2004. *The Colonization of Psychic Space: A Psychoanalytic Social Theory of Oppression.* Minneapolis: University of Minnesota Press.

Oliver, Kelly, and Steve Edwin, eds. 2002. *Between the Psyche and the Social.* Lanham, Md.: Rowman and Littlefield.

Omi, Michael, and Dana Takagi, eds. 1995. "Thinking Theory in Asian American Studies." Special issue, *Amerasia* 21 (1–2).

Omi, Michael, and Howard Winant. 1994. *Racial Formation in the United States: From the 1960s to the 1990s.* New York: Routledge.

Ong, Aihwa, and Stephen J. Collier, eds. 2004. *Global Assemblages: Technology, Politics, and Ethics as Anthropological Problems.* Oxford: Blackwell.

O'Riley, Michael F. 2004. "Place, Position, and Postcolonial Haunting in Assia Djebar's *La femme sans sépulture.*" *Research in African Literatures* 35 (1): 66–86.

Ortiz, Simon J. 2000. *From Sand Creek.* Tucson: University of Arizona Press.

Pagden, Anthony. 1995. *Lords of All the World: Ideologies of Empire in Spain, Britain, and France c.1500–c.1800.* New Haven: Yale University Press.

Palmié, Stephan. 2006. "Creolization and Its Discontents." *Annual Review of Anthropology* 35:433–56.

Palumbo-Liu, David, ed. 1995. *The Ethnic Canon: Histories, Institutions, Interventions.* Minneapolis: University of Minnesota Press.

Patai, Daphne, and Will H. Corral. 2005. Introduction to *Theory's Empire: An Anthology of Dissent,* ed. Daphne Patai and Will H. Corral, 1–18. New York: Columbia University Press.

Patterson, Orlando. 1991. *Freedom.* New York: Basic Books.

Paulin, Diana R. 1997. "De-essentializing Interracial Representations: Black and White Border-Crossings in Spike Lee's *Jungle Fever* and Octavia Butler's *Kindred.*" *Cultural Critique* 36:165–93.

Pettit, Philip. 1997. *Republicanism: A Theory of Freedom and Government.* Oxford: Oxford University Press.

Pontecorvo, Gillo, dir. 1966. *The Battle of Algiers.* Italy-Algeria.

Prabhu, Anjali. 2007. *Hybridity: Limits, Transformations, Prospects.* Albany: State University of New York Press.

Prabhu, Anjali, and Ato Quayson. 2005. "Francophone Studies/Postcolonial Studies: 'Postcolonializing' through *relation.*" In *Postcolonial Theory and Francophone Literary Studies*, ed. Donadey and Murdoch, 224–34. Gainesville: University Press of Florida.

Quijano, Anibal. 2000. "Coloniality of Power, Eurocentrism, and Latin America." *Nepantla: Views from South* 1 (3): 533–80.

Radhakrishnan, R. 2003. *Theory in an Uneven World.* Oxford: Blackwell.

Ramassamy, Ginette. 2003. "Which 'Ethics of Vigilance' to Put into Place?" In *Créolité and Creolization*, ed. Okwui Enwezor, 21–25. Ostfildern-Ruit: Hatje Cabtze.

Rancière, Jacques. 1999. *Disagreement: Politics and Philosophy.* Minneapolis: University of Minnesota Press.

Regaïeg, Najiba. 2004. "*La femme sans sépulture* d'Assia Djebar: De l'écriture de la dissidence à la dissidence de l'écriture." *Expressions Maghrébines* 3 (1): 77–91.

Rich, Adrienne. 1986. "Resisting Amnesia: History and Personal Life." In *Blood, Bread, and Poetry: Selected Prose, 1979–1985*, 136–55. New York: Norton.

Richard, Thelma Shinn. 2005/2006. "Defining Kindred: Octavia Butler's Postcolonial Perspective." *Obsidian III: Literature in the African Diaspora* 6–7 (2–1): 118–34.

Rigo, Enrica. 2007. *Europa di confine: Trasformazioni della cittadinanza nell'Unione Allargata.* Rome: Meltemi.

Rimer, Sara. 2008. "Gatsby's Green Light Beckons a New Set of Strivers." *New York Times*, February 17.

Ritte, Juergen. 2005. "Muslime in Frankreich: Symptombekaempfung statt Loesungsansaetze." *Neue Zuericher Zeitung.* April 4.

Robinson, Cedric. 1983. *Black Marxism: The Making of the Black Radical Tradition.* London: Zed.

Rosello, Mireille. 2005. *France and the Maghreb: Performative Encounters.* Gainesville: University Press of Florida.

Ross, Kristin. 2002. *May '68 and Its Afterlives.* Chicago: University of Chicago Press.

Rothberg, Michael. 2009. *Multidirectional Memory: Remembering the Holocaust in the Age of Decolonization.* Stanford: Stanford University Press.

Rushdy, Ashraf H. A. 2001. *Remembering Generations: Race and Family in Contemporary African American Fiction.* Chapel Hill: University of North Carolina Press.

Sabet, Amr G. E. 2008. *Islam and the Political: Theory, Governance, and International Relations.* London: Pluto.

Said, Edward. 1978. *Orientalism.* Harmondsworth: Penguin.

———. 1993. *Culture and Imperialism.* London: Vintage.

———. 2003. *Humanism and Democratic Criticism.* New York: Columbia University Press.

Sakai, Naoki. 1998. "Modernity and Its Critique: The Problem of Universalism and Particularism." *South Atlantic Quarterly* 87 (3): 475–504.

Sandoval, Chela. 2000. *Methodology of the Oppressed.* Minneapolis: University of Minnesota Press.

Santner, Eric. 2001. *On the Psychotheology of Everyday Life: Reflections on Freud and Rosenzweig*. Chicago: University of Chicago Press.

Santos, Bonaventura de Sousa. 2005. "General Introduction." In *Democratizing Democracy: Beyond the Liberal Democratic Canon*, ed. Bonaventura de Sousa Santos, xvii–xxxiii. London: Verso.

Sassen, Saskia. 1998. *Globalization and Its Discontents*. New York: New Press.

Sayyid, S. 2003. *A Fundamental Fear: Eurocentrism and the Emergence of Islamism*. London: Zed.

———. 2005. "Mirror, Mirror: Western Democrats, Oriental Despots?" *Ethnicities* 5 (1): 30–50.

Scad, John. 2003. Preface to *Life after Theory*, ed. Michael Payne and John Scad, ix–x. London: Continuum.

Schmitt, Carl. 1932/1996. *The Concept of the Political*. Chicago: University of Chicago Press.

———. 1985. *The Crisis of Parliamentary Democracy*. Cambridge: MIT Press.

———. 2003. *The Nomos of the Earth in the International Law of Jus Publicum Europaeum*. New York: Telos.

———. 2004. *The Theory of the Partisan: A Commentary/Remark on the Concept of the Political*. East Lansing: Michigan State University Press.

Scott, David. 2004. *Conscripts of Modernity: The Tragedy of Colonial Enlightenment*. Durham: Duke University Press.

Scott, James C. 1990. *Domination and the Arts of Resistance: Hidden Transcripts*. New Haven: Yale University Press.

Semali, Ladislaus, and Joe L. Kincheloe, eds. 1999. *What Is Indigenous Knowledge?* London: Taylor and Francis.

Seshadri-Crooks, Kalpana. 2000. "At the Margins of Postcolonial Studies: Part 1." In *The Pre-occupation of Postcolonial Studies*, ed. Fawzia Afzal-Khan and Kalpana Seshadri-Crooks, 3–23. Durham: Duke University Press.

Shadow Report on Algeria. 2000. Submitted by the CEDAW (Committee on the Elimination of Discrimination Against Women, 1999). Georgetown: Women Living Under Muslim Laws and the International Women Human Rights Law Clinic, Georgetown Law School.

Shanley, Mary Lyndon, and Carole Pateman, eds. 1991. *Feminist Interpretations and Political Theory*. University Park: Pennsylvania State University Press.

Shapiro, Ian. 2003. *The State of Democratic Theory*. Princeton: Princeton University Press.

Sharpe, Jenny. 2003. *Ghosts of Slavery: A Literary Archaeology of Black Women's Lives*. Minneapolis: University of Minnesota Press.

Sheller, Mimi. 2001. *Democracy after Slavery: Black Publics and Peasant Radicalism in Haiti and Jamaica*. Gainesville: University Press of Florida.

Shih, Shu-mei. 2003. "Globalisation and the (in)Significance of Taiwan." *Postcolonial Studies* 6 (2): 143–53.

———. 2004. "Global Literature and the Technologies of Recognition." *PMLA* 119 (1): 16–30.

———. 2008. "Comparative Racialization: An Introduction." *PMLA* 123 (5): 1347–62.

Shohat, Ella. 1998. Introduction to *Talking Visions: Multicultural Feminism in a Transnational Age*, 1–62. Cambridge: MIT Press.

———. 2002. "Area Studies, Gender Studies, and the Cartographies of Knowledge." *Social Text* 72 (2–3): 67–78.

Shohat, Ella, and Robert Stam. 1994. *Unthinking Eurocentrism: Multiculturalism and the Media*. London: Routledge.

Simpson, David. 2006. "Theory in the Time of Death." *Critical Quarterly* 48 (1): 126–35.

Singh, Ajit, and Bruce A. Weisse. 1998. "Emerging Stock Markets, Portfolio Capital Flows, and Long-Term Economic Growth: Micro and Macroeconomic Perspectives." *World Development* 26 (4): 607–22.

Singh, Amritjit, and Peter Schmidt, eds. 2000. *Postcolonial Theory and the United States: Race, Ethnicity, and Literature*. Jackson: University Press of Mississippi.

Skinner, Quentin. 1998. *Liberty before Liberalism*. Cambridge: Cambridge University Press.

Smith, Linda Tuhiwai. 1999. *Decolonizing Methodologies: Research and Indigenous Peoples*. London: Zed.

Smith, Valerie. 1998. *Not Just Race, Not Just Gender: Black Feminist Readings*. New York: Routledge.

Soysal, Yasemin. 2000. "Citizenship and Identity: Living in Diasporas in Post-war Europe?" *Ethnic and Racial Studies* 23 (1): 1–15.

Spivak, Gayatri. 1988. "Can the Subaltern Speak?" In *Marxism and the Interpretation of Culture*, ed. Cary Nelson and Lawrence Grossberg, 271–313. Urbana: University of Illinois Press.

———. 1993. *Outside in the Teaching Machine*. London: Routledge.

———. 1999. *A Critique of Postcolonial Reason: Toward a History of the Vanishing Present*. Cambridge: Harvard University Press.

Springborg, Patricia. 1992. *Western Republicanism and the Oriental Prince*. Austin: University of Texas Press.

———. 2001. "Republicanism, Freedom from Domination, and the Cambridge Contextual Historians." *Political Studies* 49 (5): 851–76.

Stewart, Charles. 2007. "Creolization: History, Ethnography, Theory." In *Creolization: History, Ethnography, Theory*, ed. Charles Stewart, 1–25. Walnut Creek, Calif.: Left Coast Press.

Steyerl, Hito, and Encarnación Guitiérez Rodríguez. 2003. *Spricht die Subalterne deutsch? Migration und postkoloniale Kritik*. Muenster: Unrast.

Stinchcombe, Arthur. 1995. *Sugar Island Slavery in the Age of Enlightenment: The Political Economy of the Caribbean World*. Princeton: Princeton University Press.

Stoler, Ann Laura. 2002. *Carnal Knowledge and Imperial Power: Race and the Intimate in Colonial Rule*. Berkeley: University of California Press.

Stora, Benjamin. 1991. *La gangrène et l'oubli: La mémoire de la guerre d'Algérie*. Paris: La Découverte.

———. 1999. *Le transfert d'une mémoire: De l'"Algérie française" au racisme anti-arabe*. Paris: La Découverte.

———. 2003. "La guerre d'Algérie dans les mémoires françaises: Violence d'une mémoire de revanche." *L'Esprit créateur* 43 (1): 7–31.

———. 2007. *La guerre des mémoires: La France face à son passé colonial*. Interview with T. Leclère. Paris: Éditions de l'Aube.

Stourzh, Gerald. 1989. *Wege zur Grundrechtsdemokratie*. Vienna: Böhlau.

Suk, Jeannie. 2001. *Postcolonial Paradoxes in French Caribbean Writing: Césaire, Glissant, Condé*. Oxford: Oxford University Press.

Suleiman, Susan Rubin. 2006. *Crises of Memory and the Second World War*. Cambridge: Harvard University Press.

Sumic, Jelica. 2004. "Anachronism of Emancipation or Fidelity to Politics." In *Laclau: A Critical Reader*, ed. Simon Critchley and Oliver Marchant. New York: Routledge.

Sun, Ge. 2000. "How Does Asia Mean? (Part 1)." *Inter-Asia Cultural Studies* 1 (1): 13–47.

Takeuchi, Yoshimi. 2005. *What Is Modernity? Writings of Takeuchi Yoshimi*. Ed. and trans. Richard Calichman. New York: Columbia University Press.

Taylor, Charles. 1994. "The Politics of Recognition." In *Multiculturalism: Examining the Politics of Recognition*, ed. A. Gutmann, 25–73. Princeton: Princeton University Press.

Taylor, Timothy D. 2007. *Beyond Exoticism: Western Music and the World*. Durham: Duke University Press.

Tilly, Charles. 2006. *Regimes and Repertoires*. Chicago: University of Chicago Press.

Torres-Saillant, Silvio. 2000. "The Tribulations of Blackness: Stages in Dominican Racial Identity." *Callaloo* 23 (3): 1086–111.

Touraine, Alain. 2000. *Can We Live Together? Equality and Difference*. Trans. David Macey. Stanford: Stanford University Press.

Trinh T. Minh-ha. 1989. *Woman, Native, Other: Writing Postcoloniality and Feminism*. Bloomington: Indiana University Press.

Trouillot, Michel-Rolph. 1997. *Silencing the Past: Power and the Production of History*. Boston: Beacon Press.

Tully, James. 1995. *Strange Multiplicity: Constitutionalism in the Age of Diversity*. Cambridge: Cambridge University Press.

Turner, Lou, and John Alan. 1978. *Frantz Fanon, Soweto, and American Black Thought*. Detroit: News and Letters.

Turner, Stephanie S. 2003. "What Actually Is: The Insistence of Genre in Octavia Butler's *Kindred*." *Femspec* 4 (2): n.p. (electronic journal).

Umozurike, U. O. 1979. *International Law and Colonialism in Africa*. Enugu, Nigeria: Nwamife.

Vergès, Françoise. 2003a. "Kiltir Kreol: Processes and Practices of Créolité and Creolization." In *Créolité and Creolization*, ed. Okwui Enwezor, 179–84. Ostfildern-Ruit: Hatje Cabtze.

———. 2003b. "Open Session." In *Créolité and Creolization*, ed. Okwui Enwezor, 199–211. Ostfildern-Ruit: Hatje Cabtze.

Wade, Robert. 1998. "The Asian Debt-and-Development Crisis of 1997? Causes and Consequences." *World Development* 26 (8): 1535–53.

———. 2004. *Governing the Market: Economic Theory and the Role of Government in East Asian Industrialization*. 2nd ed. Princeton: Princeton University Press.

Wade, Robert, and Frank Veneroso. 1998a. "The Asian Crisis: The High Debt Model versus the Wall Street-Treasury-IMF Complex." *New Left Review* 228:3–23.

———. 1998b. "The Gathering World Slump and the Battle over Capital Controls." *New Left Review* 231:13–42.

Walker, Muriel. 2008. "Femme d'écriture française: La Francographie djebarienne." *L'Esprit Créateur* 48 (4): 47–55.

Walsh, Sebastian J. 2007. "Killing Post-Almohad Man: Malek Bennabi, Algerian Islamism, and the Search for a Liberal Governance." *Journal of North African Studies* 12 (2): 235–54.

Warren, D. Michael. 2001. "The Role of the Global Network of Indigenous Knowledge Resource Centers in the Conservation of Cultural and Biological Diversity." In *On Biocultural Diversity: Linking Language, Knowledge, and the Environment*, ed. Luisa Maffi, 446–61. Washington: Smithsonian Institution Press.

White, Hayden V. 1973. *Metahistory: The Historical Imagination in Nineteenth-Century Europe*. Baltimore: Johns Hopkins University Press.

Wieviorka, Michel. 1998a. "Is Multiculturalism the Solution?" *Ethnic and Racial Studies* 21 (5): 881–910.

———. 1998b. *Le racisme: Une introduction*. Paris: La Découverte.

Williams, Raymond. 1989. *The Politics of Modernism: Against the New Conformists*. London: Verso.

Winant, Howard. 2001. *The World Is a Ghetto — Race and Democracy since World War II*. New York: Basic Books.

Wolf, Eric. 1982. *Europe and the People without History*. Berkeley: University of California Press.

World Bank. 1998a. "Priorities for a Sustainable Recovery." In *And Our Rice Pots Are Empty: The Social Cost of the Economic Crisis*, 308–37. Penang, Malaysia: Consumers International.

———. 1998b. "What Can Be Done?" In *And Our Rice Pots Are Empty: The Social Cost of the Economic Crisis*, 278–306. Penang, Malaysia: Consumers International.

Wu, Yung-Hsing. 2006. "Native Sons and Native Speakers: On the Eth(n)ics of Comparison." *PMLA* 121 (5): 1460–74.

Wynter, Sylvia. 2001. "Towards the Sociogenic Principle: Fanon, the Puzzle of Conscious Experience, of 'Identity' and What's It Like to Be 'Black.'" In *National Identity and Sociopolitical Change: Latin America between Marginalization and Inte-*

gration, ed. Mercedes Durán-Cogan and Antonio Gómez-Moriana. New York: Routledge.

Young, Robert J. C. 1990. *White Mythologies: Writing History and the West*. London: Routledge.

———. 2005. "Fanon and the Turn to Armed Struggle in Africa." *Wasafari* 44:33–41.

Yue, Ming-Bao. 2000. "On Not Looking German: Ethnicity, Diaspora, and the Politics of Vision." *European Journal of Cultural Studies* 3 (2): 173–94.

Zakaria, Fareed. 1994. "Culture Is Destiny: A Conversation with Kuan Yew." *Foreign Affairs* 73 (2): 109–26.

Zimra, Clarisse. 2003. "Mapping Memory: Architectural Metaphors in Djebar's Unfinished Quartet." *L'Esprit Créateur* 43 (1): 58–68.

Žižek, Slavoj. 1989. *The Sublime Object of Ideology*. London: Verso.

———. 1993. *Tarrying with the Negative: Kant, Hegel, and the Critique of Ideology*. Durham: Duke University Press.

———. 1996. "'I Hear You with My Eyes'; or, The Invisible Master." In *Gaze and Voice as Love Objects*, ed. Renata Salecl and Slavoj Žižek, 90–126. Durham: Duke University Press.

CONTRIBUTORS

ÉTIENNE BALIBAR is emeritus professor of moral and political philosophy at the University of Paris 10 Nanterre and distinguished professor of humanities at the University of California, Irvine, as well as a frequent seminar leader at the Centro Franco-Argentino de Altos Estudios de la Universidad de Buenos Aires and the Center for Comparative Literature and Society at Columbia University of New York. He is author or coauthor of numerous books including *Reading Capital* (with Louis Althusser) (1965), *On the Dictatorship of the Proletariat* (1976), *Race, Nation, Class: Ambiguous Identities* (with Immanuel Wallerstein) (Verso, 1991), *Masses, Classes, Ideas* (Routledge, 1994), *The Philosophy of Marx* (Verso, 1995), *Spinoza and Politics* (Verso, 1998), *Politics and the Other Scene* (Verso, 2002), and *We, the People of Europe? Reflections on Transnational Citizenship* (Princeton, 2004). Forthcoming are *Extreme Violence and the Problem of Civility* (Wellek Library Lectures, 1996), and *Citoyen sujet: Essais d'anthropologie philosophique* (Presses Universitaires de France). He is a member of Ligue des Droits de l'Homme (Paris), with a particular interest in the rights of migrants and asylum seekers. He is cofounder of the Faculty for Israeli-Palestinian Peace and acting chair of Association Jan Hus France.

DOMINIQUE CHANCÉ teaches comparative literature at the University of Bordeaux 3, Michel de Montaigne. She is the author of *L'auteur en souffrance* (2000), *Poétique baroque de la Caraïbe* (2001), *Édouard Glissant: Un traité du déparler* (2002), *Les fils de Lear: Glissant, Naipaul, Wideman* (2003), and *Histoire des littératures antillaises* (2005), which is on the different literatures of the Caribbean, in English, Spanish, Creole, and French. Her most recent works include: *Écritures du chaos (Frankétienne, Arenas, Des Rosiers)*, (2008) and *Patrick Chamoiseau, écrivain postcolonial et baroque* (2010), which gives a synthesis of her approaches to "créolité" and "créolisation."

PHENG CHEAH is professor in the Department of Rhetoric at the University of California, Berkeley. He is the author of *Spectral Nationality: Passages of Freedom from Kant to Postcolonial Literatures of Liberation* (Columbia, 2003) and *Inhuman Conditions: On*

Cosmopolitanism and Human Rights (Harvard, 2006). He has co-edited *Cosmopolitics: Thinking and Feeling beyond the Nation* (Minnesota, 1998), *Grounds of Comparison: Around the Work of Benedict Anderson* (Routledge, 2003), and *Derrida and the Time of the Political* (Duke, 2009). He is working on a book on world literature and another book on the concept of instrumentality.

LEO CHING is associate professor and chair in the Department of Asian and Middle Eastern Studies at Duke University. He is the author of *Becoming Japanese: Colonial Taiwan and the Politics of Identity Formations* (California, 2001), which has been translated into Chinese and Japanese. He is currently completing a book manuscript on anti-Japanism in postwar-postcolonial Asia and popular culture.

LIZ CONSTABLE is associate professor in women and gender studies at the University of California, Davis. She has published widely on nineteenth- and twentieth-century French and Francophone literature, culture, politics, and film, with a focus on the interdependencies of the metropolitan and the colonial, rethinking theories of postcoloniality and Francophone studies, and transnational feminist cultural studies. Her most recent publications include "Hearing Cultures: Acoustic Architecture and Cinematic Soundscapes of Algiers in Merzak Allouache and Nadir Moknèche," *Contemporary French Civilization* (September 2008), and "Balzac's Golden Triangles in the Colonial Genealogies of French Modernism," in *Disciplining Modernism*, ed. Pamela Caughie (Palgrave, 2009). Her monograph on Catherine Breillat's cinema is forthcoming in the University of Illinois Contemporary World Directors Series, 2010.

ANNE DONADEY is professor and chair of European studies and professor of women's studies at San Diego State University. She is the author of a book on Assia Djebar and Leïla Sebbar, *Recasting Postcolonialism: Women Writing between Worlds* (Heinemann, 2001), co-editor with H. Adlai Murdoch of *Postcolonial Theory and Francophone Literary Studies* (University Press of Florida, 2005), and editor of a special issue of *L'Esprit Créateur* on the works of Assia Djebar (winter 2008). She has also published articles on the current state of feminist literary studies, on antiracist perspectives in women's studies and French cultural studies, and on the works of Fatima Mernissi, Tsitsi Dangarembga, Maryse Condé, Daniel Maximin, Azar Nafisi, Octavia E. Butler, and Gloria Anzaldúa. Recent articles have appeared in *Signs: Journal of Women in Culture and Society*, *Research in African Literature*, *College Literature*, *International Journal of Francophone Studies*, and *French Review*.

FATIMA EL-TAYEB is associate professor of literature at the University of California, San Diego. Her first book, *Schwarze Deutsche* (2001), explores the relationship between race and national identity in early-twentieth-century Germany. She has published numerous articles on the interactions of race, gender, sexuality, and nation, most recently "The Birth of a European Public? Migration, Postnationality, and Race in the Uniting of Europe," *American Quarterly* 60.3 (2008). Her second book, *Queering Ethnicity. Minority Activism in Postnational Europe* is forthcoming from the University of Minnesota Press.

JULIN EVERETT is a visiting assistant professor of French at Miami University of Ohio. She received her Ph.D. at the University of California, Los Angeles, in 2010 and is the author of articles on Francophone literature, on the orphan in the postcolony, and on male homoeroticism in postcolonial literature.

BARNOR HESSE is associate professor of African American studies, sociology, and political science at Northwestern University. He is editor of *Un/Settled Multiculturalisms: Diasporas, Entanglements, Transruptions* (Zed, 2000) and author of *Creolizing the Political: A Genealogy of the African Diaspora* (Duke, forthcoming).

PING-HUI LIAO is the Chuan Lyu Endowed Chair Professor in Taiwan studies at the University of California, San Diego. He is co-editor of *Taiwan under Japanese Colonial Rule, 1895–1945* (Columbia, 2006). He is currently compiling a source book for Taiwan and its contexts.

FRANÇOISE LIONNET is professor of French and Francophone studies and comparative literature at the University of California, Los Angeles. She is the author of *Autobiographical Voices: Race, Gender, Self-Portraiture* (Cornell, 1989), *Postcolonial Representations: Women, Literature, Identity* (Cornell, 1995), and the forthcoming *The Indies, Otherwise: Creolization, Transcolonial Comparison, and World Literature*. She has edited or co-edited numerous journal special issues, including "Post/Colonial Conditions," *Yale French Studies* (1993); "Cities, Modernity, and Cultural Memory," *L'Esprit Créateur* (2001); "Postcolonial, Indigenous, and Emergent Feminisms," *Signs* (1995); "Development Cultures," *Signs* (2004); "Intra-national Comparisons," *Comparative Literary Studies* (2003); "Francophone Studies: New Landscapes," *MLN* (2003); and "Between Words and Images: The Culture of Mauritius," *International Journal of Francophone Studies* (2010). With Shu-mei Shih, she codirects the UCLA Mellon Postdoctoral Program on Cultures in Transnational Perspective and has co-edited *Minor Transnationalism* (Duke, 2005). Recent essays have appeared in *PMLA*, *Journal of Postcolonial Writing*, *French Forum, Yale French Studies*, and the volume *French Global: A New Approach to Literary History* (Columbia, 2010).

WALTER MIGNOLO is William H. Wannamaker Professor of Romance Studies and Literature at Duke University and director of the Center for Global Studies and the Humanities. His monograph *The Darker Side of the Renaissance: Literacy, Territoriality, and Colonization* (1995) was awarded the Catherine Singers Kovacs Prize at the MLA Convention of 1996. *Local Histories/Global Designs: Coloniality, Subaltern Knowledges, and Border Thinking* was published by Princeton University Press in 2000 and translated into Spanish and Portuguese. *The Idea of Latin America* (2005) received the Frantz Fanon Award from the Philosophical Caribbean Association in 2006. He co-edits *WKO*, a Web dossier, and is advisor of a forthcoming summer school seminar, "Decolonizing Knowledge: Postcolonial Studies, Decolonial Horizon."

ANDREA SCHWIEGER HIEPKO is an editor and communications manager in the fields of culture, science, and global development cooperations. After studying French, Spanish, and Latin American literature in Berlin, Paris, and Barcelona, she taught as a lecturer at the Free University of Berlin, Denver University and Fachhochschule Hildesheim. She is author of *Rhythm 'n' Creole: Antonio Benítez Rojo und Edouard Glissant—Postkoloniale Poetiken der kulturellen Globalisierung* and many articles on Caribbean literature and culture, postcolonialism, and global development.

SHU-MEI SHIH teaches comparative, Sinophone, Chinese, and Asian American literature at the University of California, Los Angeles. She is the author of two books, *The Lure of the Modern* (2001) and *Visuality and Identity* (2007), and the co-editor, with Françoise Lionnet, of *Minor Transnationalism* (2005). She has guest-edited special issues of *Postcolonial Studies* (2003) and PMLA (2008) and publishes regularly in Taiwan and China. Her research interests include Sinophone literature from around the world, the ecology of area and ethnic studies, Chinese postsocialism, world literature, transnational feminism, critical race theory, and comparative postcolonial theory. Her most recent articles will appear in *Social Text*, *positions*, and PMLA, and she is completing the co-editing of a book titled *Sinophone Studies: A Critical Reader*.

INDEX

Acculturation, 24, 262, 265

Activism, minority, 230–32, 242–48

Affect: affective imperialism, 122; definition of, 118; interiority and, 123; loss of meaning and, 119; psychoanalytic theory on, 115–16, 137; support and, 130; as traumatic, 120, 140 n. 9

African American Emancipation Day, 71

African American studies, 11, 138

Aggresivity theory, 89

Ahmed, Feiza, 235

Alexander VI (pope), 159–60

Algerian War (1954–1962), 2, 15, 17, 67, 113

Alienation, 89, 92, 96, 105, 134, 184, 243

Americanization, 16

American Revolution (1775–1783), 41, 50, 53–54

Amnesia, 68, 136–37, 228

Anamnesis, 76–79

Anthropos, 164–66, 168, 171–72, 187

Anticolonialism, 14, 45, 53–54, 68, 92

Antillanité: creolization and, 263–66; identity and, 264

Anti-Semitism, 237–38, 248

Anxiety, 20, 23, 62, 88, 179

Anzaldúa, Gloria, 182

Appiah, Anthony, 4–5, 10

Area studies, 2, 6–7, 64

Armed Islamic Group (GIA), 124

Asian American movement, 18–19

Asian American Political Alliance, 18

Asian financial crisis (1997), 96–108; autoimmunity and, 21, 105–8; capital flows and, 98–99, 101, 105–7; casino capital in, 101–2; deregulation and, 101; metaphors for, 97; physiology of power and, 99–100, 102, 105; speculative capital in, 102–3; structural adjustment policies and, 99–100; transnational capital and, 100, 104; trauma and, 96–98, 104

Assimilation, 38, 45, 63, 143, 168, 235

Autoimmunity, 21, 105–8, 109 n. 7

Autonomy: colonial imaginaries of, 38; of ego, 86; public/private, 149–50

Badiou, Alain, 9, 13

Baker, Houston, Jr., 10

Bastaroli, Pierre, 113

Beauvoir, Simone de, 26

Becoming minor, 14–15

Being and imperialism, 172

Bennabi, Malik, 29, 172–79; on dead/deadly ideas, 176–78

Bensmaïa, Réda, 10, 79 n.1

Berio, Luciano, 148–49

Best, Lloyd, 176–78

242; on diversity, 142; on entanglement, 37; on French domination, 17;
on identity, 242, 257, 259–60; interview, 255–60; on island-regions, 257;
on nationalism, 257; on racism, 258
Global decolonial thinking, 167–69,
189–91
Globalization: Africa and, 94–95; anthropological effects of, 208, 213–18; capitalism and, 5; creolization and, 24, 265;
economic, in Asia, 96–108; as expansionism, 189; forms of power, 84, 95,
99–100, 102, 105; free trade and, 215;
hyperdevelopment and, 105; inequalities and, 216; ontological paradoxes of,
208, 213–18; postcolonial theory and,
83–84
Global linear thinking, 159–60, 163, 165,
167–68, 190
Gordon, Lewis, 182
Govan, Sandra, 69
Grande, Sandy, 27
Grovogui, Siba N'Zatioula, 166
Guaman Poma de Ayala, 166
Guattari, Félix, 219, 259
Guest workers, 234–35

Ha, Marie-Paule, 14
Habermas, Jürgen, 4, 149–50, 223, 232
Haitian Revolution (1791–1804), 52, 54
Hall, Stuart, 25, 39–40, 148, 230–31, 251
n. 20
Hammerstein, Oscar, II, 144, 148, 155
Harding, Sandra, 27
Hardt, Michael, 84
Harem of Madame Osmane (film), 127
Haring, Lee, 11, 24–25
Hegel, Georg Wilhelm Friedrich, 194,
198–99, 223; on metaphysics, 28
Heidegger, Martin, 23, 28
Henderson, Mae, 65, 80
Historical narrative, rethinking, 68
Holocaust, 167, 228, 233

Homosexuality, 146, 165, 240
Honig, Bonnie, 49
Humanitas, 164–68, 171–72, 187
Humanities studies, changes in, 63
Huntington, Samuel, 168, 189
Hurcheon, Linda, 68–69
Hwang, David Henry: collaboration with
Glass, 30, 142, 144, 148, 155; on creoli-
zation, 30, 150–51, 155; masculinity and
sexuality in works, 146–47; multicul-
turalism and, 142–44, 147–48; use of
stereotypes by, 143–46, 155. *See also*
specific works
Hysteria, 87

Identity: citizenship and, 243; creolization and, 164; difference and, 244;
diversion and, 242; exclusion and,
39, 256, 258; hybrid culture and, 143;
island-regions and, 257; métissage
and, 121, 264–65; national, 9, 216;
new European, 228; as root/rhizome,
259–60
IK Movement, 27
IMF (International Monetary Fund), 95,
101
Immigrant consciousness, 183–84
Imperialism: affective, 122–23; anti-
imperialist movements, 18, 52; being
and, 172; colonial expansion, 163, 169,
173, 186, 195; global linear thinking
and, 159–60, 163, 165, 167–68; interiority and, 178; Japanese, 20, 28, 198–
203; knowledge and, 174, 187; modernity and, 195; Muslims and, 176, 178;
other and, 186, 188; place and, 174–75;
race and, 48; sovereignty and, 51, 94;
theory and, 5, 6; Western, 18, 28, 84,
164, 167, 171, 173, 181, 184–85, 188, 195,
198–203
Imperial scientia, 188
Inclusion: colonial, 126; creolization and,
144, 149, 150; geopolitical, 113, 120;

FRANÇOISE LIONNET is professor of French and Francophone studies, comparative literature, and women's studies at the University of California, Los Angeles.

SHU-MEI SHIH is professor of East Asian languages and cultures, comparative literature, and Asian American studies at the University of California, Los Angeles.

Library of Congress Cataloging-in-Publication Data

The creolization of theory / edited by Françoise Lionnet and Shu-mei Shih.
p. cm.
Includes bibliographical references and index.
ISBN 978-0-8223-4832-0 (cloth : alk. paper)
ISBN 978-0-8223-4846-7 (pbk. : alk. paper)
1. Cultural fusion.
2. Creoles.
3. Postcolonialism.
I. Lionnet, Françoise.
II. Shi, Shumei.
HM1272.C735 2011
303.48′2089—dc22
2010044967